The Private Sector in Public Office

This book addresses the long-standing puzzle of how China's private sector manages to grow without secure property rights, and proposes a new theory of selective property rights to explain this phenomenon. Drawing on rich empirical evidence including in-depth interviews, a unique national survey of private entrepreneurs, an original survey of bureaucrats, two original national audit experiments, and secondary sources, Yue Hou shows that private entrepreneurs in China actively seek opportunities within formal institutions to advance their business interests. By securing seats in the local legislatures, entrepreneurs use their political capital to deter local officials from demanding bribes, ad hoc taxes, and other types of informal payments. In doing so they create a system of selective, individualized, and predictable property rights. This system of selective property rights is key to understanding the private sector growth in the absence of the rule of law.

Yue Hou is Assistant Professor in the Political Science department at the University of Pennsylvania. Her research interests include political economy and authoritarian politics, with a regional focus on China. Her work has appeared in the *Journal of Politics, Journal of Experimental Political Science, Quarterly Journal of Political Science*, and *Social Science Quarterly*, and has been featured in the *New York Times* and *Boston Review*. She also writes articles for Chinese media outlets including the *Southern Weekly* and *Tencent ipress*.

Cambridge Studies in Comparative Politics

General Editors

Kathleen Thelen   *Massachusetts Institute of Technology*
Erik Wibbels   *Duke University*

Associate Editors

Catherine Boone   *London School of Economics*
Thad Dunning   *University of California, Berkeley*
Anna Grzymala-Busse   *Stanford University*
Torben Iversen   *Harvard University*
Stathis Kalyvas   *Yale University*
Margaret Levi   *Stanford University*
Helen Milner   *Princeton University*
Frances Rosenbluth   *Yale University*
Susan Stokes   *Yale University*
Tariq Thachil   *Vanderbilt University*

Series Founder

Peter Lange   *Duke University*

Other Books in the Series

Christopher Adolph, *Bankers, Bureaucrats, and Central Bank Politics: The Myth of Neutrality*

Michael Albertus, *Autocracy and Redistribution: The Politics of Land Reform*

Santiago Anria, *When Movements Become Parties: The Bolivian MAS in Comparative Perspective*

Ben W. Ansell, *From the Ballot to the Blackboard: The Redistributive Political Economy of Education*

Ben W. Ansell and David J. Samuels, *Inequality and Democratization: An Elite-Competition Approach*

Ana Arjona, *Rebelocracy: Social Order in the Colombian Civil War*

Leonardo R. Arriola, *Multi-Ethnic Coalitions in Africa: Business Financing of Opposition Election Campaigns*

David Austen-Smith, Jeffry A. Frieden, Miriam A. Golden, Karl Ove Moene, and Adam Przeworski, eds., *Selected Works of Michael Wallerstein: The Political Economy of Inequality, Unions, and Social Democracy*

S. Erdem Aytaç and Susan C. Stokes *Why Bother? Rethinking Participation in Elections and Protests*

Andy Baker, *The Market and the Masses in Latin America: Policy Reform and Consumption in Liberalizing Economies*

Laia Balcells, *Rivalry and Revenge: The Politics of Violence during Civil War*

Lisa Baldez, *Why Women Protest? Women's Movements in Chile*

Kate Baldwin, *The Paradox of Traditional Chiefs in Democratic Africa*

(continued after Index)

The Private Sector in Public Office

Selective Property Rights in China

YUE HOU
University of Pennsylvania

CAMBRIDGE
UNIVERSITY PRESS

CAMBRIDGE
UNIVERSITY PRESS

University Printing House, Cambridge CB2 8BS, United Kingdom

One Liberty Plaza, 20th Floor, New York, NY 10006, USA

477 Williamstown Road, Port Melbourne, VIC 3207, Australia

314–321, 3rd Floor, Plot 3, Splendor Forum, Jasola District Centre,
New Delhi – 110025, India

79 Anson Road, #06–04/06, Singapore 079906

Cambridge University Press is part of the University of Cambridge.

It furthers the University's mission by disseminating knowledge in the pursuit of
education, learning, and research at the highest international levels of excellence.

www.cambridge.org
Information on this title: www.cambridge.org/9781108498159
DOI: 10.1017/9781108632522

First published 2019

Printed and bound in Great Britain by Clays Ltd, Elcograf S.p.A.

A catalogue record for this publication is available from the British Library.

Library of Congress Cataloging-in-Publication Data
NAMES: Hou, Yue, 1987– author.
TITLE: The private sector in public office : selective property rights in China / Yue Hou.
DESCRIPTION: Cambridge, United Kingdom ; New York, NY : Cambridge
University Press, 2019. | Series: Cambridge studies in comparative politics |
Includes bibliographical references and index.
IDENTIFIERS: LCCN 2019009279 | ISBN 9781108498159 (hardback) |
ISBN 9781108705530 (paperback)
SUBJECTS: LCSH: Business and politics–China. | Businesspeople–Political activity–China. |
Entrepreneurship–Political aspects–China. | Private enterprise–Political aspects–China. |
Right of property–China. | Legislative bodies–China. | Local government–China. |
Political corruption–China.
CLASSIFICATION: LCC JQ1509.5.B8 H68 2019 | DDC 323.4/60951–dc23
LC record available at https://lccn.loc.gov/2019009279

ISBN 978-1-108-49815-9 Hardback
ISBN 978-1-108-70553-0 Paperback

献给我的家人

Contents

Figures, Tables, and Boxes

BOXES

Preface

This book addresses the long-standing puzzle of how China's private sector manages to grow without secure property rights. I propose a new theory of selective property rights to explain this phenomenon. I show that, instead of passively accepting the existing institutional arrangements, private entrepreneurs in China actively seek opportunities within formal institutions to advance their business interests. By securing seats in the local legislatures, entrepreneurs use their political capital to deter local officials from demanding bribes, ad hoc taxes, and other types of informal payments. In doing so, they create a system of selective, individualized, and predictable property rights. This system of selective property rights is key to understanding private sector growth in the absence of the rule of law.

Drawing on rich empirical evidence, including in-depth interviews, a unique national survey of private entrepreneurs, an original survey of bureaucrats, two original national audit experiments, and secondary sources, this book shows how private entrepreneurs use the status and connections associated with holding a legislative seat to protect their property. I find that, even though government predation is an endemic problem, entrepreneur–legislators are less likely to suffer its effects. I quantitatively show that entrepreneurs who have seats in the local legislatures spend, on average, substantially less on informal payments to local officials than those who do not. Experimental evidence further demonstrates that Chinese bureaucrats are significantly more responsive to business people with connections in formal institutions than to those with no political connections.

These findings challenge prominent theories of economic development and suggest that a selective property rights regime helps sustain economic growth and political stability. Adopting an "institution as resource" perspective, I show that, within authoritarian institutions, entrepreneurs can seek opportunities to advance their interests and improve their well-being, even when the powers of these formal institutions are relatively weak.

Acknowledgments

On a summer afternoon in 2012, when I was working in my graduate student office in Cambridge, MA, I received an e-mail forwarded from a friend. The e-mail was from his high school friend, who was pleading for help to save her father Mr. Zeng, a private entrepreneur who was sentenced to death for illegally fundraising billions of yuan (1 USD = 6.23 yuan in 2012). I had no connection to the Chinese legal system and I did not reply, but I started to follow the case. That same summer, Zeng's lawyer announced that Zeng's company was valued at 2.3 billion yuan but was secretly and cheaply sold to a government-owned asset management firm for 330 million while Zeng was in jail.[1] Zeng therefore missed the opportunity to sell his company in time to repay his loans. Zeng's daughter was unable to save her father. In July 2013, she posted on her Chinese Twitter (Weibo) account that he had been executed without warning. I was deeply saddened by the story. There were many details I did not know about the case, but the fact that Zeng was executed only two years after his initial guilty verdict and was not permitted to say goodbye to his daughter shows how powerless individuals are when facing a strong state. The government's devaluation and blatant takeover of private assets suggests how insecure property rights still are in China. Stories such as Mr. Zeng's motivated me to write this book, which examines how Chinese private entrepreneurs defend themselves against heavy-handed government expropriation.

[1] Sina blog entry, August 6, 2013. "Letter from Zeng Chengjie's lawyer to the Central Commission for Discipline Inspection" (*Zeng Chengjie lvshi gei zhongjiwei de xinhan*). http://blog.sina.com.cn/s/blog_d8689d1f01019rij.html. Last accessed July 26, 2018.

I have accumulated a large debt of gratitude while writing this book. First and foremost, my heartfelt thanks go to my advisors at Massachusetts Institute of Technology (MIT): Danny Hidalgo, Yasheng Huang, David Singer, and Lily Tsai. Lily has been my closest reader and has provided unparalleled guidance and support since the moment she called to welcome me to the graduate program. David, Danny, and Yasheng have all provided valuable comments and unwavering support throughout.

I reworked the book manuscript significantly since coming to the University of Pennsylvania, and my Penn colleagues have provided me with an ideal intellectual home. I thank Avery Goldstein for his scrutiny, guidance, humor, and tolerance of my many long-winded questions. My sincere gratitude also goes to Tulia Falleti and Rachel Hulvey, who closely read and commented on the entire manuscript. I am also grateful to Diana Mutz, Dawn Teele, Hanming Fang, Dorothy Kronick, Guy Grossman, Jacques deLisle, Ed Mansfield, Nicholas Sambanis, Devesh Kapur, Julie Lynch,   Dan Hopkins, Matt Levendusky, Michele Margolis, Marc Meredith, Rudy Sil, Alex Weisiger, Loren Goldman, Julia Gray, Jeff Green, Ryan Brutger, Anne Norton, Mike Horowitz, Brendan O'Leary, Dan Gillion, Ian Lustick, Jessica Stanton, Minyuan Zhao, Emily Hannum, Guobin Yang, Eunji Kim, Maria Repnikova, Sungmin Rho, Xian Huang, Mona Morgan-Collins, Binn Cho, Siyao Li, Seung-Youn Oh, Yuanyuan Zeng, and many others for their insights and friendship. Students in my authoritarian politics seminar also provided valuable comments.

Bruce Dickson, Stan Markus, Tom Pepinsky, and Kellee Tsai attended my book workshop and provided constructive feedback and much-appreciated support. At various stages of the project, I have received helpful feedback from Adam Berinsky, Sarah Bush, Lisa Blaydes, Jie Chen, Ling Chen, Fotini Christia, Chris Clary, Laura Chirot, Greg Distelhorst, Sofia Fenner, Jeremy Ferwerda, Diana Fu, Tim Frye, Jennifer Gandhi, Mary Gallagher, Chad Hazlett, Rosie Hsueh, Haifeng Huang, Yusaku Horiuchi, Jean Hong, Kyle Jaros, Junyan Jiang, Gary King, James Kung, Xiaojun Li, Krista Loose, Hanzhang Liu, Lizhi Liu, Peter Lorentzen, Xiaobo Lü, Xiao Ma, Eddy Malesky, Melanie Manion, Sofie Marien, Daniel Mattingly, Nick Miller, Andy Nathan, Ben Noble, Kevin O'Brien, Jean Oi, Jennifer Pan, Minxin Pei, Liz Perry, Meg Rithmire, Molly Roberts, Frances Rosenbluth, Dan Slater, Ben Ross Schneider, Niloufer Siddiqui, Victor Shih, Milan Svolik, Tariq Thachil, Daniel Treisman, Rory Truex, Yuhua Wang, Jeremy Wallace, Susan Whiting, Colin Xu, Yiqing

Xu, Teppei Yamamoto, John Yasuda, and Changdong Zhang. I am very grateful to my undergraduate professors at Grinnell College, especially Eliza Willis and Janet Seiz, for encouraging me to pursue a career in political science.

For my fieldwork in China, I am indebted to all my interviewees in the private sector, who generously shared their stories of successes and struggles with me, and to those in the government, who spoke about their work in great detail. Special thanks go to Biliang Hu, Junzhi He, Chuanmin Chen, Yang Zhong, Fei Yan, Minxin Liu, Qi Zhang, and Yongtao Li for sharing their knowledge and for inviting me to their institutions. I thank Yao Yao and Tingting Fan for their excellent research assistance.

At Cambridge University Press, my editor Sara Doskow has patiently guided me through the publishing process. I am grateful for the financial support of the Penn Political Science Department, the Center for the Study of Contemporary China, the MIT Political Science Department and Center of International Studies, and the Chiang Ching-kuo Foundation for International Scholarly Exchange Doctoral Grant.

This book is dedicated to my family. My grandpa, who invited – or forced – me to watch the evening news while having dinner when I was a toddler, is the earliest influence on my interest in political and social issues. My parents have accomplished many achievements in their own careers while raising me. Their work has provided me with first-hand insights on the Chinese economy, and they are always interested in learning about what I study. Peichun has been cheering me on as I approach the finish line. He has made this a finer book and will continue to make me a better scholar.

Abbreviations

ACFIC   All China Industry and Commerce Federation
CCP   Chinese Communist Party
CPPCC   Chinese People's Political Consultative Conference
LPC   Local people's congress
MP   Member of Parliament
NPC   National People's Congress
NPCSC   National People's Congress Standing Committee
PC   people's congress
PLA   People's Liberation Army
PRC   People's Repubic of China
PRI   The Institutional Revolutionary Party (Mexico)
SCIO   The State Council Information Office
SME   Small and Medium Enterprise
SOE   State-Owned Enterprise
TVE   Township and Village Enterprise
VCP   Vietnamese Communist Party (Vietnam)
VPI   Vertical Political Intergration

Introduction

In March 2015, Wu Hai, the CEO of national hotel chain Crystal Orange in China, published an open letter addressed to Premier Li Keqiang entitled "I am so frustrated after doing business for many years!"[1] The letter openly criticizes the government's preferential treatment of state-owned enterprises (SOEs) and companies with good connections, and explicitly discusses how government agencies selectively enforce laws and regulations. The letter went viral immediately and was well received by many private entrepreneurs who face similar problems. Many of Wu Hai's frustrations relate to predatory behavior by officials.

[C]an you (Premier Li) believe that whenever the "Three Festivals" take place, all relevant government agencies in City A start to become active and most of their bureaucrats are coming out to every single company to conduct the so-called inspections.[2] Of course, companies with good connections can bargain [meaning to pay less to these government agencies], and sometimes those "special taxes" can be waived.

But maybe you would wonder why among the thousands of entrepreneurs in City A, nobody dared to voice our discontent. Because we all know very well that once we do, our company will be finished.

He goes on to describe different kinds of predatory behavior through random enforcement of rules:

---

[1] *Forbes China*, March 24, 2015. "Wu Hai, the CEO of Crystal Orange, Complains to the Premier: I am too frustrated for many years" (*Juzi Shuijing CEO Wu Hai Xiang Zongli Jiaoqu: Chuangye Zheme Duonian, Wo Tai Biequ Le*). www.forbeschina.com/news/news.php?id=41541&page=1&lan=zh. Last accessed November 8, 2017.

[2] The "Three Festivals" are traditional Chinese festivals: the Duan Wu, the Mid-Autumn, and the Spring festivals. They are all Chinese national holidays.

1. Fines: "Initially, the bureau (unspecified in the letter) wanted to fine us 50,000 yuan. We found someone to lobby for us and eventually we paid a 25,000 yuan fine. What I wanted to ask is: under what condition would the fine be 2,000, and when would it be 50,000 yuan? Why not make the policy more clear-cut? If we had a more 'useful' person to lobby for us, we would only have been fined the minimal 2,000 yuan."

2. Permits: "The commission of housing and urban–rural development requires all real estate developers to use the bidding companies affiliated with the commission to bid for construction teams. Even if we have good construction teams we have worked with in the past, we are required to use their bidding company to select the construction team we have already worked with before. Otherwise we would not get the permit."

3. Identity credentials: "The police bureau requires all hotel guests and visitors to present a valid ID. It is a good policy, but the police bureau gives us all sorts of problems when implementing the policy. The police bureau can fine us hundreds or thousands of yuan as they wish. Why don't they stipulate a clear rule about how much the fines should be?" ... "There are so many ambiguous policies and regulations. There is no standard and that makes law enforcement unpredictable. We have to maintain good relationships with all relevant agencies and bureaucracies, and they create fear among us."

The Chinese economy has been growing at a spectacular rate of 9.6 percent since the 1980s.[3] By 2018, more than 50 percent of the country's total tax revenue, over 60 percent of gross domestic product (GDP), and more than 80 percent of the country's employment was contributed by the private sector (Hou 2019) and by privately owned companies such as Crystal Orange hotel.[4] Although big and successful private firms, such as Alibaba, Huawei, and Lenovo, seldom complain about government capriciousness, millions of Chinese private entrepreneurs face the heavy-handed government regulation, expropriation, and corruption described in CEO Wu's letter on a daily basis.

---

[3] According to Justin Yifu Lin's calculation. See "The Economics of China's New Era" *Project Syndicate*. www.project-syndicate.org/onpoint/the-economics-of-china-s-new-era-by-justin-yifu-lin-2017-12. Last accessed December 11, 2017.

[4] You probably have never heard of the Crystal Orange Hotels. If you ever traveled to China, chances are that you did not stay in one of the Orange hotels. Besides the international brands such as the Four Seasons and the Ritz-Carltons, China's hotel market also has many formidable domestic players such as the Wanda Group and the down-market Home Inns and Hotels Management. The Orange Hotels group is a medium-size boutique hotel chain operating in six cities in China.

As this example suggests, property rights remain unprotected in China, and the legal system does not protect private enterprises from government expropriation of property. Numerous scholars have studied how the private sector has managed to grow and prosper despite this institutional disadvantage. This book proposes a new answer: Chinese private entrepreneurs actively seek opportunities within formal political institutions that can protect their business interests. By holding seats in local legislatures, entrepreneurs use their political capital to deter local officials from demanding bribes, ad hoc taxes, and other types of informal payments. In doing so, entrepreneurs are creating a system of selective and predictable property rights.

1.1 DEFINITIONS

Identifying privately owned firms in China is a daunting task, because the ownership structure of Chinese firms is complex, and a large number of private firms "depend wholly or in part on investments or patronage by senior government officials" (Kroeber 2016, 90). Yasheng Huang suggests that characterizing a firm as either private or state owned requires carefully examining how the firm assigns its control rights, which include "the rights to appoint management, (to) dispose of assets, and (to) set the strategic direction of the firm" (Huang 2008, 13).

With these nuances in mind, I use Nicholas Lardy's definition of private enterprises: private enterprises refer to the universe of household businesses, registered private companies, and firms for which the majority or dominant owner is private. Private entrepreneurs are therefore owners of these private enterprises (2014, 4).

There are two types of property: *physical* property such as land and capital, and *intellectual* property such as patents and copyrights. I mainly study the physical property (capital) of urban Chinese private entrepreneurs.

According to Haber et al. (2003), "[a] property right consists of three, conceptually distinct rights: the right to use an asset, the right to earn income from an asset and contract with other individuals regarding that asset, and the right to alienate or sell the asset" (21). Similarly, Frye (2004) defines a property right as "a bundle of rights that include the power to consume, obtain income from, and alienate assets, such as land, labor, or capital." It is useful to distinguish *economic* property rights (which give asset holders the "ability to gain from the asset by consumption or by exchange") from *legal* property rights (which address "what the state assigns to a person") (Barzel 1989, 4). While *legal* property rights are a means of achieving *economic* property rights, legal rights are neither necessary nor sufficient for the existence of economic rights. In the absence of legal safeguards, economic rights may still be valued, but the security of property and the exchange of property need to be self-enforced (Barzel 1989, 4). This book focuses on economic rights in places where legal rights are lacking. Cull and Xu (2005) define two dimensions of the security of property rights: "the risk of expropriation by the government and the ease and reliability of contract enforcement" (118). This book studies the first dimension of secure property rights.

I study institutional change in China's property rights regime by examining how individuals creatively use existing institutional arrangements to generate individualized property rights. These choices about property rights, as Susan Whiting points out, are also shaped by the incentives of local state officials and the broader political and economic environments. Property security can be operationalized by measuring the reduction in amount of expropriation imposed by local government bureaucrats on private businesses (Whiting 2004, chapter 4). Here, I define expropriation as government bureaucrats forcefully and unlawfully confiscating or devaluing a firm's assets. In a similar vein, Johns and Wellhausen (2016) use the terms "indirect expropriation" and "creeping expropriation" to describe situations in which a government devalues assets by violating its prior commitments to firms, and in their case, foreign firms. In this definition, expropriation does not equal complete nationalization. Partial nationalization is also considered as expropriation. Throughout the book, expropriation is used interchangeably with "predation" and "extraction." In some contexts legal taxation is considered as extraction. In this book, I look only at illegal extraction. Expropriation can be direct and complete (i.e., a government confiscates all assets of a company) or partial and indirect (Thomas and Worrall 1994). In this book, I look only at partial expropriation, because all companies I study were in operation during the research period. Those that experienced complete expropriation (e.g., nationalization) would not have appeared in my sample. Nor do I study cases when a non-state actor (e.g., the mafia) expropriates from a business.

According to a recent survey in China, 51 percent of the private entrepreneurs surveyed still reported that they faced expropriation by local government to some extent.[5] The entrepreneurs I interviewed during the research for this book indicated that property insecurity is

---

[5] The ACFIC Survey (2000–2012). There was no clear change in the level of expropriation over time in this decade. See details about the survey in Chapter 5.

still a major concern. Many entrepreneurs agreed that, although local government has become more service-oriented and now treats the private sector with more respect, many lower-level bureaucrats are still "very ruthless (*ye man*) in getting what they want" and there is "nothing one could do but cooperate" (Interviews P125; P135; P137).

From the perspective of private entrepreneurs, local governments impose two types of "expropriations" (Dai 2008; Fan 1995; Li and Gong 2013). The first type is strictly illegal – bureaucrats taking property away from a firm without formal or legal causes. Bureaucrats or government officials who engage in this type of expropriation usually know that such behaviors are illegal and would prefer not to get caught.

Entrepreneurs sometimes describe a second type of expropriation as "selective enforcement of laws and regulations." In contrast to the first type, such selective law enforcement is legal from the perspective of officials and bureaucrats, because they can usually find laws or regulations to support their actions. They often selectively enforce laws or regulations on particular companies.

It is sometimes difficult to determine whether threats of expropriation are legal or illegal. Like cases in Russia and Ukraine, expropriations in China may "include a municipal court issuing an injunction paid for by a competitor; a policeman shutting down some retailers to intimidate others; a local official pressuring a firm to give a job to his relative lest the company lose its operation license" (Markus 2015, 22). Chapter 4 provides more examples I collected during my fieldwork to describe what expropriation looks like in present-day China.

1.2 THE ARGUMENT IN SUM

My core argument is that China's legislative system provides entrepreneurial actors with opportunities to advance their own interests. Chinese private entrepreneurs, who operate their businesses in an environment in which property rights are largely unprotected, seek office in the local legislatures to protect their property. In an environment characterized by asymmetric information about political connections, entrepreneurs who have a local legislative seat indicate their strong political connections with upper-level bureaucrats. This political status deters predatory behavior by lower-level bureaucrats, who fear retribution or punishment from the legislator's political network. In joining local legislatures, private entrepreneurs build a system of selective property rights.

Political participation takes different forms in different regime types. In a functioning democracy, running for public office is one of the many ways to participate in politics. V.O. Key suggests that "the nature of the workings of government depends ultimately on the men who run it. The men we elect to office and the circumstances we create that affect their work determine the nature of popular government" (Key 1956, 10). Therefore, public service in a democracy ought to be treated as "a social obligation, somehow different from other careers, and the responsibilities, duties, and personal conduct of public officials has been regarded somewhat differently from those of people holding positions in the private economy" (Lazear and Rosen 1980, 101). In addition to being motivated by the preferences and qualities of the policies, candidates are also drawn by the perks of office (Besley 2004; Callander 2008; Calvert 1985). In some established democracies, the personal benefits of holding elected offices are alarmingly large (Eggers and Hainmueller 2009; Querubin and Snyder 2013).

With limited avenues for political participation, individuals in authoritarian countries are motivated to seek political office for various reasons. In addition to gaining partial power and perquisites, my theory suggests that, in non-democracies and democracies with weak rule of law, political office provides opportunities for individuals to secure individualized rights – in the case of the Chinese congresses, property rights. Participating in politics has become a process of rights creation.

1.3 CONTRIBUTION TO THE LITERATURE

1.3.1 Property Rights and Economic Growth

Social scientists see private property rights as central to economic development (Acemoglu, Johnson, and Robinson 2001; De Soto 1990; Demsetz 1967; North and Thomas 1973; North 1981). Secured property rights restrict governments' expropriation of wealth and protect private assets. They promote investment in three ways. First, freedom from expropriation promotes investment, because individuals do not worry that others will seize the fruits of their investment. Second, more secure rights make it easier to use assets as collateral, and thus to increase liquidity in the economy and to relax the constraints on funding investment (Besley 1995). Third, secure property rights free up resources invested in protecting assets for more productive investment (Field 2007; Wibbels, Krishna, and Sriram 2016).

Yet in some cases the costs of creating a formal property rights regime outweigh the benefits, and a partial property rights system might be more conducive to growth given the poor quality of other complementary institutions (Trebilcock and Veel 2008). When the market environment is highly uncertain, the regulatory environment is unclear, and the transaction costs of creating rights are high, ambiguous property rights might be more efficient than unambiguously defined private property rights (Li 1996).

Accepting these premises, scholars such as Dani Rodrik argue against the simplistic "best-practice" approach to development and propose that developing countries might instead need "second-best" mindsets and institutions that are context specific (Rodrik 2008). To cope with the absence of property rights, entrepreneurs in Russia and Ukraine form alliances with various stakeholders around their firms (Markus 2015), and/or have frequent contacts with private protection rackets (Frye and Zhuravskaya 2000). In Peru, property is secured not by formal but by all sorts of informal and extralegal arrangements. In countries like Ghana and Vietnam where legal recourse is lacking, firms rely on relational contracting to build long-term and personalized relationships and sustain cooperation through repeated interactions (Rodrik 2008).

In China, despite the under-development of secure property rights and the rule of law, the economy has still managed to grow at a rapid rate. Yingyi Qian reasons that China's "transitional institutions" have been able to "improve economic efficiency by unleashing the standard force of incentives" (Qian 2002).[6] My book advances this literature in two ways: first, it carefully describes a selective property rights system and provides micro-level evidence that such a system sustains economic growth in the short (and even medium) run. Second, although I concur that at a certain stage in a country's development, full property rights increase economic efficiency, I argue that a selective property rights regime might not just be a "transitional institution." Given other institutional constraints, such as an uncertain regulatory environment, a selective property rights regime could be the first-best solution.

---

[6] On the other hand, Yasheng Huang argues that China's growth experience is more conventional than others have suggested. In the 1980s, even if there was little protection of property security, there was "security of the proprietor" (Huang 2008, especially see chapter 2).

1.3.2 Property Protection

The view of an authoritarian state as "the grabbing hand" and a "stationary bandit" is not unique to China: scholars of business–state relations have identified violations of property rights by state agencies in many economies (Frye and Shleifer 1997; North et al. 2013; Olson 1993; Tilly 1985). Friedman and colleagues, using data from 69 countries (many of them developing economies in Eastern Europe and Latin America), find that entrepreneurs in countries with heavy burdens of corruption and bureaucracy are more likely to divert some resources to the unofficial economy to avoid extortionate and arbitrary demands (Friedman et al. 2000). More nuanced country-level studies have been conducted on specific cases (Gans-Morse 2017b; Markus 2012; Rithmire 2015; Shleifer and Vishny 2002, chapter 9). In these systems in which property rights are weakly secured, how do firms fend off the grabbing hands of local bureaucrats? Previous studies have documented various ways in which private firms defend their property rights from expropriation by the state or powerful elites. In these cases, since formal protection is usually either unavailable or ineffective, firms usually resort to one of the following informal means.

First, when formal institutions fail to function, one default option is to resort to *private or corrupt force,* such as the criminal protection rackets and private security agencies that played a central role in property security in early 1990s Russia. Corrupt force includes protection rackets provided by bureaucrats and law enforcement officials, which in Russia replaced criminal protection rackets by the late 1990s. Using state resources, these protection rackets provided private clients with property protection (Gans-Morse 2017b).

Second, firms may resort to forging *informal connections and exchanges.* David Wank documents that in the 1980s China, private firms invited "backstage bosses" – public officials – to join their firms as advisors, shareholders, and board members so that these bosses could assist their businesses with information on business-related policy, lowering tax bills, and preventing government expropriation (Wank 1999).[7] Another important channel of connection is kinship, which provides

---

[7] These "backstage bosses" can still be observed in the current Chinese economy. In 2011, 49.3 percent of all SOE firms listed in the Chinese stock market have hired retired government officials. See *the Southern Weekly* for a news report at www.infzm.com/content/60155. Last accessed August 1, 2016.

entrepreneurs with access to resources (Ruf 1999). Entrepreneurs with relatives in government share similar privileges with entrepreneurs who hired backstage bosses.

Third, private actors might use *non-state arbitrators*, such as business associations, to enforce property rights. In the late medieval period, merchant guilds helped protect their members from abuses by city governments by coordinating punitive actions against predators (Greif, Milgrom, and Weingast 1994). In a similar fashion, business associations in Russia provide property security exclusively to their members by establishing norms of transactions and resolving disputes when necessary (Gans-Morse 2017b).

Fourth, firms sometimes creatively construct *partial ownership structures* and forge *sponsorships* that protect their property and property rights. For instance, in China, "backyard profit centers" of state agencies are entities registered as independent public enterprises that are managed by incumbent or former public officials or persons they trust. These relatively undocumented entities receive favorable regulatory and funding treatment from, or with the help of, their government-sponsoring agencies and *de facto* state protection for their private property rights (Lin and Zhang 1999). In the 1990s, entrepreneurs could also seek partial local government ownership of their businesses, which helped limit state predation (Che and Qian 1998; Oi 1992). This method of ownership disguise ceased to be necessary when the private sector was officially recognized first in the 15th party congress in 1997 as "important component" of a socialist market economy and in the country's constitution in 1999 (Dickson 2008, 39).

Fifth, firms can make *alliances with stakeholders* such as foreign investors, regional communities, and organized labor to protect property rights through exerting pressure on the state (Markus 2012; 2015). This strategy points to the conceptual watershed among different protection strategies discussed in the literature: joining the state (either formally or informally) versus counterbalancing the state (through stakeholder alliances or business associations).

In present-day China, private entrepreneurs have a toolbox of strategies to protect themselves. They still actively engage in informal connections and exchanges (Chen 2018; Kennedy 2005; Pei 2016); they sometimes use political connections to facilitate the use of the courts (Ang and Jia 2014; Wang 2015); they creatively register themselves as foreign investors and use "round-tripping" to avoid heavy taxation and regulation (Xiao 2004); they continue to partner with the state and foreign investors (Huang 2005); they obtain Chinese Communist Party (CCP) memberships to develop ties with the party elites (Dickson 2008); and they rely on organizations such as business associations (Kennedy 2005). In this book, I do not dismiss any of these strategies as ineffective or unimportant. Instead, I propose an important addition to the "toolbox" of strategies: Chinese entrepreneurs, in addition to using many informal coping strategies, join legislatures to protect their property from predation.

Ishow that this strategy is different from others in two important respects. First, compared to strategies that rely heavily on informal political connections, the strategy of using one's legislator status to protect property can be purely formal. An entrepreneur does not have to go through any informal exchange to establish or enhance his political capital once he has a seat in the legislature. In this process, legislators use their political position to defend their property rights as well as to legislate. A second distinction is its relatively cost-effective nature. Although securing a legislative seat might incur high costs, once an entrepreneur has a seat in the legislature, his position serves as a signaling mechanism to deter potential predators without any additional investments. The informal strategies described above, such as forging informal connections or relying on partial ownership, can only be sustained through iterated and costly interactions between entrepreneurs and other political entities.

In contrast to existing approaches that view the emergence of property rights as outcomes of efficiency pursuits or state mandates, this book contributes to a new theoretical approach that sees the emergence of and changes in property rights regimes as outcomes of political interactions (Haber, Razo, and Maurer 2003; Rithmire 2015). This approach better explains why property rights are sometimes provided as private goods rather than public goods and how a selective property right system does not necessarily sacrifice efficiency in the short or even medium run.

1.3.3 Authoritarian Institutions

Earlier scholarship on authoritarian institutions views authoritarian legislatures as "rubber-stamp" institutions that are symbolic but have little impact on policy. Rustow (1985) sees legislative elections as a merely "political tactic" that "pay[s] homage to virtue" in the authoritarian Middle East. Magaloni (2006) argues that elections help the Institutional

Revolutionary Party (PRI), Mexico's dominant party, to establish an "image of invincibility" and deter potential opponents from entering the political market. In the same vein, Geddes (2008) argues that rubber-stamp parties and elections remind potential opponents of the difficulty of overthrowing the regime and thus help deter coups.

In the midst of the recent "institutional turn in comparative authoritarianism," there has been a surge in scholarly work attempting to explain how elites use political institutions to structure political power (Pepinsky 2014). A rich body of literature suggests that authoritarian institutions co-opt the opposition or potential opposition by making policy concessions and by sharing power and rents (Blaydes 2011; Boix and Svolik 2013; Gandhi and Przeworski 2007; Gandhi 2008; Lust-Okar 2006; Magaloni 2008; Malesky and Schuler 2010; Svolik 2009). An emerging line of scholarship views authoritarian legislatures as an important source of information on regime stability, public opinion, and policy implementation. Compared to government officials in democratic regimes, autocrats face greater challenges in collecting information about the behavior of their local agents, public approval of policies, and sources of discontent (Lorentzen 2013). Autocrats respond to these informational challenges with a variety of information-gathering institutions including partially free media and selective censorship (Distelhorst 2013; Egorov, Guriev, and Sonin 2009; King et al. 2013; Lorentzen 2014; Stockmann 2013), technological and human surveillance (Morozov 2012), public opinion polling (Henn 1998), constituency services (Distelhorst and Hou 2017), and limited electoral contests (Xu and Yao 2014). Moreover, legislatures in authoritarian regimes matter not only to regime survival but also to policy outcomes. Legislatures and elections could introduce the opposition's reform agenda and help broaden the support of such agenda (Falleti 2011). Policy reforms, in the event of decentralization, have consequences "on the posterior processes of institutional reform" (Falleti 2011, 158).

By bringing in the perspective of "institutions as resources" (Hall and Thelen 2009), this book enriches the discussion of comparative authoritarianism. Rather than examining how institutions serve autocrats' objectives, I study how muchless powerful individuals participate in nominally democratic political institutions and use these institutions as resources to advance their interests. I show that institutions in authoritarian contexts can serve a purpose that their creators do not foresee.

1.4 METHODOLOGY AND DATA

I collect information on Chinese legislatures and legislators, private entrepreneurs, and their strategies to protect property using a mixed-methods approach. I combine quantitative survey data with 108 in-depth interviews and two audit experiments. Each method covers a variety of regions in China. I supplement these materials with official documents, news reports, and secondary sources. The chapter appendices provide additional details: on the conduct of the interviews (appendix to Chapter 4), on the surveys (Chapter 5), and on the experiments (Chapter 6).

To understand the business environment of private entrepreneurs and state–business relations in China, I conducted 108 in-depth and semi-structured interviews with Chinese private entrepreneurs, government officials, scholars, and journalists during 16 months of field research between 2012 and 2016, across five provinces in China. These interviews were arranged through a combination of local government and academic contacts, as well as my own solicitations. All interviewees were guaranteed anonymity. These interviews were conducted in Chinese, semi-structured, and each lasted between 30 minutes and a few hours. The four provinces – Zhejiang, Guangdong, Hunan, Guizhou – and Beijing and Shanghai were selected to reflect important differences between coastal and inland provinces in terms of economic and private sector development, as well as regional differences in institutional arrangements and government capacity. Zhejiang and Guangdong Provinces, located in coastal China, are the richest provinces in the country,[8] and both have a vibrant and sizable private sector. Local governments in these provinces have a reputation for being "business friendly" and "service oriented." Hunan and Guizhou Provinces, located in central and western China, respectively, have smaller economies and less-developed private sectors. Governments in these provinces are reputed to be less friendly towards businesses.[9] I also spoke with local scholars studying similar topics in Beijing and Shanghai. These in-depth interviews not only helped me develop a deep understanding of everyday business–state

---

[8] *The Phoenix Finance News*, February 2, 2015. "Local GDP Once Again Add Up to 4.8 Trillion Yuan Higher than the National GDP, Smallest Discrepancy in Recent Years" (*Gedi GDP Zaichao Quanguo 4.8 Wanyi, "Shuifen" Yishi Jinnian Zuishao*). http://finance.ifeng.com/a/20150202/13475261_0.shtml. Last accessed November 8, 2017.

[9] For one example, see the Institutional Indices in Li, Meng, and Zhang (2006).

FIGURE 1.1 Provinces and cities where I conducted interviews

Note. Provinces and cities where I conducted interviews are: Beijing, Shanghai, Zhejiang Province, Hunan Province, Guangdong Province, and Guizhou Province. They are highlighted on the map.

interactions and a theory of property protection in the Chinese context, they also highlighted broad patterns and scope conditions for my theory on property protection in transitional economies.

After developing a basic understanding of business–state interactions based on observations in these locations, I next use a nationally representative survey of private entrepreneurs to exploit variation in entrepreneurs' political participation in China across space and industry and over time (2000–2012) and industry in order to make generalizations about private entrepreneurs and property protection for a broader range of locales. The survey has been conducted every other year jointly by the All China Industry and Commerce Federation (ACFIC), the China Society of Private Economy at the Chinese Academy of Social Science, the United Front Work Department of the Central Committee, and the Communist Party of China ("ACFIC survey" hereafter). The ACFIC survey sampled private entrepreneurs from 31 provinces and all major industries, and is by far the most commonly used Chinese private entrepreneur survey by scholars (e.g., Ang and Jia 2014; Li et al. 2006; Sun, Zhu, and Wu 2014). The questionnaire asks about private entrepreneurs' political statuses, as well as their personal and business backgrounds. Importantly, entrepreneurs were asked how much expropriation by local government they had experienced. Direct interviews were conducted using a questionnaire. The richness of this dataset allows me to analyze the determinants and severity of, as well as the degree of variation in, local-level expropriation. The survey also provides important information on private entrepreneurs' political participation in a variety of political organizations, including congresses, people's political consultative conferences, and other government-affiliated organizations and associations. Such data allows me to compare the effectiveness of political participation in different channels.

With the help of local collaborators, I conducted an original survey in 2013 of local government officials and bureaucrats in ten prefectures in China. The survey covered three provinces in the eastern region and three provinces in the west-central region. A total of 3,120 bureaucrats from the government administrative units and CCP local offices were surveyed, and 2,372 returned our survey, yielding a 76 percent response rate. The survey measured the perceived importance of the private sector in the local economy and invited subjects to discuss the motivations of private entrepreneurs who become involved in politics. Although respondents were clearly informed about the academic nature of the survey, public servants are a particularly risk-averse and politically sensitive population, and readers should interpret their self-reported answers cautiously. Nevertheless, this survey provided a valuable perspective of potential "predators," whom private entrepreneurs often accuse of acting based on their self-interests regardless of property rights.

To further investigate the causal link between formal office and property protection, I conducted two original audit experiments in 2013 and 2014 on Chinese bureaucrats to observe how local bureaucracies respond to citizens with connections to formal institutions in a real-life context. These experiments involve directly contacting officials in order to investigate how they respond to realistic messages from putative private entrepreneurs. Data generated from the experiments allow me to examine behavioral outcomes and, more specifically, officials' preferences regarding individuals with different political statuses and ties, as well as to evaluate whether the signaling mechanism I proposed in the theory is in fact at work.

1.5 LOOKING AHEAD

Chapter 2 elaborates the logic of selective property rights in authoritarian regimes. Drawing on theories of property rights and economic growth, it discusses why autocrats might prefer a system of selective and predictable property rights to universal property rights. I illustrate that profit-maximizing property holders do not necessarily need to conduct their business where property rights are fully protected. If the expected return on asset is large enough to offset the risk of expropriation, a property holder might choose to stay and invest in a country with insecure property rights. This selective rights system, if designed well, produces sustained revenue for the state and rents to political elites, benefits a select group of asset holders, and generates economic growth and political stability. However, the implicit contract between political elites and economic elites can be difficult to sustain. Since property holders lack legal protection, they must seek alliances with political elites and find ways to enhance their property security on an individual basis. The argument delineates how private entrepreneurs use legislative office to secure property rights and generates important observable implications about the characteristics of political economies under authoritarian rule.

Chapter 3 studies private entrepreneurs in legislative office. How much time do these part-time legislators spend on legislative duties and tasks? Do they actively participate in congressional meetings and hearings? Do they carve out time to interact with their constituents? Besides answering these questions, this chapter also traces the development and examines the functions of China's legislative system. It describes how local legislators are elected and how competitive this process is. It also discusses legislators' responsibilities and rights, and shows that their formal power is still largely nominal. This chapter also introduces the Chinese People's Political Consultative Conferences (CPPCC), the "lower house" of the people's congresses. While CPPCCs also provide networking opportunities for private entrepreneurs, entrepreneurs can build much stronger political connections in the people's congresses.

Chapters 4–6 test three empirical implications derived from my theoretical argument and illustrate how Chinese private entrepreneurs use legislative office to deter expropriation and secure property rights. Chapter 4 focuses on the motivations of private entrepreneurs joining politics. The chapter shows that private entrepreneurs believe that holding a legislative seat protects their property from expropriation, and this protection effect is one of their main motives for entering into politics.

Drawing on interviews with private entrepreneurs who are legislators and also those who are not, this chapter establishes the empirical observation that entrepreneurs see predation as a major problem in developing businesses in China, and that securing property has become a main motivation for them to seek legislative office. This chapter closes by surveying a small but valuable sample of legislative and policy proposals from entrepreneur–legislators. This analysis shows that legislators intentionally avoid discussing issues related to property rights. Property rights security has not yet become a collective issue among these well-connected entrepreneurs.

Is holding a legislative seat an effective way to protect individual property? Chapter 5 evaluates the "effectiveness" implication, that is, whether legislator status indeed provides property protection for entrepreneur–legislators. I evaluate this argument by using a large national survey of private business owners combined with original survey and interview evidence. My analysis of a national survey of private entrepreneurs shows that those who serve in the local legislatures save a significant portion of business expenses on informal payments to local governments. A legislative seat protects private businesses from government expropriation, and local legislatures generate selective property rights. Finally, I propose an "insurance premium" framework to describe entrepreneurs' decisions to enter a local legislative race: the price individuals pay to secure congressional seats buys them "insurance" against complete expropriation.

How exactly do entrepreneurs marshal their political capital when dealing with government officials and receive preferential treatment? Chapter 6 answers this question, first through interview evidence and case studies, by showing that the formal power associated with holding a legislative seat is insufficient to explain a legislator's ability to deter expropriation from local bureaucrats. I then argue that the key mechanism is the political capital associated with their position: legislative membership sends a credible signal of high political connectedness to low-level bureaucrats, deterring them from expropriation. I test this mechanism with two original national audit experiments in which I directly contacted prefectural tax collectors and examine how they respond to information requests from local entrepreneurs with and without political connections to local congresses. This evidence sheds further light on how entrepreneurs use their political titles to signal strong political capital and protect their assets.

The concluding chapter offers an overview of the argument and reviews the main empirical findings. It closes by discussing what the model of selective property rights means for China's long-term growth and prospects for political reform.

2

Selective Property Rights

A system of fully protected property rights is usually associated with strong economic growth: it enhances individuals' investment incentives, increases their access to credit, and generates efficiency gains by freeing up producers' time that was previously devoted to solidifying informal claims (Acemoglu, Johnson, and Robinson 2001; Besley 1995; De Soto 2000; Field 2007; Frye 2004; Johnson, McMillan, and Woodruff 2002; North 1973; Olson 1993). Any government or political elite interested in delivering economic growth should be motivated to grant property rights to their producers and investors. Haber (2008) suggests that understanding the relationship between property rights and economic growth is imperative for understanding the logic of authoritarianism. But there is a fundamental economic dilemma, stated most clearly by Barry Weingast: "[a] government that is strong enough to protect property and enforce contracts is also strong enough to confiscate the wealth of its citizens" (Weingast 1993). Especially in an autocratic state, political elites who control the government represent a constant threat to the property of those who lack political rights (Ansell and Samuels 2014).

Instead of granting individuals property rights, a government can also revoke all property rights and generate revenue from those properties. It is difficult for leaders in a democracy to do so, because they face electoral as well as legal and institutional constraints. The law might prohibit them from expropriating or nationalizing private property, and voters can punish them by voting them out. The calculation is trickier for leaders in autocracies. They usually stay, or at least expect to stay, in power for an extended period of time. This time horizon prevents them from expropriating all property and destroying the economy to achieve short-term gains, which is what a "roving bandit" would do (Olson 1993).

Autocrats can thus best be described as "stationary bandits": they are more expropriatory than their democratic counterparts because there are no electoral and fewer institutional checks on their power, but they must sustain economic growth in order to ensure a steady stream of income and therefore resist nationalizing all private property. It is rational for autocrats to grant property rights only to a small portion of the economy, ideally the most productive sectors, and to expropriate from those that are less productive. Thus rather than enforcing property rights universally, autocratic governments can selectively grant such rights to property holders as private goods.

This chapter elaborates the logic of selective property rights in authoritarian regimes. The theory can also be extended to developing democracies with weak property rights. I illustrate that profit-maximizing property holders may find it more profitable to conduct their business in countries where property rights are only protected selectively. This partial rights system, if designed well, produces sustained revenue for the state and rents for political elites, benefits a select group of asset holders, and generates economic growth and political stability. However, the implicit contract between the political and economic elites can be difficult to sustain. Since property holders lack legal protection, they must seek alliances with political elites and find ways to enhance their property security on individual bases. My argument then delineates how private entrepreneurs use legislative office as a new "red hat" to secure property rights in China.

2.1 WHY PROPERTY HOLDERS ACCEPT INCOMPLETE PROPERTY RIGHTS

Where universal property rights are guaranteed, asset holders feel safe to produce and invest. Yet all property holders do not necessarily demand universal property rights: a selective but predictable property rights system might benefit an asset holder even more if his own property is protected but his competitors' properties are not. A high risk of expropriation makes a competitor's assets less liquid and valuable; property insecurity might even drive a competitor out of the market. In this scenario, the protected asset holder could make a higher profit than he could under a system of full property rights, because this partial system disadvantages his competitors.

Therefore, instead of a "second-best" solution, a selective but predictable property system could present a first-best institution for an autocrat and a select group of asset holders. This institution supplies the autocrat with a steady stream of income from the protected sectors and individuals, as well as rents extracted from those who do not have property rights. This select group of asset holders enjoys exclusive protection of their property rights, and their assets are likely to grow more valuable. If this group happens to be the most productive sector of the economy, this selective property rights system could be relatively efficient as a whole.[1] Of course, this system does not benefit those with unprotected assets, and it produces negative welfare consequences in terms of the distribution of income. Therefore, it is not necessarily a Pareto-improving solution compared to a system of no property rights, because those who are not protected might face more severe expropriation.[2]

Actors in this system of selective property rights face a central challenge: the commitment problem. If an autocrat does not grant everyone property rights, how would any property holder trust that the autocrat would honor his commitment? The nature of a selective property rights system means that rights are unlikely to be protected under or by the law; most likely there is not a trustworthy system of rule of law. Haber, Razo, and Maurer (2003) propose ways in which such a commitment can be made credible between an autocrat and an asset holder. The first is "when the government earns more from imposing the profit-maximizing tax rate than it would earn from abrogating the asset holder's property rights and running the industry itself" (24). This self-enforcing mechanism is difficult to sustain, because it assumes that the autocrat acknowledges that he is less capable than asset holders to run the industry efficiently, and is humble enough to operate accordingly.

Another solution is to have a third party to enforce the commitment. This third-party actor would have to be incentivized and capable of punishing the government in the event of a breach of contract. The incentive, for instance, could be rents in exchange for enforcing the contract. As Haber et al. (2003) point out, it is difficult to strike a balance between the third party, the government, and asset holders. If the third party is too

---

[1] Trebilcock and Veel (2008) point out that in certain cases, the costs of creating a formal property rights regime outweigh the benefits, especially when other supporting institutions are not in place.

[2] A Pareto improvement is any change to the economy that leaves everyone at least as well off and someone strictly better off.

weak, it cannot credibly threaten to punish the government; if it is too powerful, it will also be a threat to asset holders. Further, the third party could collude with the government and jointly expropriate the assets (28).

Haber et al. (2003) describe a partial property rights regime called the Vertical Political Integration (VPI) system, in which the government and property holders are so integrated that the line between the government and private asset holders becomes blurred. In a VPI regime, the government might ask a select group of asset holders to write or advise on business policies or hold leadership positions in executive agencies. The integration could also be informal: a dictator could simply choose his cronies and lend his ear. The VPI model alleviates the commitment problem because a small group of asset holders could potentially shape economic policies and closely monitor the government to ensure it does not alter these policies (31).

By their account, the partial property rights system was crucial in facilitating Mexico's economic take-off during the term of President Porfirio Diaz (1876–1911). Haber et al. (2003) document how Diaz defined and protected the property rights of a select group of property holders. The Diaz government gave special privileges to a small group of individuals and created barriers to entry for all others. It also encouraged local political leaders to enter business, and turned political enemies into third-party property rights enforcers; companies that received preferential treatment routinely invited politicians to serve on their boards of directors to facilitate the transfer of rents (chapter 4). In this partial property rights system, government commitments were not made according to the rule of law, but based "on the generation and sharing of rents among a coalition of economic and political elites" (Haber et al. 2003, 51).

This VPI system makes it more costly for the government to deviate from its contracts with asset holders, but it does not solve the commitment problem. The government cannot credibly commit not to dissolve its commitment to protect the property rights of the select group of asset holders.

In post-Soviet Russia and Ukraine, where threats to property remain severe, firms secure their property rights through alliances with stakeholders, such as foreign investors and local communities (Markus 2015).[3]

---

[3] Gans-Morse (2017a) documents that firms in Russia are increasingly using formal legal channels to secure property rights.

Foreign stakeholders help strengthen firms' property security through backdoor lobbying and leveraging international courts and legal structures against domestic predators, while domestic alliances often involve high-ranking officials to sanction their predatory subordinates (Markus 2015, chapter 6). Not all companies have access to such valuable resources, and as Markus shows, alliances do not always succeed in protecting firms. Nevertheless, firms that have more domestic and international alliances feel that their properties are more secure. Firms still operate their businesses in an economy with insecure property rights, and the state does not promise not to abrogate their property rights. Yet capable and connected firms build an alliance-based defense mechanism that decreases the risk of being expropriated and increases their perception of property security.

2.2 AUTOCRATS CANNOT COMMIT CREDIBLY BUT CAN BE PREDICTABLE

These cases illustrate that in a partial property rights system, it is very difficult for the government to make a credible commitment to protect a group's property rights. The solutions of a third-party enforcer or blurring the line between the government and business are unstable, because the government is not bound by legal institutions, and autocracies lack an electorate to hold the government to account for honoring its commitments to property holders. If property holders are aware of this commitment problem, why would they choose to keep their assets in the country and continue to produce, given the constant threat of expropriation?

A property holder constantly runs the risk that his property rights may be abrogated against the benefit of staying in the country and earning an income from his property.[4] Consider Entrepreneur Erik, who owns assets worth $100. In country A, Erik's assets are expected to yield an annual return of $10. In country B, they are expected to yield an annual return of $50, and in country C, the expected yield is $55 per year. Now, let us assume that country A enjoys full protection of property and thus the risk of expropriation is zero. In country C, there is no property protection and expropriation is rampant, while in country B, the government made

---

[4] I only use male pronouns to describe entrepreneurs, politicians, and bureaucrats, because the majority of them are male. Unspecified gender pronouns also help protect the identities of my interviewees.

an implicit contract with Erik not to expropriate his assets, but he has to give the government a $5 side payment. Let us also assume that there is no tax in any of the three systems, and that Erik plans to sell his business after one year. In country A, Erik is expected to make $10 after one year, after which his total asset value will be $110 ($100 + $10). In country B, Erik is 80 percent confident that the government will honor the contract not to expropriate his assets. His total expected asset value a year from now is $125 ($100 * 0.8 + $45). In country C, Erik is worried that the government will nationalize his property any time: he believes there is a 50 percent probability that it will do so during the course of the year. Therefore, his expected total asset value is $105 ($100 * 0.5 + $55). Country B gives Erik the highest expected total asset value in a year. As a rational profit-maximizing business owner, Erik would choose to operate his business in a partial property rights system (country B) over a system with full property rights (A) or one with very little protection of property rights (C). This example might explain why some investors choose to start a business in China instead of the United States or Chad.[5]

This example demonstrates that profit-maximizing property holders do not necessarily choose to operate their business in a country that guarantees the full protection of property rights. Given a certain level of return on asset, an entrepreneur would always prefer a system in which the likelihood of expropriation is low, but the probability does not have to be as low as zero. If the expected return on asset is large enough to offset the risk of expropriation, a business owner might even choose a system with insecure property rights (country B over A, in the example above). In an autocracy or a developing democracy where the government has no credible commitment to bind its hands, a property holder might lower his assessment of the risk of expropriation if two conditions are met: (i) the government is predictable in its expropriatory behavior (see also Stasavage 2002) and (ii) he observes that property owners with certain characteristics are less likely to be expropriated.

In the remainder of the book, I show that during the reform period (1978–present), the Chinese government is expropriatory, but predictable in its expropriatory behaviors. This predictability gives entrepreneurs

---

[5] According to the World Bank "Doing Business Report" published in 2017, Chad ranks 180th on the ease of doing business, China ranks 78th, and the United States ranks 8th. Available at www.doingbusiness.org/reports/regional-reports. Last accessed September 12, 2017. China has steadily moved up in the ease of doing business ranking: in 2019, China ranks 46th in the same World Bank "Doing Business Report".

some confidence that their property will be secure. In the earlier years, private entrepreneurs camouflaged their firms as collective entities or joined the Chinese Communist Party (CCP) to protect their properties; now they compete for seats in local congresses in order to deter expropriation. These individualized responses to insecure property rights generate a system of selective and predictable property rights in China.

2.3 SELECTIVE PROPERTY RIGHTS AND EXPROPRIATION IN CHINA

Since the late 1970s, China has produced an impressive record of economic growth despite a legal system that does not provide secure property rights. Although there have been profound developments in the legal system, law making and law enforcement powers have been concentrated in the hands of the CCP and the governments. The economic reforms remain partial and unfinished (Brandt and Rawski 2008). Property rights are fundamentally unprotected from state predation: there is no credible commitment to prevent national and local governments from expropriating property from private enterprises (Che and Qian 1998; Haggard and Huang 2008; Pei 2016; Whiting 2001).

How did the private sector manage to grow in an environment of insecure property rights? State policy towards the private sector has alternated between "harshness and leniency" (Solinger 1984, 157). This section reviews the private sector development and policy changes in the reform era and surveys forms of institutional and individual responses to insecure property rights.

1978–1989: The pivotal Third Plenum of the Eleventh Central Committee of the Communist Party of China in 1978 marked the beginning of the country's economic reforms. The focus of this initial reform period was on running the state sector in a more efficient manner. In 1981, the State Council established provisions "governing private investment in the form of individual household firms (*getihu*) ... limiting the number of employees to seven" (Clarke, Murrell, and Whiting 2008, 388). Larger private enterprises were still not legitimized until 1988, when the State Council passed the Provisional Regulations on Private Enterprises, which legitimized sole proprietorships, partnerships, and limited liability companies with eight or more employees (Tsai 2006, 128; Whiting 2001, chapter 4).

Private entrepreneurs had two responses to these property rights restrictions, both of which created a partial property rights system that granted a subgroup of entrepreneurs more secure property rights. The first response is the emergence of the township and village enterprises (TVEs), which became the driving force of growth during this period. While private firms were forbidden to operate until 1981, TVEs were relatively unconstrained because of their politically acceptable collective status: community governments are their de facto executive owners (Whiting 2001; Xu 2011). The share of TVEs involved in the country's industrial output increased from 9 percent in 1978 to 27 percent in 1993, while the share of state-owned enterprises declined from 78 to 43 percent (Che and Qian 1998, 467–468).

Jean Oi attributes the rise of TVEs to fiscal reforms and the introduction of the new tax responsibility system, under which local governments submitted a portion of their revenues to upper-level government and kept the rest (Oi 1992, 103). These fiscal arrangements provided local officials with a huge incentive to promote rural industries. Growth allowed officials to get rich without resorting to corruption, and it made their jobs easier by alleviating public budget constraints (Oi 1992, 114). Oi argues that local governments were essentially assigned property rights over income, and that local governments took on the characteristics of a business corporation, with officials acting as the equivalent of a board of directors (Oi 1992, 100). Yasheng Huang contends that these TVEs were essentially private companies in disguise (Huang 2008).

Why would the national government assign property rights to the local government-owned enterprises? Jiahua Che and Yingyi Qian argue that it is in the national government's interests to do so: compared with private enterprises, which have huge incentives to hide revenue in systems without the rule of law, enterprises such as TVEs provided more revenues to governments and spent more on local public goods, which could help increase future revenues and improve social stability (Che and Qian 1998).

Private entrepreneurs' second, more individualized, response to this system is to "wear a red hat": the practice of privately managed and owned enterprises registering as collective ones (Dickson 2008, 37; Oi 1999, 133; Tsai 2006). This arrangement is usually associated with providing a payment to the local government "for protection against predation and to qualify for various benefits available only to the public sector" (Clarke, Murrell, and Whiting 2008, 389). By 1988, when private enterprises were permitted, half a million enterprises were already operating under a red hat (Tsai 2006, 129). Similar to TVEs, wearing a red hat gave private entrepreneurs the legal status to operate where private businesses were not officially allowed, and were at constant risk of being extorted.

1992–present: The Tiananmen Square crisis halted the private sector growth for a couple of years, but the sector started to grow again shortly after Deng Xiaoping's Southern Tour in 1992. In the 1990s, the number of registered private businesses increased 32.8 percent annually, and the rate of employment in the private sector grew 29.2 percent per year (Tsai 2006, 129).

During this period, there has been a series of legal developments and government recognition that further support the development of the private sector. The CCP recognized the private sector as an "important component" of the economy, which was a significant step-up from a "supplemental component." In 2001, Jiang Zemin formally invited private entrepreneurs to join the party. A series of laws were also passed during this time: the Corporate Law (1993); Price Law (1997); Securities Law (1998); Contract Law (1999); Law on Individual Wholly Owned Enterprises (1999); and Property Law (2007).

Despite the profound legal development in recent decades, the current legal system still does not provide a secure system of property rights: "[s]ecure legal rights cannot exist when there is a bewildering array of bodies that have the right or the practical power to make overlapping rules of varying degrees of binding effect and no authoritative body to resolve conflicts" (Clarke, Murrell, and Whiting 2008, 399). Private entrepreneurs are still subject to arbitrary treatment and harassment by tax officials and other bureaucrats on a daily basis, and state and collective businesses continue to receive favorable treatment in terms of tax, bank loans, and the use of land (Tsai 2006, 129).

With the legalization of private enterprises, the TVEs started to privatize and consolidate. By the mid-2000s, more than 90 percent of the TVEs were registered as private enterprises, and the TVE phenomenon "had run its course" (Dickson 2008, 50). This new era has ushered in a new type of "red hat": the rise of "red capitalists" – entrepreneurs who are also CCP members.

Private entrepreneurs were banned from joining the party between 1989 and 2001, yet many CCP members participated in the non-state sector throughout the period of the 1990s (and even during the 1980s). Having a CCP membership made it safer for entrepreneurs to run their businesses (Tsai 2006, 132). These "red capitalists" have easier access to credit, licenses, permits, and many other benefits and resources, and are more likely to "avoid the interference of party and government organizations in their business affairs" (Dickson 2008, 94). Thus compared to firms owned by non-CCP members, those owned by red capitalists usually generate higher sales revenues, hire more employees, and own more fixed assets.

Starting in 2001, the party began to formally welcome private entrepreneurs. Not only do private entrepreneurs become party members, they also set up party units to organize existing members and expand memberships in their companies. Initially, entrepreneurs voluntarily set up party cells within their companies as a gesture of loyalty to local government and party committees. Soon afterwards, the Party Constitution and the Corporate Law of China stipulated that any company with three or more CCP members had to establish a party unit. By mid-2017, party organizations existed in nearly 70 percent of all private companies (Martina 2017).[6]

2.4 USING LEGISLATIVE OFFICE TO PRODUCE PROPERTY RIGHTS

While private entrepreneurs in China have not secured property rights as a group during the reform era, some have secured property rights individually using a variety of methods: they disguised themselves as collective enterprise owners, and became "red capitalists" by joining the CCP and setting up party units within their companies. In Wank's term, they "produced property rights" through innovative actions (Wank 1999, 249). Their property rights are not granted legally or institutionally, but entrepreneurs in these groups enjoyed some degree of confidence that the government would not expropriate their properties. Therefore, they operated their businesses in an environment in which the expected expropriation risk was lower than the market average. Expropriation has become more observably predictable: TVEs and entrepreneurs wearing a red hat are less likely to be expropriated.

This book describes a new method that Chinese private entrepreneurs have invented to produce individualized property rights: seeking local legislative offices. Holding a local legislative seat becomes a new "red hat" strategy: it signals significant (and increasing) levels of political

---

[6] The State Council Information Office (SCIO) states that "company party organizations generally carry out activities that revolve around operations management, can help companies promptly understand relevant national guiding principles and policies, coordinate all parties' interests, resolve internal disputes, introduce and develop talent, guide the corporate culture, and build harmonious labor relations." But Xi's recent mandate to strengthen the party's role in private and foreign companies has caused concern that the party will increase its influence on business operations and decisions (Martina 2017).

capital, which deters government bureaucrats from expropriating the assets of these entrepreneur–legislators. Legislatures thus systematize selective and individualized property security: a seat in congress helps protect an entrepreneur's assets and deters expropriation.

Here, I differentiate protection from rents: unlike other types of economic payoffs, protection from expropriation is not inherently built into the congress system; therefore the ruling elite cannot distribute it to buy the loyalty of the business class. Unlike in Mexico (1876–1911), where Diaz built a rent-sharing system to allocate property rights to a small group of political entrepreneurs (Haber 2008), the CCP does not promise that having a legislative seat translates into property security. Rather than a top-down process, individualized property security is the result of a bottom-up process in which private entrepreneurs invent and experiment as they participate in the political institution. Normatively, rights are also different from rents: in a functioning and just market economy, all business people should have property rights, while no entrepreneur should deserve higher material payoffs (rents) from the government just because of his political connections. Private entrepreneurs in China seek rights as well as rents when they enter politics.

Next, I discuss the preferences of the three main actors in the argument: low-level bureaucrats, high-level bureaucrats, and private entrepreneurs. The strength of an entrepreneur's political connections to high-level officials varies. The entrepreneur knows the strength of his own political connectedness, but low-level bureaucrats do not. Low-level bureaucrats infer the type of entrepreneurs from their political statuses and decide who is safe to extract from. A low-level bureaucrat extracts from an entrepreneur if he believes the entrepreneur's political connections are

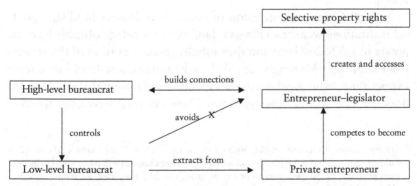

FIGURE 2.1 How entrepreneurs produce property rights using legislative office

weak, and avoids extracting from an entrepreneur if he believes the entrepreneur's political connections are strong. Entrepreneurs with high political capital reveal their type by sinking the cost of running for deputy seats in the local people's congress. The political status of a people's congress deputy delivers a credible signal of strong political connectedness to these low-level bureaucrats, therefore deterring them from expropriations. High-level bureaucrats allow low-level bureaucrats to expropriate from local businesses, but they might punish their subordinates if they expropriate from entrepreneurs with whom they have a friendly relationship.

2.4.1 Low-Level Bureaucrats

Low-level bureaucrats are the agents of their high-level principals. In this book, I define low-level bureaucrats as subnational government bureaucrats who interact with local businesses across all relevant agencies. These bureaucrats are distinct from congressional deputies – they are usually too low-ranked to be a deputy in any local congress. In this stylized argument, I assume that these bureaucrats have two main objectives: to get promoted and to extract rents when possible.[7]

The public choice literature commonly assumes that local bureaucrats have "grabbing hands" – that is, they engage in various forms of corruption to profit personally from their positions (Krueger 1974; Olson 1965; Shleifer and Vishny 2002). While a significant number of local bureaucrats in China are publicly spirited and serve their constituents, many are exploitative and extract rents from local businesses. Many argue that Chinese civil servants naturally seek to supplement their comparatively low salaries by engaging in corrupt practices (Chan and Ma 2011; Lu 2000).

In rural China, the inclusion of community leaders in village political institutions weakens villagers' land rights – village officials have the power to reallocate land and they usually retain a portion of the revenue from land sale (Mattingly 2016). In urban areas, low-level bureaucrats extract rents from local businesses by imposing informal taxes, fees, and fines through ad hoc investigations. These informal payments are often

---

7 On this assumption, one might object that some Chinese local bureaucrats could be publicly spirited, pursuing justice and acting according to moral and ideological principles, even at some cost to their wealth or career prospects. In those cases, we would observe a very low level of extraction.

called *tanpai*, and range from "protection fees" paid to local bureaus, to "pre-paid" taxes collected by local taxation bureaus, and from "forced donations" to, for example, building a new road in the village to ad hoc fines and payments.[8] Kellee Tsai observes that "[i]n any given week, the typical factory owner may be approached by dozens of different agencies requesting seemingly random user charges, surcharges, and contributions for local projects" (Tsai 2004). Chapter 4 presents more examples of such expropriations.

A potential predator could come from any one of many local government bureaus, such as the local taxation bureaus, the administrations for industry and commerce, the environmental protection agencies, administrations of work safety and coal mine safety, administrations of quality supervision, the inspection and quarantine administrations, and the police bureaus. An estimated 2.5 percent of China's population is employed in the local public sector, which is more than twice the global mean of 1.1 percent (Ang 2012). Of these local-level civil servants, 61.8 percent frequently or occasionally interact with local businesses (according to a survey conducted by Hou, Meng, and Yang 2014). Therefore, in a typical Chinese prefectural city with an average population of three million residents, 46,375 local bureaucrats could be potential predators on local businesses.

Income from extraction can either end up in the pockets of line bureaucrats' or be directed to local governments' budgets to support the legitimate provision of public goods (Tsai 2004). It is perhaps more justified to extract from local businesses if this income is invested in public projects, but from the perspective of entrepreneurs, extraction is undesirable and is considered an infringement on their property, regardless of where the money goes.

Yuen Yuen Ang provides an institutional explanation for the prevalence of predation at the local level:

... China's fast-growing economy has not been governed by a purely salaried civil service. Instead, Chinese bureaucracies still remain partially prebendal; at every level of government, each office systematically appropriates authority to generate income for itself. Such a bureaucratic form normally invites predation and hinders capitalism. (Ang 2009, iv)

---

[8] Jia and Mayer (2016) translate *tanpai* as "designated shares" and "unauthorized levies." They find that these levies or financial contributions were "illegal" but distinct from corruption.

Some low-level bureaucrats might have more information than others about the local elite network, but given the large number of entrepreneurs and the possibilities of making connections with different high-level officials, low-level bureaucrats have limited information about each entrepreneur: who might know my boss? Who is politically connected and powerful? Who has friends in his network who might be able to protect him? The answers to these constitute mostly private information unknown to low-level bureaucrats. Facing information constraints, low-level bureaucrats usually find it costly and often impossible to map all business–government connections. In this limited information environment, bureaucrats have to make careful decisions about from whom they might extract rents. A local congress membership is a signal of one's strong local political network. An entrepreneur who is a legislator requires an extensive political network to get elected in the first place, and by holding this position, enhances his access to upper-level officials and the elite network. But since the full extent of that political network is not *observable* to low-level bureaucrats, a low-level bureaucrat is likely to avoid extracting from the business of an entrepreneur–legislator, for fear that the connected entrepreneur might marshal his political capital to retaliate, for example, by reporting to high-level bureaucrats.

Local bureaucrats look for opportunities to extract rents, but they do not want to be reported for preying on businesses and to develop a bad reputation with their superiors. They are more likely to be reported if they expropriate from individuals who have access to high-level bureaucrats who are their principals. Although high-level bureaucrats might not necessarily punish extractive behavior by low-level bureaucrats, complaints from legislators can affect low-level bureaucrats' likelihood of promotion.

2.4.2 High-Level Bureaucrats

High-level bureaucrats are the superiors of low-level bureaucrats.[9] Principals (high-level bureaucrats) assign agents (low-level bureaucrats) specific tasks and evaluate these agents based on their performance. Just like

---

[9] Here, the terms "superior" and "high-level" are relative. For example, when I study county-level tax collectors, their higher–level bureaucrats would be their direct superiors – county-level tax bureau heads, and their indirect superiors – officials working at the prefectural, provincial, and national tax bureaus. However, when I study prefectural-level tax collectors, the very same "high-level" prefectural tax bureau officials become "low-level bureaucrats" in this case, and their higher–level superiors include their direct superiors – prefectural tax bureau heads, and indirect superiors – officials working at the provincial and national tax bureaus. Indeed, high-level bureaucrats can also engage in extractive activities.

any principal–agent relationship, principals cannot always successfully monitor the behavior of their agents and suffer from problems of hidden information and hidden actions. In this context, a main concern of these principals is that lower-level agents sometimes exploit their offices for private gains.[10] While high-level officials allow subordinates to expropriate from local businesses to a limited extent, they have developed a toolkit of methods to monitor and evaluate their agents to make sure they do not expropriate too much (Edin 2003; Landry 2008; Lü and Landry 2014; Shih, Adolph, and Liu 2012).

Local businesses, as Scott Kennedy points out, are "central to accomplishing government objectives such as a growing economy, stable prices, high employment, and expanding tax receipts" (Kennedy 2009). In resource-scarce areas, business elites represent especially important sponsors for public projects and the functioning of local administration (Lu 2000; Sun, Zhu, and Wu 2014). Patron–client ties are also built based on personal connections. Kennedy observes that "[o]fficials provide entrepreneurs access to scarce goods, credit, government and overseas markets, and protection from onerous regulations. Entrepreneurs, in return, provide officials with payoffs and gifts, employment, and business partnerships" (Kennedy 2005, 10).

High-level bureaucrats have plenty of opportunities to befriend entrepreneurs, but they must choose their relationships carefully. It is "safer" for them to have a friendly relationship with entrepreneurs who serve in the congress. Local legislatures provide a formal channel through which high-level bureaucrats can interact with other legislators, many of whom are successful and therefore rich entrepreneurs. Local political and business elites make connections through formal and informal lectures, parties, meetings, and get-togethers organized by various government bureaus, associations, and individual business elites (Wank 1996). Some of these entrepreneurs already are friends with these high-level bureaucrats, and a legislator status legitimizes an entrepreneur's interactions with high-level officials. New connections are also formed and nurtured through plenary sessions, meetings, visits, tours, and other events related to local congresses, providing opportunities for formal business–government interactions (Sun, Zhu, and Wu 2014). For example:

---

[10] Again, forced payments can go to public projects, too, and in those cases, high-level bureaucrats would not punish low-level bureaucrats for executing expropriation.

Box 2.1 Who are high-level and low-level bureaucrats?

High and low levels are relative concepts given the multiple layers of the Chinese government. For example, in a county-level local taxation bureau, low-level bureaucrats include county bureau tax collectors who collect taxes from local businesses on a regular basis. Their direct superior is the county bureau head; their indirect superiors include the prefectural bureau head, the provincial bureau head, and the national bureau head. All these superiors are considered "high-level" bureaucrats. The county head and the county party secretary are also direct superiors. An entrepreneur's political connections with the county bureau head, the county head, and the county party secretary are likely to help deter expropriation. Connections with the prefectural- and provincial-level officials are also helpful.

In a prefectural-level local taxation bureau, the low-level bureaucrats are prefectural tax collectors who collect taxes from local businesses. Their direct superiors are the prefectural local taxation bureau head, the mayor, and the prefectural party secretary. To deter expropriation, it is the best to build political connections with these direct superiors. Indirectly, the provincial bureau and the national bureau heads are also their supervisors. The county local taxation bureau head, who is a high-level bureaucrat in the context of a county-level taxation bureau, is not a high-level bureaucrat in the prefectural-level bureau. Nor is he considered a low-level bureaucrat in this case, because he does not directly engage in expropriation as a county head.

County-level Local Taxation Bureau

Low-level bureaucrat: county bureau tax collector

High-level bureaucrat: county bureau head; county head; county party secretary prefectural bureau head; prefectural mayor and party secretary provincial bureau head;... national bureau head;...

Prefectural-level Local Taxation Bureau

Low-level bureaucrat: prefectural bureau tax collector

High-level bureaucrat: prefectural bureau head; prefectural mayor and party secretary provincial bureau head; ... national bureau head; ...

Local officials play mahjong with businessmen on a regular basis ...They only invite people's congress deputies to play with them ...Of course, local officials always win the game and make money off those rich businessmen. (a local official, interview G127)

If a government official is observed having dinner with a private entrepreneur at an expensive restaurant, it might be perceived as a bad thing. But if the entrepreneur is a people's congress deputy, then others might think that they are having dinner together to discuss (congressional) committee work. The fact that they both serve at the congress is a useful facade. (an entrepreneur–legislator, interview P136)

In this framework, high-level bureaucrats either have *high* or *low* connections with individual private entrepreneurs.[11] All entrepreneurs enhance their political capital after they become legislators by interacting more with high-level bureaucrats.

2.4.3 Private Entrepreneurs

Entrepreneurs want secure property rights so that they can focus on developing their businesses and generating profits. They are aware that local bureaucrats are extractive, and they understand low-level bureaucrats are more likely to seek rents from companies with weak political connections. An entrepreneur's strength of political connection is one's private information unknown to low-level bureaucrats (but known to high-level ones), but he can reveal his "type" – his political connectedness – to those bureaucrats. I argue that running for and being a legislator sends a strong signal to uninformed bureaucrats about one's high political connectedness, therefore deterring expropriation.

This signal is highly costly. Becoming a legislator is expensive in China: in some cases it entails bribery to secure a seat[12]; it is expensive to socialize with other deputy "friends,"[13] and there may also be opportunity costs associated with time spent on collecting public opinion information, writing legislative proposals, and attending meetings.

If an entrepreneur is a member of a local congress, his business is likely to be an established and profit-making enterprise; it is also

---

[11] In Chapter 4, I discuss which entrepreneurs are more likely to have stronger political capital prior to their running for office.

[12] A recent vote-buying scandal reveals that an entrepreneur candidate could spend as much as three million yuan to secure a seat at the Hunan provincial congress.

[13] The monetary costs of maintaining connections with government officials are carefully documented by Sun, Zhu, and Wu (2014).

likely to be a major taxpayer and an important job creator in the local economy. Relatedly and most importantly, he almost certainly has strong connections with local elites – both those that helped him get elected and new relationships developed through the local congress (i.e., through attending plenums, collaborating in working groups, and participating in legislature-related events). In Chapter 5 I show that entrepreneurs who sit in local congresses are also more likely to be CCP members and to have worked in governments and state-owned entrepreneurs in the past, all of which suggest a strong and existing political network.

A low-level bureaucrat would therefore be particularly careful when deciding whether to extract rents from an entrepreneur–legislator, since the entrepreneur could contact high-level bureaucrats in his network (potentially including the bureaucrat's direct superior) to report or complain about the incident. A high-level bureaucrat is not obliged to respond to such a report, and would likely choose to ignore it if he ordered or approved the activity. However, high-level bureaucrats are more likely to take reports from a fellow legislator seriously and take action, which could range from an oral warning to a serious investigation.

In summary, how entrepreneurs strategically use the congress to shield their property – which is changing the structure of the property rights regime in China – bears a strong resemblance to what Kellee Tsai describes as informal institutional change in China:

[E]ven in nondemocratic contexts where truly representative formal institutions do not exist, state and non-state actors may collaborate to manipulate the formal rules of the game in a manner that serve their interests and, eventually, lead to more fundamental reform or change of formal institutions that neither of the parties fully intended. (Tsai 2007, 43)

Our arguments share the same premise that "formal institutions comprise a myriad of constraints and opportunities that may motivate everyday actors to devise novel operating arrangements that are not officially sanctioned" (Tsai 2006). My argument departs from Tsai's account in that I find individual actors do not resort to informal means when formal institutions do not function. Instead, individuals innovate and repurpose one formal institution to serve the function that other formal institutions are supposed to serve: private entrepreneurs use legislatures to create a new system of selective property rights.

2.4.4 Other Actors

Autocrats in Beijing

The ruling elite in Beijing exercises the most power and establishes the rules of the game. This group includes the General Secretary of the Communist Party/the President of China, his peers at the Politburo Standing Committee, and a small group of political and business elites who surround them. Consistent with major theories on authoritarianism, this book assumes that the primary interest of the ruling elite is to stay in power.

Autocrats in Beijing created the people's congress system for a variety of purposes, and the benefits for participants have evolved over time. Local congresses provide information regarding public approval of policy implementation, and report the behavior of local agents to their superiors (Lorentzen 2013; Manion 2016). Through legislative plenums and proposals, autocrats not only acquire information on public opinion and on the behavior of low-level bureaucrats (Birney 2007).[14] The ruling elite also uses legislatures to share spoils with other elites. For instance, Truex (2014) carefully documents the "return to office" to members of China's national congress and estimates that companies that have a national legislator as a top executive enjoy an average of 1.5–2 extra percentage points in returns and a 3–4 percentage point boost in operating profit margin, compared with similar companies that do not have a national legislator.

According to existing theories, autocrats almost always maximize their utility within institutions of their creation, and other actors in the system simply comply. Scholars rarely study the institutional by-products created by actors other than the ruling elite.[15] Individualized property security is one such by-product of Chinese local legislatures that is largely created by private entrepreneurs through a bottom-up process.

Charles Tilly describes governments' provision of protection to their citizens as "racketeering," because governments create a threat and then charge for its reduction (Tilly 1985, 171). Although Tilly mostly refers to violence and organized crime, Margaret Levi similarly characterizes most rulers as predatory: they "design property rights and policies meant to maximize their own personal power and wealth" (Levi 1981, 438). In this

---

[14] Chapter 3 thoroughly examines the evolution of the people's congress system.

[15] Blaydes (2011) briefly mentions that there might exist "endogenous by-products" of institutional equilibrium that could potentially undermine the stability of the regime.

book, I clearly differentiate between levels of government agents in China and posit that government agents at the very low levels are predatory. But I do not focus on the types of predatory behavior in which autocrats in Beijing might engage.[16] That said, I argue that the individualistic strategy of property protection exercised by these private entrepreneurs is incentive compatible with the ruling elite, whose utility function includes both economic growth and personal wealth growth. Therefore, the ruling elite would allow other actors to exploit existing institutions for multiple purposes. Again, if entrepreneurs who successfully win seats in the local legislatures are more productive than other entrepreneurs, this selective property rights system is relatively efficient: protected entrepreneurs contribute to growth in total output and government revenue, while unprotected and less productive entrepreneurs are expropriated by low-level bureaucrats.[17] This outcome would be desirable to autocrats in Beijing.

The Citizenry

Citizens are not involved in higher-level legislative elections, but they directly elect their own legislators at the district and county levels. Their political participation takes two forms: casting a vote and nominating individuals as "voter nominees." Contrary to the stereotypical image of citizens in a strong authoritarian state, Manion (2017) finds that, at the very local levels Chinese voters can use their electoral power to select "good types," that is, legislators who reliably represent local interests, by collectively nominating candidates as "voter nominees." How Chinese citizens use their limited power to influence electoral and policy outcomes is an extremely interesting topic, but it is beyond the scope of this book. In the case I study, private entrepreneurs are usually nominated as "party nominees," rather than "voter nominees," and citizens have very little influence on local party committee' nominees. There are also few cases in which a private entrepreneur has made it onto the ballot but has been voted down by citizens at the very local level. Therefore, the citizenry plays a minimal role in my argument.

---

[16] Predatory behavior exists at the highest level of governments in what Minxin Pei terms "China's crony capitalist order" (Pei 2016, 6).

[17] Data in Chapter 4 provides some support to this claim: entrepreneur–legislators' firms are bigger, older, make higher profits and pay more taxes. I do not have a productivity measure to rigorously assess the productivity claim, but the high-level autocrats might not, either. Their impressionistic estimation of how these entrepreneurs are doing might be enough for them to conclude that the people's congress is protecting the "right" group.

2.5 A SIGNALING GAME

Next, to illustrate how entrepreneurs use legislative seats to signal polit-ical connection and to avoid expropriation, I present the entrepreneur–bureaucrat interactions as a stylized signaling game of incomplete infor-mation (Figure 2.2). Chapter 6 provides more empirical evidence to show how the "legislative seat as signal" logic works on the ground.

The sequence of the game is as follows. Nature moves first and assigns an entrepreneur to be either the connected type (C) with probability P, or the unconnected type (UC) with probability $1-P$. After nature's move, the entrepreneur, who knows his type, chooses "to run" (R) or "to not run" (NR) for a people's congress seat. The low-level bureaucrat does not know the entrepreneur's type, but observes whether the entrepreneur plays "run" (R) or "not run" (NR). The bureaucrat chooses either to "expropriate" (E) or to "not expropriate" (NE).

This game is stylized, and I make a number of simplifying assumptions. The starting point is that an entrepreneur is connected (C) or unconnected (UC) in the local political network. Both types of entrepreneurs make the same amount of revenue r, but their costs of running for a people's congress seat are different. The cost is much higher for an unconnected

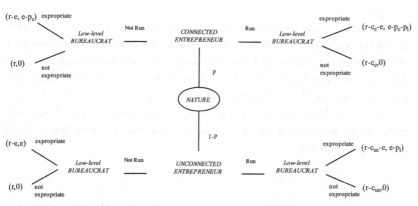

FIGURE 2.2 Signaling game between entrepreneurs and low-level bureaucrats

Note. The payoffs are as follows. For the entrepreneur, r represents the revenue from running the business; c_c is cost of running for connected entrepreneurs; c_{uc} is the cost for the unconnected entrepreneurs; e is the amount expropriated. For the low-level bureaucrat, e is the amount gained from expropriation, p_c represents the amount of punishment from his superior when the bureaucrat expropriates from a connected entrepreneur; and p_l represents the amount of punishment when he expropriates from a legislator.

entrepreneur compared to that of a connected one: $c_c < c_{uc}$, because the unconnected entrepreneur needs to exert more effort to get himself on the ballot by making friends in the government. I assume that all entrepreneurs who run for a seat get the seat in this game. Besides using the legislative seat as a signal, entrepreneurs who gain a seat also enhance their political connectedness. In this game, the enhancement of political connections results in stronger punishment to the low-level bureaucrat as illustrated below.[18]

I assume that the low-level bureaucrat expropriates from an entrepreneur for a fixed amount of e, regardless of the type of the entrepreneur. The bureaucrat does not know whether an entrepreneur is the connected or the unconnected type.[19] If the bureaucrat expropriates from a connected entrepreneur, the bureaucrat faces punishment from the superior in the amount of p_c. If the entrepreneur is a legislator, the bureaucrat faces an extra amount of punishment from the enhancement of political connections in the amount of p_l, regardless of the type of the entrepreneur. Because bureaucrats observe running and not running, they observe p_l. Finally, because a bureaucrat refrains from expropriation sometimes, he has to be deterred from doing so in certain situations. Therefore, I assume the worst possible punishment he will receive is greater than his expropriation income, that is, $e < p_c + p_l$.

The game has a separating equilibrium when $c_c < e < c_{uc}$ (see appendix for proof).[20] In this equilibrium, the connected entrepreneur always runs for office and the bureaucrat avoids expropriating from the entrepreneur–legislator; the unconnected entrepreneur does not run for office, and the bureaucrat expropriates from the unconnected entrepreneur. Running and being a legislator sends a signal of high political connectedness to the predatory bureaucrats and deters them from expropriation.

---

[18] In reality, the enhancement of political connections should also increase an entrepreneur's payoff, for instance, in the forms of government contracts, or easier access to land and credit. Because this model only looks at expropriation, the enhancement of political connection is only reflected in the higher punishment to the extractive bureaucrat.

[19] In reality, some bureaucrats may have more information about an entrepreneur's type than others.

[20] The model produces the same equilibrium if I set p_l to zero, and the deterrence effect only comes from signaling. I keep p_l in the model because in real life the deterrence effect could come from both signaling and political capital enhancement.

2.6 OBSERVABLE IMPLICATIONS

If the system functions as described, private entrepreneurs compete for seats in the local congresses, and these seats protect their assets from being expropriated by low-level bureaucrats; low-level bureaucrats expropriate from local businesses, but avoid those owned by legislators; high-level bureaucrats interact with entrepreneur–legislators, and collect information on low-level bureaucrats' behavior.

On the macro (institutional) level, we expect individuals' political participation in China to enhance a selective property rights regime in which a select group of property holders has more secure property rights than others. All entrepreneurs, having observed how this selective property rights system works, update their beliefs about how likely their own business is to be expropriated. This creates a new institutional equilibrium in which expropriation is more predictable than before.

This institutional-level implication leads to three individual-level implications, and I label them as: motivation, effectiveness, and political capital.

First, while private entrepreneurs are *motivated* to enter politics for a number of reasons, such as gaining material payoffs, policy influence, social standing, the authoritarianism literature has previously overlooked the goal of securing a seat in the local legislature to protect their property from expropriation. I closely assess this implication in Chapter 4.

Second, if the strategy of using legislative office to protect property is *effective*, we would not only observe that private entrepreneurs want to join the institution, but also that there are real benefits after a private entrepreneur becomes a legislator. We should observe that entrepreneur–legislators are less likely to be expropriated by local bureaucrats than entrepreneurs who do not serve in a local congress. I assess this implication in Chapter 5.

Finally, I closely examine possible mechanisms underlying the strategy of protecting property by entering congresses. I argue that the *political capital* associated with holding a legislative seat best explains why legislators are less likely to be expropriated. Becoming a legislator requires a significant amount of political capital, and once an entrepreneur becomes a legislator, he further enhances his political capital by making connections within congress. Low-level bureaucrats do not observe entrepreneurs' political capital, and they can only make inferences based on available information. Entrepreneurs' deputy status delivers a credible signal to local officials about their levels of political connectedness, and therefore deters expropriation. Chapter 6 explores this implication empirically.

APPENDIX

I show a separating perfect Bayesian equilibrium (PBE) exists in this game where the connected entrepreneur runs and the unconnected does not run. Note that I do not argue that this is necessarily the only equilibrium.

All entrepreneurs make a revenue of r. The cost of running for office for the connected is c_c, and the cost for the unconnected is c_{uc}. If a bureaucrat extracts from an entrepreneur, the amount of expropriation is a fixed value of e. If the bureaucrat expropriates from a connected entrepreneur, the punishment is p_c; if the expropriated entrepreneur is a legislator, the punishment is p_l, regardless of the type of the entrepreneur. There is no punishment if the bureaucrat expropriates from an unconnected entrepreneur who does not run for office.

In a separating PBE, each entrepreneur type chooses a different message, so that the message perfectly identifies his type. In this case, if there exists a separating PBE, it must be that the connected entrepreneur plays "run" (R) and the unconnected type plays "not run" (NR). In other words,

$$\sigma_e(t) = Run \quad \text{if } t = C$$
$$\sigma_e(t) = Not\ Run \quad \text{if } t = UC$$

Let $\mu(t_i|A)$ be the probability that the bureaucrat assigns to type i after observing action A.

If the bureaucrat sees that the entrepreneur plays R, he will assign probability 1 to type C. This is the only belief consistent with Bayes' rule, because both the left-hand and the right-hand information sets are reached with positive probability along the equilibrium path.

To see this, recall Bayes' rule:

$$\mu(C|R) = \frac{P(R|C)P(C)}{P(R)} = \frac{P(R|C)P(C)}{P(R|C)P(C) + P(R|UC)P(UC)}$$

We know from the structure of the game that,

$$P(R|C) = 1 \quad \text{and} \quad P(R|UC) = 0$$

Plugging this into the above and we get:

$$\mu(C|R) = 1 \quad \text{and} \quad \mu(UC|R) = 0$$

In the same way, we solve for

$$\mu(C|NR) = 0 \quad \text{and} \quad \mu(UC|UR) = 1$$

Next, we discuss best responses for the bureaucrat. If the bureaucrat observes "R", his expected utility from playing E and NE are:

$$EU_b(E, R) = \mu(C|R) * U_b(E, R; C) + \mu(UC|R) * U_b(E, R; UC)$$
$$= U_b(E, R; C) = e - p_c - p_l$$

and

$$EU_b(NE, R) = \mu(C|R) * U_b(NE, R; C) + \mu(UC|R) * U_b(NE, R; UC)$$
$$= U_b(NE, R; C) = 0$$

Therefore, observing "Running," the bureaucrat's best response:

$$BR_b(R) = E, \quad \text{if } e - p_c - p_l > 0$$
$$BR_b(R) = NE, \quad \text{if } e - p_c - p_l < 0$$

We assume that $e - p_c - p_l < 0$, hence

$$BR_b(R) = NE$$

If the bureaucrat observes "NR", his expected utility from playing E and NE are:

$$EU_b(E, NR) = \mu(C|NR) * U_b(E, NR; C) + \mu(UC|NR) * U_b(E, NR; UC)$$
$$= U_b(E, NR; UC) = e$$

and

$$EU_b(NE, NR) = \mu(C|NR) * U_b(NE, NR; C)$$
$$+ \mu(UC|NR) * U_b(NE, NR; UC)$$
$$= U_b(NE, NR; UC) = 0$$

Therefore, observing "Not Running," the bureaucrat's best response is:

$$BR_b(NR) = E, \text{ because we assume that } e > 0$$

Therefore, the bureaucrat's best response is always to "expropriate" (E) when observing NR.

Because the bureaucrat's beliefs are Bayesian by construction, and his strategy is a best response given those beliefs, an equilibrium exists if and only if (iff) neither type of entrepreneur has an incentive to deviate.

First, let us look at the connected entrepreneur. The assigned strategy is to play R with the payoff

$$U_c(R, NE; C) = r - c_c$$

If he deviated and played UR instead, the bureaucrat's beliefs would continue to be as above; that is, he would believe, upon seeing UR played, that the entrepreneur was of the UC type with probability 1, and would therefore play E. The entrepreneur's payoff from deviating would therefore be

$$U_c(NR, E; C) = r - e$$

Therefore, the connected entrepreneur would not deviate iff $r - e < r - c_c$, that is, $c_c < e$.

Next, let us look at the unconnected entrepreneur. The assigned strategy is to play NR with the payoff

$$U_{uc}(NR, E; NC) = r - e$$

If he deviated and played R instead, the bureaucrat would believe that the entrepreneur was of the C type with probability 1, and would play NE. The entrepreneur's payoff from deviating would be:

$$U_{uc}(R, NE; NC) = r - c_{uc}$$

The unconnected entrepreneur would not deviate iff $r - c_{uc} < r - e$, that is, $e < c_{uc}$.

Therefore, both types of entrepreneur would not deviate iff $c_c < e < c_{uc}$.

In this separating equilibrium, the connected entrepreneur always runs for legislative office and the low-level bureaucrat does not expropriate from the entrepreneur; the unconnected entrepreneur does not run for office, and the low-level bureaucrat expropriates from the entrepreneur.

3

Private Entrepreneurs in Legislative Office

Of all the entrepreneurs I met, Mr. Qian left the strongest (and the most immediate) impression. I first met him at a coffee shop in Hunan, because he moved his company from Hunan to Beijing and no longer had office space in Hunan. At the time, he was still serving in the Hunan Provincial Congress and flew back several times each year to attend meetings. I arrived a few minutes late and found him working on a legislative proposal about regulating the province's taxi industry. I was pleasantly surprised: most entrepreneur–legislators I met told me they were so busy running their businesses that they hardly had any time to fulfill their legislative duties beyond attending meetings, and here I find a businessman writing a legislative proposal! It became only natural for us to discuss his legislative office. A few days later, Qian even invited me to a hearing where he and a few legislator colleagues presented their findings and policy recommendations to a panel of government officials.

Qian runs a successful interior design company. He also served two terms in the provincial congress for a total of ten years. He proudly mentioned that he was awarded an "excellent deputy" title and never missed any meeting except for emergencies. Attending all meetings requires taking about 11 days off work per year. He submits one or two legislative proposals or policy suggestions every year, and each proposal takes about 30 hours of research time and 20 hours of writing time.

Qian believes that not all of his fellow entrepreneur–legislators take the job as seriously as he did, but many entrepreneurs in office invest a significant amount of time and energy into fulfilling their legislative responsibilities. How does a private entrepreneur become a legislator in China, and how competitive is it? What process do they have to go through? How costly is it to enter politics? What legislative tasks do entrepreneurs accomplish while in office? How much time do they spend in office? This chapter answers these questions. The first section provides an overview of the Chinese legislature – the people's congresses. It describes how entrepreneur–legislators are elected and the competitiveness of this process. It also discusses legislators' rights and responsibilities, and shows that their formal power is still largely nominal. The next section surveys the history of the people's congress system. The party uses the legislatures to mobilize cadres, to discuss and implement new policies, to gather feedback on developing problems, and to show the public that it does not run the country in total secrecy. The CCP has strong control over local legislatures, and legislators have little influence over local policy-making and lawmaking. The chapter then briefly discusses the functions of the Chinese People's Political Consultative Conferences (CPPCCs), which are political advisory institutions. While CPPCCs also provide networking opportunities for private entrepreneurs, entrepreneurs can build much stronger political connections in the people's congresses. The last section provides a case study of private entrepreneurs in office using a recent survey of local legislators from one province. I find that, like Qian, many entrepreneur–legislators in this province are committed to public service and fulfill their legislative duties as much as their non-entrepreneur colleagues. They regularly attend local congressional meetings and hearings, spend time researching and writing legislative proposals and policy suggestions, and carve out time to interact with government officials and constituents. The private sector has a notable presence in public office.

3.1 THE CHINESE LEGISLATURES: A SNAPSHOT

The institutional focus of this book is China's local legislatures – the local people's congresses. Local congresses are established in the following administrative levels: (1) provinces and municipalities directly under the Central Government (*zhixia sheng/shi*), (2) prefectures and prefectural districts, (3) counties and autonomous (ethnic) counties, and (4) townships (Article 95 of the Constitution).[1] When I discuss "subnational" or "local" legislatures, I refer to congresses below the national level. Some levels of subnational congress have more power than others – the biggest

---

[1] At the village level, the villagers' assemblies represent "a form of direct democracy that would supplement the indirect democracy of the people's congresses" at higher levels (Oi and Rozelle 2000).

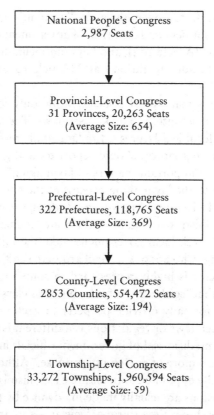

FIGURE 3.1 Hierarchy and sizes of China's legislatures

difference is that congresses at the provincial and prefectural levels have the power to make laws, while the rest do not. All levels of local legislatures share many similar functions.

As stated in Article 2 of the Constitution, "[t]he National People's Congress and the local congresses at various levels are the organs through which the people exercise state power." Article 3 states that "the National People's Congress and the local people's congresses at various levels are constituted through democratic elections. They are responsible to the people and subject to their supervision."[2] National and subnational

[2] The Chinese Constitution. www.npc.gov.cn/npc/xinwen/node_505.htm#45. For an English translation, see the official website of the National People's Congress at www.npc.gov.cn/englishnpc/Constitution/2007-11/15/content_1372965.htm. Last accessed November 8, 2017.

legislators exercise state power through "law and regulation making" (Article 99), "appointment and dismissal of government officials" (Article 101), "supervision" (Article 104), and "appointment, dismissal, training, assessment of public administration staff" (Article 107, see Appendix for more detail).

Local legislatures make local policies, while only legislatures above the county level are permitted to make local laws. The autonomous lawmaking power of local legislatures is fundamentally restricted because in principle "Chinese legislatures should report to, and get prior approval from, the CCP in all important matters of lawmaking" (Cho 2009, 20).[3] Moreover, similar to the lawmaking process at the national level, where the lion's share of legislative initiative, and drafting has been "the responsibility of the administrative organs of the State Council" (Tanner 1999, 118), at the local level, local governments take the initiative in agenda setting and drafting (Cho 2009, 42; MacFarquhar 1998). As a result, even if the business sector is highly represented in some local legislatures, it remains unlikely that legislators from the business class can initiate laws or regulations to formally provide property protection. And of course, enforcement of such laws or regulations is a different issue on its own.

Appointment and dismissal of government officials and public administration staff is also more of an "empty promise." Although government officials are formally appointed and, in rare cases, dismissed by local congresses, these decisions are usually made in advance by the party and the local governments. From time to time, legislators do appoint or dismiss government officials at their own will. Local legislatures also have the power to "supervise the work of the people's government." Supervisory power is regarded as the most important role of the local legislatures (Cho 2009).

The congresses were invited to oversee policy implementation in the 1980s (O'Brien 1994b). As a result, people's congress deputies have been slowly gaining a new reputation as "legitimate complainers" or "remonstrators," who identify and bring problems "to the attention of officials and request a response" (O'Brien 1994a). During this period, the party has come to consider legislative supervision as "a useful means of checking and preventing corruption in governments" (Cho 2009, 47). Legislative supervision has since played an increasingly important role in local pol-

---

3 Tanner (1999, chapter 4), on the other hand, has argued that the CCP's control over lawmaking has experienced an erosion in post-Mao China.

itics, making officials more accountable to the people (Almén 2005; Xia 2000).[4]

Deputies supervise governments through two methods: examining the enforcement of laws and appraising government officials. And there are two types of appraisal: self-evaluation and deputies' appraisal. The first type of appraisal usually happens during the congressional annual plenums, whereas the deputies' appraisal can happen at any time of the year. Congressional deputies at all levels attend hearings, and during those hearings, they review and question government work reports. Deputies also can take part in special investigative commissions on government bureaus and officials. A county-level congress in Guangdong Province, for instance, dismissed six local officials from their posts in 2010. Similar dismissals by local legislators have also happened in Yunnan, Zhejiang, Sichuan, and Hunan (Cho 2009; Xia 2000). Since the deputies have the power to dismiss government officials from their posts and to appoint new ones, they can use their formal power to significantly affect officials' career prospects. The "power to dismiss" could trigger government officials' preferential treatment of congressional deputies and their friends. The "power to appoint" creates an incentive for government officials to treat people with political connections differently. Dickson (2008), for example, argues that the appraisal process gives deputies "some degree of influence and oversight" (172).

The second type of appraisal is deputies' appraisal. Deputies are sometimes assigned into "appraisal or supervision groups," and one group usually corresponds to one specific government agency. In theory, the group should conduct investigations for several months, visiting relevant officials and interviewing residents (Cho 2009, 59). In fact, these supervisory groups usually visit the assigned agency once a year, when the agency hosts a focus group meeting and discusses their work. The supervisory group then evaluates the quality of the agency's work and writes up an appraisal report to the people's congress standing committee. The report is delivered to the party committee and, if a majority of the supervisory group members do not approve the officials or agencies supervised, an official will face punishment, including possible dismissal.

In sum, on paper these forms of formal appraisal processes are powerful, but in practice, they are rarely independently performed. In this

---

[4] To the contrary, some scholars of China have also argued that "local people's congresses play virtually no role in supervising policy implementation of county and township/town government" (Zhong 2003, 154).

chapter and in the latter part of this book I will show that (i) these formal processes do not deter expropriation and therefore are not the reason entrepreneur–legislators are protected from the grabbing hand, and (ii) these nominal functions are not powerful enough to motivate individuals to run for office. But before we get into these claims, let us first take a closer look at the legislators.

3.1.1 The Deputies

Legislators in the congresses are called people's congress deputies. According to Article 97 of the Constitution, people's congress deputies at the county, prefecture without districts, prefectural districts, and township levels are directly elected by the constituents. Deputies at the provincial and prefectural levels are elected by their lower-level congresses. The Constitution vaguely states that local deputy quotas and electoral processes should be regulated by "law." The term of local congress deputies is five years, but the Constitution does not specify a term limit (Article 98).

Deputies are elected either by constituents at the county level and below, or by electoral units at the higher levels. Constituents or electoral units have the right to dismiss deputies according to a specified process (Article 102).

Being a legislator in China is a part-time job.[5] It is clearly stated in the Deputy Law that deputies shall not "be separate from their own production and work." But when they attend congressional meetings and other events and activities organized by local congresses during the off-meeting period, deputies should give priority to their legislative duties, and arrange their work accordingly.

To ensure that deputies exercise their rights, the Deputy Law stipulates a set of "guarantees" or "privileges" for deputies, and "immunity" and "responsiveness to proposals" deserve highlighting:

Box 3.1 Privileges enjoyed by deputies (the Deputy Law)

Article 32: [Immunity]
Deputies at the county level or above cannot be arrested or prosecuted, unless the people's congress presidium (in sessions) or standing committee (off sessions) issues a permission.

---

[5] Part-time legislators are definitely not a China-specific phenomenon. For instance, in Texas, the state legislature met "in a regular legislative session in Austin once every two years" (Besley 2004).

> Article 42: [Responsiveness to proposals]
> Relevant government bureaus and organizations should take deputy proposals, critiques, and suggestions seriously. It is required to reply to them within 3–6 months.

Recall I argue that entrepreneurs join local legislatures to protect property from expropriation. The "immunity" privilege provides an alternative reason for entrepreneurs to join the legislatures: private entrepreneurs seek seats in legislatures in order to get immunity from prosecution. Literature shows that immunity has been one of the main motivations for individuals in autocracies to seek office. For instance, in Egypt, the strong guarantee of parliamentary immunity is particularly appealing to business elites, who seek protection from arrest, detention, or charges of criminal activity (Blaydes 2011, 10). In Chapter 6, I describe an incident in which a prefectural entrepreneur–legislator used his immunity privilege to successfully escape possible criminal charges. But overall, we do not observe such cases very often in China. If the local government or local party committee wishes to press charges against a legislator who has immunity privilege, it would be easy to strip him of his legislator status first before pressing charges.

3.1.2 Composition, Selection, and Competition

One consensus from the studies of legislative recruitment is that "opportunities to serve in legislatures are quite unevenly distributed in all societies" (Matthews 1985). It is very much the case in China.

Local congressional deputies come from a variety of industries, sectors, and occupations. A quota system ensures that major occupations are represented in the legislatures, but entrepreneurs are overrepresented in the system. At the national level, around 17 percent of NPC deputies are CEOs or leaders of companies of some form, whereas the population average is close to o. About 27 percent are small business owners and entrepreneurs, compared to the population average of 9 percent (Truex 2016). At sub-national levels, private entrepreneurs take up about 11 percent of total seats at county congresses (Manion 2016). My survey of provincial congresses reveals that half of all provincial congresses have private entrepreneurs taking up at least 15 percent of their seats. As expected, coastal provinces, where the private sector is more developed, in general have a higher concentration of private entrepreneurs in local congresses than inland provinces. Non-coastal

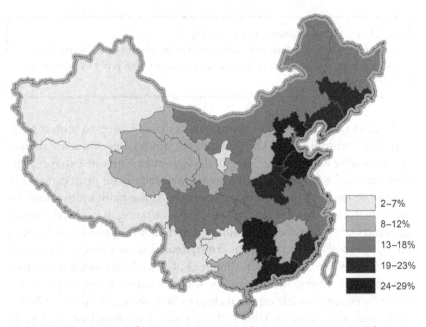

FIGURE 3.2 Percentage of private entrepreneur deputies across provincial congresses

Note. This map displays the percentage of private entrepreneur deputies in each provincial congress. A lighter color indicates a lower percentage of private entrepreneur deputies in that province. This data was collected in December 2016 and reflects the 12th provincial congress membership. All provincial congresses ran new elections in the spring of 2017.

provinces in the east have higher percentages of private entrepreneurs than provinces in the west (see Figure 3.2 and Table 3.2).

The most represented occupations in Zhejiang provincial congress, for instance, are government, military and the CCP officials (35.6 percent), peasants and workers (20.6 percent), and private entrepreneurs (17.6 percent) (Table 3.1). The percentage of private entrepreneur deputies is similar to a county congress in Hunan (21.1 percent), a district congress in Guangdong (22.0 percent), and much higher than counties in Guizhou (<10 percent).[6] These numbers also correspond to the percentage of

---

[6] The information on these local legislatures is not public, therefore I am anonymizing the names of the locations. Usually, local congress websites publish deputy names, party affiliations, gender, and perhaps a picture. Occupation and detailed contact information are usually not public.

TABLE 3.1 *Deputy composition of Zhejiang's 12th Provincial Congress*

	Number	Percentage
Government, Military, and CCP Officials	226	35.6
Private Entrepreneurs	112	17.6
SOE Entrepreneurs	13	2.0
Peasants and Workers	131	20.6
Other	153	24.1
Total	635	

Note. Numbers of private enterprises and SOE represented are subject to measurement error, because the ownership structure for some of the firms is unclear based on the information provided on their websites. Occupation information comes from the website "Zhejiang Online" at http://zjnews.zjol.com.cn/05zjnews/system/2013/01/19/ 019099130.shtml and http://blog.sina.com.cn/s/blog_a3f2f5990101hp2h.html. Last accessed November 8, 2017.

entrepreneurs represented in the NPC, which is about 26.9 percent (Truex 2016, 100).

Entrepreneurs from the state sector also take a large number of seats in most provincial congresses. Beijing and Shanghai are the only two congresses where business deputies from the state sector comprise more than 20 percent of total seats. The incentives and behavior of entrepreneurs from the state sector are beyond the scope of this book, but according to my interviewees, once an SOE candidate was chosen, the process of vetting and electing a SOE deputy is much easier than that of vetting and electing a private entrepreneur deputy.

Getting a seat in the local legislature is a complex and competitive process. According to the 2010 Electoral Law, county- and district-level legislators are directly elected by their local constituents, and legislators at the prefectural, provincial, and national levels are elected by their lower-level legislatures. The total number of seats at each level is stipulated in the Electoral Law.[7] A temporary party-led election committee, the majority of whose members come from the local Communist party committee, is formed prior to elections to manage the electoral process. To ensure broad representation, the election committee assigns quotas specifying that each congress should have a certain proportion of government and party officials, entrepreneurs, peasants, intellectuals, and deputies

---

[7] Electoral Law of the People's Republic of China for the National People's Congress and Local People's Congresses (2010 Amendment) [Effective]. PKU Law. en.pkulaw.cn/ display.aspx?cgid=127960&lib=law. Last accessed November 8, 2017.

TABLE 3.2 *Provincial congresses: percentage of entrepreneurs from private and state sectors*

Province	Private Sector %	State Sector %	Total %
Hunan	29	9	38
Guangdong	24	7	31
Shandong	24	11	35
Jilin	20	14	34
Liaoning	20	12	32
Hebei	26	8	34
Fujian	20	7	27
Henan	19	10	29
Zhejiang	18	2	20
Hubei	18	12	30
Heilongjiang	17	11	28
Anhui	16	10	26
Shannxi	16	6	22
Sichuan	15	3	18
Inner Mongolia	15	2	17
Chongqing	15	8	23
Jiangsu	14	9	23
Tianjin	13	15	28
Gansu	11	1	12
Guangxi	11	2	13
Shanxi	11	9	20
Beijing	10	21	31
Jiangxi	10	5	15
Hainan	9	4	13
Qinghai	8	2	10
Shanghai	8	26	34
Guizhou	7	4	11
Xinjiang	7	4	11
Ningxia	7	2	9
Yunnan	6	0	6
Tibet	2	1	3

Note. Data collected in December 2016, reflecting deputy composition of the 12th provincial congress of each province. Lists of provincial congressional deputies come from official websites of local congresses (if available) or are results of internet searches. Ownership information was collected from www.tianyancha.com. Last accessed December 2016. In some cases, the company's ownership status was not entirely clear to my research assistant and me, and we had to make educated guesses. Therefore, these numbers are best estimates.

representing other occupations (O'Brien and Li 1993). According to the Electoral Law, the ballot must list 1.33 to 2 candidates per legislative seat, and the election committee decides on the final number (Manion 2017).[8]

Since this book focuses on entrepreneur–legislators, I mainly discuss how a private entrepreneur obtains a seat in a local legislature. The process works somewhat differently for candidates from the government, the party, and the military, since these candidates are, for the most part, vetted by the local party organization department. These seats, therefore, are not competitive once a candidate is chosen. In contrast, campaigns for seats set aside for private entrepreneurs are competitive.

If a private entrepreneur wishes to get elected, the first thing he must do is to get nominated. Nominations are made either by the corresponding organization department (*zuzhi bumen*) of the local communist party committee, the united front work department (*tongzhan bumen*) of the party committee together with satellite parties, or collectively by ten or more voters. The former are usually referred to as "party nominees" and the latter as "voter nominees" (Manion 2017).

Private entrepreneurs are usually nominated through the "united front work" channel.[9] The concept of the united front work, first developed by Mao, is a set of strategies to harness the support of noncommunists to help achieve the goals of the CCP. Given the facts that the communists are always a minority of the population, the CCP needed to "devise a program that the vast majority of people could support to move things toward the desired outcome" (Lieberthal 2004, 72–73). The united front work department under the party's committee is set to implement these programs. Kevin O'Brien sees these deputies as "honorary deputies" chosen by the party symbolically for breadth and representativeness considerations, at least in the pre-Deng period (O'Brien 1990, 63).

Starting in 2011, a select group of local congresses experimented with a new form of nomination: independent candidate nomination. Here, a local legislator candidate can be on the ballot as an "independent candidate" if he is nominated by a certain number of constituents, and formal endorsement from any party or government-affiliated organizations is

---

[8] For an overview of the election procedure, see Almén (2005, chapter 6) and Manion (2016, chapter 2).

[9] In some local congresses, private entrepreneurs can also be nominated as voter nominees, but usually the party organizations "worked the system" and got them nominated through the "united front" channel as "party nominees" (Interview O161).

not necessary. In 2011, 11 percent of the total number of independent candidates in thirteen selected locations were entrepreneur–candidates (He and Liu 2012). Independent candidates rarely win elections (Manion 2016, chapter 5), and they are not included in my analysis.

Manion (2016, 53) describes the candidate selection and election process in the lowest congresses – the township and county congresses, where party-led election committees select candidates from nominees and voters directly elect winners. In the higher-level congresses, candidate selection follows a similar process: the organization and united work front units of the local communist party committee select nominees. These nominees, together with independent candidates,[10] are vetted by a local communist party-led election committee, which selects candidates from nominees. Elections in prefectural and provincial congresses are different from elections in township and county congresses in that candidates are elected by lower-level deputies instead of voters in the district.

Individuals interested in a position invest time and money both in the "candidate selection" and the "election" stages. In order to get nominated, they lobby the local party committee, the personnel at the local congress standing committee, and other organizations such as the local satellite party committee or the local ACFIC office. If they manage to get on the ballot, candidates continue to work on getting elected, either by voters from the district (township and county-level congress) or by their respective lower-level deputies (all higher-level congresses). The congressional election scandal in Liaoning, described at the beginning of Chapter 5, for instance, involves vote-buying at the election stage.

Let us consider an example of how a private entrepreneur might get elected as a provincial congressional deputy. Imagine a provincial congress with 700 seats. Among these 700 seats, 100 seats are directly nominated by (allocated to) the party committee according to a quota requirement. The remaining 600 seats are allocated to voting districts (i.e., prefectural and the People's Liberation Army [PLA] units) at the next level within the province. The communist party committee in these districts then decides how to allocate the seats. If a voting district, that is, a prefecture, were allocated 60 among the 600 seats, the prefectural party committee would first directly nominate some

---

[10] Independent candidates rarely survive candidate selection and appear on the ballot, so they are more like "independent nominees" rather than "independent candidates." (Manion 2016, chapter 5). Following the literature and the media, I also label them as independent candidates.

candidates and then distribute some seats to the voting district at the next level down – the districts and counties. After several rounds of distribution and allocation, a county might receive a number of allocated seats. Assuming that a county receives five allocated seats, it is a given that one seat would go to a local party or government leader, presumably the county party secretary or the county head, and one seat would go to a female candidate, and three remaining seats are open (Interview G151). If a private entrepreneur is thinking of running for a provincial legislative seat, he should think carefully whether he has a shot at one of the three seats; if a female entrepreneur wishes to run, she might want to discuss with relevant sources, such as the local people's congress standing committee chair or local party committee members, regarding whether she has a good chance at securing the seat designated for a female candidate.

In sum, to be elected as a provincial legislator, a private entrepreneur first needs to be nominated either by the provincial party committee, a prefectural party committee, or a county or district party committee, all of which together make the final nominations but receive recommendations from democratic party committees, local governments, and various organizations. After the entrepreneur makes it onto the ballot, he is to be voted on by the corresponding prefectural legislators. Because the number of candidates is required to be 20–50 percent higher than the total number of seats, an entrepreneur candidate usually engages in some form of campaign to secure votes. In some cases, these campaigns incur high costs, and might even entail bribery.

All of these strategic calculations and decisions are usually made by the entrepreneur candidate, the election committee, the local communist party committee officials (especially those at the organization department and the united front work department), personnel at local congress standing committee offices, and other organizations that might be involved in nominating candidates (Interview G151). As one can imagine, a significant amount of informal lobbying is common during and even before the nomination process.

The entrepreneur–legislators I interviewed usually refrained from talking about the campaign and the lobbying process, but contrary to the standard assumption that deputy seats are "arranged" and tightly controlled (Chen 1999, 67), many of my interviewees believe that securing a seat is "highly competitive" (Interviews O126; P1311), "costly" (Interviews P124; P1222), "too much work" (Interview P1212), and especially so if a legislator wants to go one level up, for instance, if a county-level deputy aspires to become a prefectural-level deputy (Interview P134). Cho reveals that influential regional figures, including entrepreneurs, "have asked legislative leaders to help them to become deputies since the mid-1990s" (Cho 2009, 84). Finally, while spending money to secure a seat is important, it is essential for entrepreneur–candidates to secure endorsements from the local congress standing committee and the local party committee. Political scientist Changdong Zhang, who studies the people's congresses, describes a case where a private entrepreneur who has spent three million yuan and had already secured a seat in the prefectural congress in 2011, had to renounce his deputy title because he did not seek the endorsement from the county-level people's congress standing committee. The county people's congress chair and the county tax bureau head visited his office and offered him the option of getting audited by the tax bureau or renouncing his title. It was likely that getting audited would have cost him more than three million yuan, and he essentially had no choice but to quit the bid for a prefectural congressional seat (Zhang 2014).

3.2 A HISTORICAL OVERVIEW OF THE PEOPLE'S CONGRESS

3.2.1 Pre-reform Period

The CCP has traditionally been an "anti-capitalist" party. In the 1950s, it initiated a land reform that redistributed lands from landlords to peasants; the welfare of the peasants was the objective of the Communists' program and the basis of their political power. The fact that landlords and rich peasants were killed in tens of thousands hardly suggests the CCP began as a capitalist-friendly party (Chang 1951). Forms of "capitalist exploitation" were also to be curbed. Such policies stifled industrial production. Mao's fear that "capitalism will be restored" and "the whole of socialism will be done away with" launched the Cultural Revolution (1966–1976), which threw the Chinese political system into chaos (MacFarquhar and Schoenhals 2006).

The people's congress system has its roots in the first civil war period, with several organizations emerging as embryonic forms of the people's congress system. These groups included the CCP-led peasants associations, the Sheng Gang strike workers' association (*shenggang bagong gongren daibiao dahui*) in 1925, the Citizens Congress (*shimin dahui*), and the Shanghai mayoral government after the successful 1927 workers' revolution (Zhang and Chen 2002, 304).

The Chinese People's Political Consultative Conferences (CPPCC, discussed further in the section 3.3) functioned as the "temporary Congress" from 1949 until 1954, when the Constitution set up the people's congress as China's legislature. The people's congress system was closely modeled after the Soviet legislature. The 1954 set-up of the people's congress system was modeled after the Soviet system based on the 1936 Soviet Constitution, which certainly did not have a "pro-capitalism" element (Cai 1992, 17–18).

It was clear from the beginning that the people's congress would not be a liberal democratic legislature (O'Brien 1990, 25). Between October 1954 and the end of 1957, the standing committee of NPC held a total of 89 meetings, averaging two to three meetings per month. During this period the NPC discussed and decided critical issues facing the new republic, selected state leaders, and stipulated a set of important laws and statues (Zhang and Chen 2002, 317).

Sinologist John Fairbank observed the activities of Beijing's first congress meeting in 1949:

When I stepped into the conference hall, I saw many people: They were wearing uniforms, work clothes, short sleeves, *Qi Pao* (traditional Chinese dresses), western suits, traditional Chinese long suits, and someone wearing a skullcap. All these different looking individuals were discussing (political and social) issues together. … then I looked up and saw the word "deputy." Representativeness! Beijing is a diverse city. If deputies all look the same, how could they be representative! (Zheng 2014)

However, the liveliness of the people's congresses did not last long. During the first wave of the Anti-Right Movement (1957), 62 NPC members were labeled and purged as "rightists" due to their criticisms of and suggestions to the party and the government. As a result of this purge, deputies no longer exercised the power given to them by law, and did not dare to discuss politics and policies. Legislative and policy proposals from NPC deputies dropped from 243 in the fourth plenum of the first NPC to only 46 proposals in the second plenum of the third NPC. Between 1959 and 1966, the NPC did not make a single law, and the party "took over most important issues" (Zhang and Chen 2002, 319).

During the Cultural Revolution, the Chinese congresses completely stopped functioning, and any previous efforts to strengthen and develop the people's congress system were "basically down the drain" (Jiang 2009).[11] By then, the NPC's reputation was "a mere formality that the

---

[11] Also, see O'Brien (1990, chapter 3) for a comprehensive account of the early development and struggle of the NPC.

people mock as a rubber stamp; in the people's eyes the people's congress system exists in name only; people regard the NPC as a phony organ or idle talk" (O'Brien 1990, 60).

3.2.2 The Reform Period

The reform period has witnessed the expansion of the private sector. In the early reform years, the legal basis of the private sector was insecure, and private firms had to disguise and register as collective enterprises. While continuing to pay lip service to the concept of socialism, the party started to reduce its "emphasis on its traditional bases of support" and to embrace a "modernist paradigm" (Dickson 2003).

In the revised 1982 Constitution, the CCP remained "anti-capitalist." The Constitution stated that "[t]he proletariat dictatorship will inevitably replace the dictatorship of bourgeoisie ... the socialist system has incomparable superiority over the capitalist system." In the late 1980s, the party embraced the private sector with the announcement of then Premier Zhao Ziyang that "cooperative, individual and private sectors of the economy in both urban and rural areas should all be encouraged to expand ... [W]e must formulate policies and enact laws governing the private sector as soon as possible, in order to protect its legitimate interest" (cited in Tsai 2006, 131). Zhao also proposed the "separation of party and enterprise," but the idea was abandoned with Zhao's fall from power in 1989 (Nathan 2003).

During the 1990s, entrepreneurs continued to be excluded from the party, partly because many had supported the demonstrators in 1989, although some local party officials "quietly co-opted entrepreneurs" (Dickson 2007; 2008, 119). Their status started to change more dramatically around 1995, when the SOE reform ("grasping the large, letting go of the small") offered new opportunities for private firms to enter new markets and to buy up SOE assets (Kroeber 2016, chapter 5).

The formal incorporation of the private sector by the party did not happen until 2001, when then-party general secretary Jiang Zemin introduced a new guiding theory for the CCP called the "three represents" (*sange daibiao*). This called for the party to represent advanced social productive forces, advanced culture, and the greatest majority of the people. This new theory "paved the way for a renewed recruitment of entrepreneurs into the party" (Lardy 2014, 119). In 2002, Jiang Zeming announced that the party is "determined to encourage, support and guide the development of the nonpublic sector" at the 16th CPC National Congress, followed by a series of constitutional revisions to legitimize and to protect the private sector (Guo et al. 2014; Tsai 2006). The party now even encourages its members to go into business (Dickson 2007). The party's effort to integrate the private sector can be seen as a combination of both intentionally co-opting an emerging group (Dickson 2007; 2016) and accepting the informal rules of the game that party members had already been playing in the private sector (Tsai 2006).

In the reform period, the compositions of the NPC, local congresses, and their committees were to include members of formerly disparaged social groups, including "tails of capitalism," and party leaders expected them to "penetrate society, to build legitimacy, and to contribute to system maintenance" (O'Brien 1990, 8). However, two factors have limited the congresses from becoming a genuinely attractive institution for elite co-optation in the reform period: the party's tight control of the people's congress and the lack of power among individual legislators while the power of congress committees strengthened.

First, the party insisted on having a tight control over the congresses, from nomination of legislative candidates to agenda setting in the congressional meetings. The 1982 Constitution made it clear that the party controls the congresses and that strong party leadership of and oversight over congresses persist today. Jiang (2009) believes that the party's leadership of the legislatures is essential in ensuring the "socialist characteristics" of the legislative system. Cai Dingjian, a legal scholar who has worked in the National People's Congress and the Shenzhen prefectural people's congress for more than ten years, argues that a main political reform within the congress system should be to "separate the party from the people's congresses" (Cai 2011). Otherwise, legislators are simply "writing laws that are already written, deciding on issues that are already decided, dismissing individuals who are already dismissed by the organization department, and supervising issues already supervised by (party) leaders" (Cai 2011). Kevin O'Brien commented in 1990 that NPC deputies "often discussed improving one-party rule" but "few suggested ending it" (O'Brien 1990, 6). Truex's 2016 book suggests that it is still true after more than two decades.

Relatedly, the party leadership again rejected the proposal of a bicameral legislature system, which was supposed to divert more power to the legislature from the CCP. It was first proposed in 1954 by Zhang Bojun, the then-president of the China Democratic League, and it was not received well (Liu 2004). When the Constitution was revised in 1982, the discussion came up again, and the majority of the NPC deputies were supportive of a bicameral legislature. Among the many advocates was

Hu Qiaomu, a member of the Politburo, who proposed that the NPC should reduce its size from 3,000 deputies to 1,000, and split into two congresses. Hu argued that having 500 deputies in one congress would make it easier for quality discussions and debates to take place, and the new set-up would give people less of an impression that the National People's Congress was simply a "rubber stamp" (Cai 2006, 91–2).[12] With a smaller NPC, deputies would play a larger role in law making, supervision, and representation (O'Brien 1990, 137). This proposal, although originating high in the CCP leadership, was again rejected by Deng Xiaoping, who believed that coordination costs would be too high for two congresses when disagreement arose. Deng's decision was backed by other party leaders such as Ye Jianying, who proposed a stronger people's congress standing committee as an alternative solution to the rubber stamp image problem (Cai 2006, 91–92; O'Brien 1990, 137).

Second, the 1982 Constitution increased the power of people's congress standing committees instead of increasing the power of people's congress deputies. According to the revised Constitution, local people's congresses at the county level or above should be able to establish their own standing committees. These committees have the right to discuss and decide important local issues and policies and to supervise local governments. Standing committees at the provincial level have the power to issue and enact local laws and regulations (Cai 2007; Zhang and Chen 2002). Scholars argue that the NPC and LPC standing committees act as "second chambers" in view of their independent authority to pass laws or local regulations alone (Zhang 2012, 53). The establishment of local congress standing committees and the push for more professionalized standing committees was an important reform, but it did not grant deputies more power.

In the first few congressional sessions in the reform era, the party's goal was primarily to bring things back to normalcy. Zhang Qianfan, a prominent legal scholar, comments that "there were genuine efforts at institution-building at the beginning of the reform period, with the intention of making the NPC a fully functioning legislature. From the time of the first NPCSC Chairman, Peng Zhen, who personally suffered from lawless persecution during the Cultural Revolution, the status of the People's Congresses gradually improved" and that "the People's

---

[12] Defenders of the status quo argued that a bicameral system would further weaken the NPC (O'Brien 1990, 138).

Congresses are still 'rubber stamps,' but occasionally they do surprise those who take such an image for granted" (Zhang 2012, 123).

Further, there is no official quota for entrepreneurs in the people's congress system. In Communist Poland, for instance, the Polish United Workers' (Communist) party intended to "introduce to the Sejm [Parliament] a significant group of 25 percent of Catholic deputies" with the goal of broadening "the political base" (Gandhi and Przeworski 2006). In China, such quotas usually guarantee that individuals from ethnic minorities, women, the military, returnees from abroad, industrial workers, peasants, and intellectuals are represented in the legislatures, but formally there is no guarantee that entrepreneurs take a certain percentage of the seats (Cai 1992, 129–134; Interview G161).[13]

In sum, to answer the question of why, if it seldom has performed any legislative functions, the people's congress exists at all, Kevin O'Brien concludes that "for thirteen of its first twenty-four years, NPC sessions were not held, and in other years, it was dormant for long stretches of time. It appeared on the political stage mostly to mobilize cadres and mass activists to take part in implementation of new policies and to gather feedback on developing problems." Another important function in its earlier years was to "relax habitual secrecy and to announce changes to the attentive public" (O'Brien 1990, 86). In Cai Dingjian's work, he argues that theoretically the high concentration of power in the people's congress system was a response to the highly state-controlled economy in its earlier years (Cai 1992, 17–21).

To compare legislatures in other authoritarian contexts, we see that in Jordan, the government allocates "an unofficial quota for parliamentarians' relatives and acquaintances to avoid friction with deputies, and better still, to secure safe haven from the deputies' comments and criticism" (Lust-Okar 2006). In Iran, MPs have "authority over how money is spent" within their district (Mahdavi 2015). In Mexico under the PRI, legislators distributed pork to constituents in exchange for votes (Magaloni 2006). In Egypt under Mubarak, targeted spending increased so much that it raised inflation prior to elections (Blaydes 2011).

---

[13] Informal quotas which give a certain number of seats to entrepreneurs exist at some local legislatures, as described in O'Brien and Li (1993). In Chaohu Prefecture of Anhui Province, for example, the prefectural party secretary promised two provincial PC seats (and the possibility of NPC seats) to two private entrepreneurs in exchange for local investment (Zhang 2014).

In contrast, Chinese legislators have much less institutional power and resources than legislators in these nondemocratic or semi-democratic regimes. Because the party continues to have a tight grip on the decision making of the congresses and the system grants legislators so little power, the congresses do not seem to be the most effective option to co-opt business elites.

3.3 CHINESE PEOPLE'S POLITICAL CONSULTATIVE CONFERENCES

A discussion of the Chinese legislatures is not complete without mentioning the Chinese People's Political Consultative Conferences (CPPCC). Annual national and local CPPCC sessions and people's congress sessions usually happen back to back, and they are usually referred to jointly as "the two conferences" (*liang hui*). According to the Constitution, the CPPCC is "a broadly representative organization of the united front," including deputies from the CCP, eight democratic parties, non-partisan public personages, people's organizations, ethnic minority groups, and patriotic personalities from all walks of life, including compatriots of Taiwan, Hong Kong, Macau, and overseas Chinese.[14] The CPPCC operates at every level where there is a congress. The two main functions of the CPPCCs are "political consultation" and "democratic supervision." CPPCC deputies practice their rights mostly through policy consultation proposals, and respective government agencies are required to respond to their proposals within a given time frame.[15] Unlike the people's congress deputies, the CPPCC deputies are nominated by democratic parties and other organizations without any broad electoral process, and they are voted on internally by the CPPCC standing committee members. A local commentator has argued that the CPPCC deputy selection method is in fact an "invitation-only" process, which discounts the consultative and supervision functions of the CPPCC, therefore making it more like an "honors club."[16] He and Thogersen (2010) also argue that CPPCCs lack "either the power of decision or veto" when it comes to policy discussions.

---

[14] Charter of the Chinese People's Political Consultative Conference (2004 Revision) [Effective]. See http://en.pkulaw.cn/display.aspx?cgid=51997&lib=law. Last accessed May 21, 2015.

[15] The National CPPCC website. www.cppcc.gov.cn/2011/09/27/ARTI131710219875 1744.shtml. Last accessed May 13, 2015.

[16] China.org Shandong Channel. January 14, 2015. "How to become a CPPCC deputy" (*Ruhe Dangxuan Zhengxie Weiyuan*). http://sd.china.com.cn/zhuanti/2015/changshi_0124/511.html. Last accessed May 21, 2015.

Deputies coming from the CCP constitute a small percentage of the total number of deputies in the CPPCCs. Other deputies come from a wide spectrum of sectors and organizations. The 834 deputies of Shanghai's 12th CPPCC, for instance, were nominated by 32 different parties and organizations. Among the organizations eligible to nominate was the CCP Shanghai party committee, which contributed 30 CCP party officials. The rest of the deputies came from other democratic parties and a variety of organizations and sectors. For example, the Shanghai office of the ACFIC nominated 39 deputies to the CPPCC, and they were mostly private entrepreneurs.[17] Deputies from the "economic sector" took 92 seats, and a significant portion came from the private sector as well. It appears that besides the 30 CCP deputies who work in government agencies and the CCP party committees, the vast majority of other CPPCC deputies come from the business sector, academia, and democratic party committees.

In several studies of political connections in China, scholars have treated a CPPCC membership as the equivalent of a people's congress membership (e.g., Li et al. 2006; Li and Zhou 2005; Stuart and Wang 2014). However, from the perspective of private entrepreneurs, at the same level, it is much more difficult and requires significantly higher political capital to get into a local people's congress than getting into a local CPPCC. The opportunities to network with relevant government officials within the CPPCC are more limited compared with those within the congress at the same level. The CPPCC still provides a valuable platform for entrepreneurs to socialize with other business and political elites, and some entrepreneurs see the status of "CPPCC deputy" as a stepping stone towards a congressional membership (Interview P154).[18]

The rest of this book focuses primarily on private entrepreneurs' engagement within the people's congresses, but CPPCC memberships and their networks were sporadically mentioned during my interviews and are discussed throughout the book. To some extent, a "CPPCC membership" is a weaker signal than a "people's congress membership" in terms of the political network the membership is associated with. In Chapter 5,

---

[17] The Official Shanghai CPPCC website does not provide occupation information about its deputies. The occupation information is extracted from an unofficial Chinese politics blogpost: http://blog.sina.com.cn/s/blog_a3f2f5990101g0xq.html, thus the data reliability should be taken with a grain of salt. Last accessed May 13, 2015.

[18] It is also possible for a people's congress candidate to be "arranged" to become a CPPCC deputy. See MacFarquhar (1998, 664) for an interesting example from Shandong Province.

I further test whether a CPPCC membership has any "protective effect" on private entrepreneurs' property using survey evidence.

3.4 PRIVATE ENTREPRENEURS IN OFFICE

What do private entrepreneurs do in office? How much time do they spend on office-related duties? Do they take time off from running their businesses? Mr. Qian (discussed at the beginning of this chapter) was a dedicated legislator, but does he represent other entrepreneurs in office? A recent legislative survey of 187 provincial legislators from one southern province sheds light on some of these questions.[19] The survey asked legislators about how they do their job, how they seek information, how much time they spend on legislative duties and tasks, and so forth. The survey questionnaires were sent out to all provincial legislators in one province in September 2017, and respondents were asked to mail back their responses in a pre-paid envelope. The overall response rate was 33.8 percent.

The survey results suggest that legislators in this province are very active. Recall that Qian submits one to two legislative proposals or suggestions (including joint submissions) each year, and in this province, legislators submit an average of 9.7 proposals or suggestions per year. Entrepreneur–legislators are even more active than the average, submitting 11.4 proposals or suggestions per year. They are also more likely to initiate fieldwork or research trips and are more likely to make their contact information publicly available. On other aspects of the role, including attending government-organized hearings, visiting government officials, and receiving constituents, there seems to be little difference between entrepreneur–legislators and non–entrepreneur legislators (Table 3.3). All answers are self-reported, and we can safely assume that some legislators have inflated their numbers to appear more dedicated to the public office than they actually were. In addition, these results come from a survey of legislators from one province, which might not be representative of the rest of China.

With these caveats in mind, this survey shows that entrepreneur–legislators are as committed to their legislative office as their non-entrepreneur colleagues: they take time off work to attend meetings, to write legislative proposals and policy suggestions, to interact with

---

[19] As requested by the survey principal investigators, the name of the province is kept confidential.

TABLE 3.3 *What legislators do in office*

Legislative duties in the past year	All legislators	Entrepreneur–legislators
Legislative proposals/suggestions submitted (total no.)	9.7	11.4
Self-organized fieldwork/research*	0.9	1.3
Attended hearings/discussions organized by government*	1.5	1.5
Visited government officials*	0.5	0.6
Received constituents*	0.9	0.9
Voiced opinions on social media*	0.5	0.4
Published contact information (e-mail or phone no.)	71.1%	83.3%
Total observations	184	25

Note. Provincial survey of legislators conducted in 2017. All values are self-reported, and the table only reports the mean values. * 0-none; 1-once; 2-twice or more in the past year.

government officials, and to assess public opinion. In the next chapter, I describe what some of those legislative proposals and policy suggestions submitted by entrepreneur–legislators look like.

3.5 DISCUSSION

The people's congress system has undergone significant changes, especially during the reform era. In contrast to its "rubber-stamp" image, the Chinese legislatures have become a platform for lawmaking and policy discussion. The system has also begun to serve as a channel to collect feedback on local problems from citizens. Despite this notable progress, the people's congresses have limited power, as the party still tightly controls all important decisions they make, from lawmaking and policymaking to government appointments.

As China's private sector is gaining its legal status, private entrepreneurs are running for and winning seats in the legislatures. In this chapter, I show that private entrepreneurs are gradually taking up more seats in the local congresses and are spending time fulfilling their legislative duties. Contrary to the perception that these congressional seats are "arranged," private entrepreneur candidates compete to get on the ballot and to win elections. Throughout the process, they engage in costly and mostly informal lobbying and networking activities to win the support of relevant party and government officials. If a legislative seat does not bring individuals power or influence, why do these entrepreneurs exert so much effort to run for office? The next chapter unpacks their motivations.

Box 3.2 State power exercised by the congresses

Article 99 [Law and Regulation Making]
Local people's congresses at various levels ensure the observance and implementation of the Constitution and other laws and the administrative regulations in their respective administrative areas. Within the limits of their authority as prescribed by law, they adopt and issue resolutions and examine and decide on plans for local economic and cultural development and for the development of public services.

Local people's congresses at or above the county level shall examine and approve the plans for economic and social development and the budgets of their respective administrative areas and examine and approve the reports on their implementation. They have the power to alter or annul inappropriate decisions of their own standing committees.

The people's congresses of nationality townships may, within the limits of their authority as prescribed by law, take specific measures suited to the characteristics of the nationalities concerned.

Article 101 [Appointment and Dismissal of Government Officials]
Local people's congresses at their respective levels elect and have the power to recall governors and deputy governors, or mayors and deputy mayors, or heads and deputy heads of counties, districts, townships and towns.

Local people's congresses at or above the county level elect, and have the power to recall, presidents of people's courts and chief procurators of people's procuratorates at the corresponding level. The election or recall of chief procurators of people's procuratorates shall be reported to the chief procurators of the people's procuratorates at the next higher level for submission to the standing committees of the people's congresses at the corresponding level for approval.

Article 104 [Supervision]
The standing committee of a local people's congress at or above the county level discusses and decides on major issues in all fields of work in its administrative area; supervises the work of the people's government, people's court and people's procuratorate at the corresponding level; annuls inappropriate decisions and orders of the people's government at the corresponding

level; annuls inappropriate resolutions of the people's congress at the next lower level; decides on the appointment or removal of functionaries of State organs within the limits of its authority as prescribed by law; and, when the people's congress at the corresponding level is not in session, recalls individual deputies to the people's congress at the next higher level and elects individual deputies to fill vacancies in that people's congress.

Article 107 [Appointment, Dismissal, Training, Assessment of Public Administration Staff]
Local people's governments at or above the county level, within the limits of their authority as prescribed by law, conduct administrative work concerning the economy, education, science, culture, public health, physical culture, urban and rural development, finance, civil affairs, public security, nationalities affairs, judicial administration, supervision, and family planning in their respective administrative areas; issue decisions and orders; appoint or remove administrative functionaries, train them, appraise their performance and reward or punish them.

People's governments of townships, autonomous townships, and towns execute the resolutions of the people's congresses at the corresponding levels as well as the decisions and orders of the State administrative organs at the next higher level and conduct administrative work in their respective administrative areas.

The People's Congress Deputy Law further specifies the rights and responsibilities:[20]

Box 3.3 Rights enjoyed by deputies

Article 3 Deputies enjoy the following rights:

1. To participate in the people's congress sessions and to participate in the deliberation of all bills and proposals, reports and other issues, and putting forward their opinions;
2. To propose legislation, inquisition and collective dismissals, in accordance with law;
3. To advise, critique, and suggest on all aspects of works;

---

[20] "Law of the People's Republic of China on Deputies to the National People's Congress and Deputies to Local people's congresses" (2010 Amendment) [Effective]. Law Info China. http://en.pkulaw.cn/display.aspx?cgid=139687&lib=law. (last accessed May 19, 2015).

4. To participate in elections (of upper-level people's congress deputies) if applicable;
5. To participate in all votes held by the people's congresses at corresponding levels;
6. To acquire information and guarantees necessary for their performance of duties according to law; and
7. To enjoy other rights stipulated by law.

Box 3.4 Responsibilities of deputies

Article 4 Deputies shall perform the following duties:

1. To play an exemplary role in abiding by the Constitution and laws, to guard state secrets, to assist implementation of the Constitution and law in the production, work, or public activities which they take part in, to assist the implementation of the Constitution and the laws;
2. To attend people's congress sessions on time, to earnestly deliberate and assess bills, proposals, reports, and other topics, to express opinions, and to accomplish all tasks during the sessions;
3. To actively participate in organized visits, research trips, investigations, and other activities related to deputy responsibility;
4. To develop and enhance further study and research ability, and to enhance their capacity for performing their duties as deputies;
5. To keep close contact with constituents and electoral units, to listen to them and to collect their opinions and demands, and to serve the people;
6. To consciously abide by social morality and be clean, self-disciplined, impartial, decent, and diligent; and
7. To serve other duties stipulated by the law.

4

Motivations to Run

Most local congress websites have a page called "A Glimpse of Deputies" (*Daibiao Fengcai*), which contains profiles of selected congressional deputies. This page exhibits deputies' manifestos, which usually state that they see their people's congress deputy status as an honor and describe how they fulfill the duty that comes with that honor. The manifesto of Cheng Tianqing, a deputy in the Changzhi prefectural congress in Shanxi Province, is a typical manifesto from an entrepreneur–deputy (Figure 4.1). It was published in January 2010 under the title of "Cheng Tianqing: it is a glorious responsibility for a deputy to make sure every single proposal is of good quality." Cheng is described as "a prefectural congress deputy; Chairman of the board at the Shanxi ZhongDe Plastic-Steel Profile Co., LTD." It starts with the following statement:

In 2003, I was elected as a prefectural congress deputy with great honor. I understand that in order to be a qualified people's congress deputy, I have to represent people's interests, to bring people's wishes (to the meetings), and to follow the Constitution and the law. Not only do I have to be a role model at work and at public events, I also need to enhance my understanding of theories related to the people's congress, to develop my study skills, and to understand what the masses care about. I will devote myself completely to serving the people.

He then states that "a small enterprise belongs to an individual, but a big enterprise belongs to the society" – an expression that many entrepreneurs use, which usually expresses their unyielding willingness to contribute to the government's tax revenue and to public projects. His manifesto showcases donations his company has made in recent years and policy proposals he submitted as a deputy to local governments, and ends by emphasizing that "great honor comes with great responsibility."

FIGURE 4.1 "A glimpse of deputies"

Note. A screenshot of "A glimpse of deputies" page on the Changzhi prefectural congress website. The word "national" in the header was a typo.

These kinds of manifestos are not interesting to read – they are highly monotonic; the deputies always describe their role as a great "honor" and a "glorious" moment for themselves and for their companies, and they always stress that they represent the people. They never talk about other, less altruistic, motivations for being a people's congress deputy.

Do individuals compete for seats in congresses for the honor and to serve the public? Or are there other, more selfish, reasons to join a legislature? I argue in previous chapters that private entrepreneurs believe that being a legislator makes their property more secure. This chapter assesses this implication. The first section provides a more detailed discussion of the definitions and interpretations of the term "expropriation," a central concept of the book. Using interview evidence, I establish that private entrepreneurs perceive predation as a major problem associated with operating a business, and that securing property is a main motivation for them to seek legislative office. The chapter then uses survey data to demonstrate that government officials acknowledge the predation problem and recognize that entrepreneurs have a valid need to use legislative office to protect their businesses and property. A final section surveys a small sample of legislative and policy proposals from entrepreneur-legislators. I show that although property security has been a main concern for entrepreneur–legislators, they seldom formally discuss this issue when they submit legislative or policy proposals. In those rare cases when they do talk about property security, entrepreneur–legislators are very careful with their language to avoid triggering a political backlash.

4.1 EXPROPRIATION: MORE EVIDENCE

Chapter 1 defined expropriation and discussed how it occurs in China. This section draws evidence from my fieldwork in China to give readers more concrete examples of the types of expropriation that typically occur.

4.1.1 Interview Data and the Issue of Desirability

In China, localities vary substantially in the degree of (and support for) private sector development (Tsai 2007, chapter 6). Therefore, I carefully chose my fieldwork locations to represent different levels of private sector development and different kinds of business–state relations. Between 2012 and 2016, I conducted 108 in-depth interviews with entrepreneurs and government officials in four provinces and two provincial cities in China: Zhejiang and Guangdong on the east coast, where the private economy thrives and local governments are relatively market-oriented; Guizhou in southwestern China, a province with the lowest GDP per capita in the nation, which has a small and developing private sector; and Hunan, a province in central China with medium-level private sector development. The two provincial-level cities are Beijing and Shanghai. The Appendix provides detailed information on these interviews.

I was mostly interested in interviewing entrepreneurs who are local legislators, and entrepreneurs who are equally successful in their businesses but did not make it to the local legislatures. I also interviewed some entrepreneurs who do not belong to either of these camps. The ideal sampling strategy is to randomly select a representative sample of legislator-entrepreneurs and non-legislator-entrepreneurs in a given location. This strategy, however, was unrealistic, because local legislators' information is largely private, and it is difficult to successfully schedule an interview with the manager or other top executives of a company that is represented in the local legislatures without an introduction. Therefore, I had to rely on introductions from colleagues and friends to access the appropriate subjects. I also collected perspectives from government officials who frequently interact with local businesses. Similarly, the sample of officials is non-random and was assembled via introductions. Finally, I interviewed

Chinese scholars who conduct research on business–state relations in Beijing, Shanghai, and Zhejiang.

Although neither the entrepreneur nor the government official samples were a random sample, I tried to get an entrepreneur sample that represented the main industry and a representative variety of industries in each location, and a government official sample that represented a wide variety of bureaucrats and officials who interact with local businesses on a regular basis. These samples ensured that a wide range of views were expressed. Introductions through trusted connections ensured that respondents were more open and forthcoming.

The main purpose of the qualitative analysis is to substantiate the argument by presenting a variety of perspectives. Several findings emerged from the open-ended interviews. First, private entrepreneurs live with arbitrary expropriation every day, and they do not feel that their property is secure. This finding is consistent with Kellee Tsai's 2002 survey of private entrepreneurs: 71 percent of her respondents reported that "laws protecting property rights" need further improvement (Tsai 2007, 81). Second, different types of private entrepreneurs experience different levels of expropriation. Owners of small firms, who usually have few channels for making connections with local officials, are at the greatest risk of expropriation, and have few options except to comply. By contrast, private entrepreneurs who are local legislators, and whose companies are large and successful, do not worry too much about arbitrary predation. They usually have friends in different bureaus in local government to whom they report problems with local bureaucrats. A third group of entrepreneurs is situated between the powerless and the powerful entrepreneurs. Their businesses might also be quite successful, and they might have a few friends in various local government bureaus. Yet they are not local legislators, and they must use other channels to network and sustain their relationships with local officials, who can help the entrepreneurs shield their businesses from expropriation. While entrepreneur–legislators can use their office to efficiently build connections to multiple government agencies, this third group of entrepreneurs has to build individual connections with each government agency, which is much more time consuming and costly. Finally, the interviews revealed that both legislator– and non-legislator-entrepreneurs believe that having a legislative seat ensures greater property security.

Social desirability and political sensitivity are potential issues in the context of this study, and they could bias the findings of this study. For example, entrepreneurs whose businesses have been expropriated by local

bureaucrats might exaggerate the frequency and severity of local predation, while entrepreneurs could under-report levels of expropriation out of
fear of retribution, especially if they do not trust the interviewer. Likewise,
government officials and bureaucrats lack a strong incentive to truthfully
report their behavior to me because expropriation is mostly informal
or illegal.

Therefore the structure of the open-ended interview process and the
way I conducted the interviews were designed to try to alleviate these
potential problems in two ways. First, when I began collecting the qualitative data, I was unaware of the extent to which entrepreneur–legislators
are protected from local predation. I mostly asked entrepreneurs about
their opinions on the current business environment; property security
issues emerged naturally from these conversations with no prompting.
Therefore, confirmation bias due to my own prior beliefs is not a major
concern (Nickerson 1998). Second, my interviewees were usually introduced to me by trusted acquaintances, which ensured relatively open and
honest conversations. All interviews were conducted in Chinese. As a
native speaker, I tried my best to avoid using terms with any political
connotations.

4.1.2 Small Enterprises and Local Predation

I loosely define firm size. If a firm is one of the leading companies in an
industry, or represents a main contributor to local tax revenue, I treat it as
a large and successful enterprise. If a firm has fewer than 100 employees
and is regarded as a small business in the local economy, I treat it as a
small enterprise.[1]

Small business owners usually believe that they have "no chance" of
becoming a local legislator, and that they have little influence over local
policy. They are also usually cynical and believe that local legislators have
no say in local policy making or legislation. When asked if he would be
willing to run for office in the local legislature, Mr. Wong, a small business owner in the firecracker manufacturing industry in Hunan Province,
quickly replied "no" – "political status of a local legislator is an empty
title" and it is "useless" (Interview P137). Similarly, when asked this ques-

---

[1] The official definition of SME, according to the National Bureau of Statistics, is an
enterprise that has less than 0.4 billion yuan in total assets and less than 0.3 billion yuan
in sales (Shen et al. 2009).

tion, Mr. Wu, a small online commerce business owner in Hunan, laughed at the impossibility of himself securing an office (Interview P122).

Interviewer: Have you ever thought of running for district legislator?

Mr. Wu: No way. I am a grassroots entrepreneur and I would have zero influence over government policy and decisions.

Many of these entrepreneurs believe that their businesses are at a high risk of being expropriated by local bureaucrats. As illustrated, they see themselves as "non-influential" in the local political economy, and their properties are usually "unprotected." Such local expropriation takes a variety of forms, including bureaucrats taking products for free or forcing entrepreneurs to grant them a discount. Mr. Zhang, the co-owner of a small drugstore in Hunan, is often visited by tax collectors, who take the Chinese medicines produced by his company for free (Interview P1377). Mr. Xu, who runs a small retail clothing shop in Hunan Province, has also frequently received tax collectors who force him to give them discounts (Interview P1378). Local expropriation could also entail governments forcing companies to make particular purchases. For example, the district government in Zhejiang Province ordered Mr. Liu, an entrepreneur in Zhejiang Province, to purchase an optional business insurance (Interview P1222). Local expropriation could also occur in the form of "public goods project donations," "protection fees" collected by the local police station, or "extra tax payments" collected by the local taxation bureau (Interviews P135; P1373; P1375).

Not only do these small business owners experience regular harassment by local bureaucrats, they are also well aware that expropriation is discriminative. During a focus group session, I spoke with ten representatives from small ceramic manufacturing companies who unanimously agreed that the industry leader and firms with congressional deputies would never be arbitrarily inspected and were unlikely to be expropriated by local bureaucrats (Interview P135).

These small enterprises are not the main focus of my research. While they are crucial economic actors and operate in the same business environment as large enterprises, they are more vulnerable to local expropriation than larger, better-connected companies. Interviews with them helped me understand the local business environment and business–state relations. But for analytical purposes, since my "treatment group" consists of entrepreneur–legislators, my "control group" should be comparable to the "treatment group," meaning that this group consists of private entrepreneurs who run sizable businesses, who could potentially win a seat in the local legislatures but have not, for whatever reason.

4.1.3 Entrepreneur-Legislators and Low Predation

Private entrepreneurs who have a seat in the local legislatures usually own, or are in the top management of, large and successful companies in the region. In contrast to small business owners, they usually do not see local predation as a big problem for their businesses. They believe that being a legislator helps their business development, but they also generally do not think that they are in any position to influence policy through the legislative process.

Some entrepreneurs are "invited" to join local legislatures, while others have gone through a competitive process to obtain a seat. While it is difficult to obtain information on how exactly each legislator obtained his seat, the interview evidence suggests that entrepreneurs who are invited into local legislatures are usually those whose companies that are essential to the local economy (e.g., the biggest taxpayer, a main job creator, etc.). Most entrepreneur–legislators have successful enterprises, and they usually have some political capital. Mr. Tan, the chief financial officer of a major manufacturing company in Hunan, was invited by the prefectural congress standing committee to join the prefectural legislature; thus he faced little competition getting in. His understanding was that his company has a guaranteed seat in the prefectural congress, and even in the provincial congress.[2] The board of directors decides who among them occupies the seat in a given term (Interview P1217).

Other legislators face more competition when running for office. Mr. Qian, the owner of a large interior design firm in Hunan, told me in vague language that he had to do "a lot of work" with the local ACFIC office in order to get nominated. He was also frustrated that he was not going to be a prefectural congress deputy for a second term, despite the "effort" he continues to put in (Interview P131). Qian refused to comment when I asked more specifically what kind of efforts he exerted. The message behind this vague language is that nurturing a good relationship with the local ACFIC office and being nominated usually

---

[2] He told me that it was originally his boss (the chairman of the board of directors) who was invited to be a member at the prefectural congress. His boss did not want to do it, and "gave" the position to him. It is unclear whether Mr. Tan's claim that the company would always have a seat in the prefectural or even provincial congress is true.

involves money and is very costly. I inferred from the conversation that Qian has spent quite a lot of money on banquets and gifts.

Mr. Kang, a real estate developer and a local legislator from the central province of Henan, reported that legislative elections are becoming increasingly competitive. Although he did not elaborate on why and how he believes this, I gathered from our conversation that as more entrepreneurs are becoming interested in obtaining a legislative seat, the price of these positions rises. When I asked him how exactly he obtained his seat, he told me that it involved a lot of "management" and "handling" (*yun zuo*), a vague term frequently mentioned by entrepreneurs to describe how they manage their relations with government officials and how they get nominated and elected as legislators (Interview P1311).

Entrepreneur–legislators generally think that their legislative or policy proposals are "unimportant," and are never "treated seriously by corresponding governments." Mr. Zhou, a second-term district-level legislator in Hunan, is one such nonbeliever in the system (Interview P1218):

Interviewer: Have you ever submitted any policy proposals?

Mr. Zhou: Many times! I have always proposed for tax reductions. I do not believe in other tax rebate or tax return policies (*shuishou fanhuan zhengce*). They are mostly for show and useless. I think the most straightforward way to help us entrepreneurs is direct tax reduction. But I am frustrated that my proposals are never adopted by local governments. Not even once!

Mr. Zhao, the CEO of a pharmaceutical company in Guizhou, also believed that proposals are "useless," and that his main responsibility in the congress meetings is "to clap hands" (Interview P126). Mr. Ma, the owner of a trading firm in Zhejiang, believes that political connections obtained through the congress are "way more important" than the power to propose legislative bills or policy suggestions (Interview P1222).

Legislator–entrepreneurs, although unable to influence legislation, do see one main benefit of office: they are usually less likely to face expropriation by local bureaucrats. Most of the entrepreneur–legislators I interviewed believe that they are "protected from predation" as legislators (Interviews P1312; P136; P123). Mr. Sun, a entrepreneur–legislator in Hunan, calls local bureaucrats "selective predators." As a legislator, he has never been "selected" as prey.

The above mentioned Mr. Qian, who has been doing business in the same province for more than 20 years, recalled that his company was frequently inspected by the local taxation bureau before he became a legislator (Interview P124).

Mr. Qian: The situation in the past was much worse. Those tax collectors were relentless *(ye man)*, and they would just come to my company to take stuff. Eventually my wife and I could not stand it and we decided to take it to the court.

Interviewer: Really? Take civil servants to court?

Mr. Qian: Yes. There was this one specific tax collector who was so hated by many entrepreneurs in the district and we decided to do something together.[3] We were not sure what the results would be though.

Interviewer: How about now? Are tax collectors less relentless?

Mr. Qian: Inspection and random check-ups seldom happened anymore soon after I became a prefectural legislator. It might be that the business environment has improved. Or it might be those tax people knew that I am more powerful and connected now.

Zhou (a friend of Qian who happened to be with Qian and who is also a private entrepreneur): No. The tax collectors are not much better. They still come to my (yoga) studio at random to cause trouble.

Zhou did not specify what kind of trouble tax collectors were making. We had just met, and he was reluctant to talk about expropriation with a total stranger. But because we had been talking about tax collectors and expropriations before he spoke, I could safely conclude that the "trouble" Zhou referred to would be some form of expropriation similar to what Qian had experienced in the past.

Mr. Gao, the owner of a large computer and electronics resale store in Hunan, has also experienced such a difference in treatment before and after he obtained a seat in the county congress (Interview P139).

Interviewer: I heard expropriation is a common problem here. Has your business ever been affected?

Mr. Gao: Yes, it happened in the past. I forgot which government bureau it was, but there was this one time when a few officials came to my store and asked me to give them a few computers for free as a contribution to the government. It was not too much and I just gave them a few computers for free.

Interviewer: Do you think it would happen again?

Mr. Gao: I don't think so. But it is not a big deal. If they come again, I will give them what they want. I would even invite them to lunch or dinner.

---

[3] This was the only time when one of my interviewees discussed some sort of "collective action" or legal action. How often entrepreneurs resort to courts to settle disputes is an empirical question beyond the scope of this project. For a related discussion, see Ang and Jia (2014).

Gao does not think being a legislator will always protect him, but this conversation suggests that he believes that becoming a legislator has resulted in less expropriation.

Not only do legislator–entrepreneurs experience less severe expropriation, they may sometimes even reject expropriation-like requests without facing repercussions from the government. For instance, Mr. Zhao once refused to contribute to a government-sponsored charitable foundation when asked for an involuntary donation.

Some legislators even impose business on other companies through the congress network. Mr. Zou, a prefectural legislator and the manager of an entertainment business in Guizhou, bragged about his good connections with the local tourist administration bureau and how he managed to convince the bureau to send all local travel agents' customers to see shows produced by his company (Interview P128).

4.1.4 Big Enterprises and Non-legislators, Some Expropriation

Entrepreneurs who are not local legislators have other ways to build connections with local bureaucrats and to protect their property, but it is costly for them to make friends with officials and bureaucrats in every bureau. These firms present good opportunities for predation by local bureaucrats.

Owners of large and successful companies have diverging opinions about their local congresses. Mr. Deng, the owner of a well-established, million-yuan IT business in Guizhou, usually has contracts with the local government. He insisted that he would not enjoy "sitting through the congress plenums," although he had not been to one. He also believed that business–government relations are determined by local governments rather than by local legislatures (Interview P1215). Other entrepreneurs stated that a congressional seat represents a privileged status for the whole company rather than an individual, and that it is possible to send a colleague as a replacement to congressional meetings, or to have them run for the legislative seat instead (Interviews P1217; G136). Although Deng is not a local legislator, he is the founder of a local IT business association, which helps him maintain close ties with local governments (Interview P1215).

Interviewer: Does your company experience any expropriation from local bureaucrats?

Mr. Deng: Connections matter a lot. A company can avoid arbitrary inspections and fines if it maintains good relations with local bureaucrats. I have been running my business in this district for almost ten years. I use the business association I started to interact with local bureaucrats.

Interviewer: Let's imagine a hypothetical scenario. If the neighboring district issues a new tax policy that is more favorable towards IT companies, would you consider moving your company to that district?

Mr. Deng: Absolutely not. Even if I save 10 percent on tax payments, I might actually lose more, since I would know nobody in the new district taxation bureau.

Interviewer: What is the loss?

Mr. Deng: You know, some arbitrary tax collection by tax collectors.

Deng has used his business association to expand his political network, and has built up enough political capital to protect his property from expropriation. Mr. Tao, a young and savvy entrepreneur who started an online travel agency a few years ago in Hunan, claims he already has a "very good relationship" with various local government bureaus, even though he is not a legislator or a CPPCC deputy. He also has friends working in the local taxation bureau in a neighboring district who informed him about a new tax refund policy that was going to be implemented the following year. He then worked to convince the taxation bureau in his own district to "selectively enforce the policy early," and thus enjoyed a lower tax rate that was supposed to become effective one year later. He did not want to tell me how he established this solid relationship with the local taxation bureau, but he suggested that not all firms could persuade the taxation bureau to allow them to enjoy this benefit. Although he has good friends in the district taxation bureau, he does not have any friends in the local administration for industry and commerce, which forced him to join some local business associations and to pay significant membership fees (Interview P133). In Tao's case, his political capital helped him to enjoy a new policy benefit, but was not enough to deter predatory behaviors from other bureaus.

Mr. Sang, a medium-size real estate developer in Guizhou, talks about the difference between his company and other real estate developers who have seats in the local legislatures. "Those companies and SOEs are different from us. When they start a new development, even the provincial party secretary will show up [to support their new project]. They also get better policy from the government. We just cannot compete with them." When I asked him how he develops his connections with the local government, he was vague: "We have to do informal things. If we are totally formal, we would not have any good policy or good land (for real estate development)." What Sang meant by "formal" is to have a formal political title, such as "people's congress deputy." Although for "personality reasons" Sang did not want to enter into politics, he has other entrepreneur friends in the congress who he can "ask for help from" if he is "in trouble" (Interview P1211).

Mr. Ouyang, a vice president of a big brand attire manufacturing company in Zhejiang, proudly described his company as the second-largest tax contributor in the county. Because of its importance in the local economy, the company receives considerable support from the local government.

Interviewer: What kind of support can you get?

Mr. Ouyang: Our company recently built a new factory space and purchased new facilities which are all connected above the factory floor space. The factory space arrangement did not pass inspection from the local work safety bureau, but there was actually no way to rearrange the equipment so that it meets the safety standard. Of course we did not want to pay a fine, and I decided to talk to one of the vice county heads, who oversees the safety bureau. We know each other and I managed to solicit his support. In the end, our company did not have to pay a fine, while keeping the facility as it is.

Interviewer: Can other manufacturing firms get a similar deal?

Mr. Ouyang: I think it might be really difficult for smaller companies to secure such a deal. They do not have as great a relationship with the local government as we do.

Although his company is a local government's favorite, it is not exempt from all arbitrary inspections by local government agencies, especially the taxation bureau. Ouyang referred to the taxation bureau as "relentless," and his company has to comply whenever tax collectors decide to drop by and collect "extra tax." Again, in these cases, entrepreneurs who own large companies and do not yet have legislator status usually resort to other means to protect their property.

4.2 COUNTING MOTIVATIONS

The above qualitative illustrations provide clear evidence that Chinese entrepreneurs are experiencing various types and levels of expropriation, and that entrepreneurs who are local legislators feel less worried that their property will be expropriated. Because most of these interviews are open-ended, the topic of "motivation to run for office" did not come up during every conversation. It was discussed in the interview with Mr. Pan, an entrepreneur–legislator:

Interviewer: Do you think writing policy proposals will result in anything concrete in local policies?

Mr. Pan: Of course not. I wrote proposals every year asking for better roads connecting our prefecture to the nearby ones. The only response I received from the government was "do not propose this anymore." My entrepreneur friends in the congress all share the same perspective [that proposals do not matter]. I believe 80–90 percent of them wanted to join the legislature simply because they were looking for a "protective umbrella."

Interviewer: Do you belong to the 80 percent?

Mr. Pan: No, I do not. I join because I hope I can represent the interests of my district.

[Pan clearly forgot what he just said regarding the "ineffectiveness" of policy proposals.]

Similarly, Mr. Lang, a prefectural legislator and the owner of a trading company, uses an interesting metaphor (Interview P154):

Mr. Lang: Doing business in China is like sailing a small boat in a turbulent sea. The government is a giant boat sailing nearby. A small boat should sail next to the big one, but it should not go too close – that will be very dangerous. When a business owner joins politics, s/he will make the boat sail much more smoothly.[4]

Individuals have multiple and diverse motivations for joining politics, and there are optimists who believe that their voices can sometimes be heard during legislative and discussion sessions. Mr. Gao, for instance, joined the district legislature mainly because he was "interested in understanding local politics and policy," and thinks some of his policy proposals have "been considered by some leaders," but he also admits that due to his higher social status, local bureaucrats "respect" him more than his peers, and that government inspections and check-ups became "more standard-ized" after he became a legislator (Interview P139).

To analyze these interview texts more systematically, I performed a simple text analysis on all my interview transcripts, counting different motivations to run for legislative office mentioned by the entrepreneurs interviewed. A second coder who is a native speaker of Chinese performed the same task to reduce any individual coder effect. Table 4.1 presents the count of the primary motivations mentioned in the interviews.

---

[4] Chinese entrepreneurs love to use metaphor, and usually reject my request to give more concrete examples.

TABLE 4.1 *Motivations to run for local legislative office*

Motivation	N	Percentage
To help develop business	32	67
To build connections with local elites	38	79
To protect business from local predation	20	42
To represent local interests	2	4
To understand local policies	1	2
To influence policy	1	2
Total	48	

Data source. Author's interview data. Individuals sometimes discussed multiple motivations to run for office, therefore the total percentage adds up to more than 100%.

Such data should be taken with a grain of salt: some individuals might be more outspoken and honest than others, and some entrepreneurs might be more risk-averse than others. But the fact that almost no one stated that their main motivation for joining the local congress was "to represent local interests" or "to influence policy" should give readers some confidence that they spoke their minds.

Entrepreneurs pointed out that one of the main motivations for them to compete for legislative office is to protect their business from local predation (Table 4.1). The top three most mentioned reasons or motivations to run are "to help develop businesses," "to build connections with local elites," and "to protect business from local predation." These reasons are highly correlated: of the 20 individuals who reported that they ran because a legislative office "protects their business," many also stated that such an office helps develop businesses, and builds and enhances connections with local elites.

A few important caveats are necessary here. First, "developing business" is a direct translation from Chinese, and its meaning is a little different from the English term "business development." In Chinese, business development could either mean organic business development or aggressive development through informal means. Second, "building connections with local elites" could be a means to many ends. Stronger connections could help with many aspects that are related to "business development." Entrepreneurs use these connections to bring more government contracts or to bid for a newly vacated parcel of land. Entrepreneurs also understand that their stronger connections help fend off expropriations. In other words, the motivation to build connections with local elites explains how entrepreneurs may use legislative office to "help develop business" and "ensure property security." These answers echo the findings of Bruce Dickson's 2005 survey, which asked private entrepreneurs why they joined the Chinese Communist Party (CCP): 54.3 percent of the subjects reported joining because of the "economic benefits to themselves or their firms." Other motivations included "to avoid the interference of party and government organizations in their business affairs," to "gain better protection from economic competitors," and to have "easier access to material resources and financial and tax benefits" (Dickson 2008, 93–4). In Chapter 6, I show that the benefits of being a CCP member have become increasingly marginal, but the mechanisms that explain how entrepreneurs take advantage of their party membership are relevant to understand how entrepreneurs use legislator status to protect their business.

Although I argue that property security is the *main* motivation for private entrepreneurs to run for office, it is not the only reason. Cho (2009) observes that deputies from the private sector seem to aspire to political status the most, because they hope to "make up for their weak and unstable political status" (108). Truex (2014) argues that rent-seeking is a main motivation, and estimates a two-percentage-point increase in returns for entrepreneurs who are National People's Congress deputies. However, he also argues that "rents that are too extravagant could crowd out representative norms and even engender public unrest" (Truex 2016, 188). Similar to my argument, Li et al. (2006) suggest that an entrepreneur's decision to enter politics in China can be explained by the underdevelopment of the market and market-supporting institutions, and Dickson (2008) suggests that a legislative seat protects individuals from government seizures of land and property, and in general helps further cultivate personal relationships with leaders. Last but not least, many entrepreneurs believe holding a congressional seat is "a great honor." Such accounts usually appear in the media and on official congressional websites.[5] My legislator–entrepreneur interviewees rarely mentioned "honor," "prestige," or "social status" as a main motive, but it does not mean they do not see the positions as an "honor." In fact, many of them

---

[5] For instance, see a statement by a local legislator from Pingdingshan prefectural people's congress, published on January 17, 2013. "Pingdingshan Legislator: Taking the Honorable Responsibility and Lawfully Practising my Duties" (*Pingdingshan Renda Daibiao: Dandang Guangrong Shiming Yifa Luxing Zhize*). http://news.dahe.cn/2013/01-17/101927309.html. Last accessed November 8, 2017.

spoke with pride when they mentioned their political positions, and at least two entrepreneurs displayed pictures in their offices of themselves posing with other people's congress deputies.

4.3 SELECTIVE PREDATORS

The discussion thus far has mostly focused on the perspective of private entrepreneurs. How about government bureaucrats, who are often accused of being the "predators"? Bureaucrats, for obvious reasons, do not use the words "predation," "expropriation," or "exploitation" when they refer to their interactions with local businesses. Instead, government officials frequently use alternative phrases such as "irregular check-ups" (*tuji jiancha*), "additional income," and "the need to accomplish goals" (*wancheng renwu*). Tax collectors usually avoid additional inspections on firms led by congressional deputies in order to "avoid troubles" (Interviews G133; G131). Mr. Qi, a tax officer in a prefectural-level tax bureau in Hunan, sees a congressional deputy status as a "protective umbrella" (*baohu san*) for entrepreneurs.

Interviewer: How exactly does this "protective umbrella" work?

Mr. Qi: Most taxation bureau heads are congressional deputies at some level, and entrepreneur–deputies are likely to be friends with these bureau heads. We, naturally, will treat friends of my boss nicer and be more cautious.

Interviewer: Do entrepreneur–legislators have better companies so that you do not need to inspect them as much? [I was trying to get at "arbitrary inspections."]

Mr. Qi: Yes, it is less likely that we inspect deputies' companies. My superiors sometimes suggest that I should check up on these companies after I inspect everybody else, or at least after the annual plenum of congress [so that deputies interact less, and Qi's boss would be less likely to encounter and to deal with entrepreneur–deputies who have complaints].

Mr. Lee, another tax collector in Hunan, sees legislators as "the privileged class" who are "annoying" to deal with. After a few encounters with those entrepreneur–legislators, he decided to avoid unnecessary interactions with them, since they can "easily phone [his] bosses" (Interview G133). Qi and Lee did not use the word "signaling," but they both infer that a legislator status is associated with strong political connections, and they both suggest that they are less likely to inspect companies with strong political connections.

In some cases, local governments are not financially able to deliver public goods projects, and they sometimes collect money from local entrepreneurs for non-personal purposes. Consistent with the findings in Sun, Zhu, and Wu (2014), my interviewees suggest that entrepreneur–legislators are more likely to donate to these projects, but some also "have the guts to say no" (Interviews G1213; G1214). Saying no is usually not an option for most entrepreneurs, because bureaucrats could easily find legitimate reasons to authorize collecting money from these companies in any case. However, bureaucrats are less likely to unnecessarily visit entrepreneurs who have seats in the legislature or are known to be friends with local officials.

4.3.1 Surveying Local Bureaucrats

During my interviews, I quickly realized that it was much more difficult to talk with government officials than with entrepreneurs about expropriation, or even more generally, about business–state relations. These topics naturally make people think of corruption, and sometimes our conversations came to an abrupt stop, or led to questions from my interviewees about the "real intention" of my research. Therefore, I bring in an additional source of data to analyze the perspective of local officials, especially about entrepreneurs who enter into politics.

The *China Youth Survey*, which took place in the fall of 2013, is one of the first large-scale academic surveys of government and party leaders in China.[6] A total of 3,120 surveys were distributed, and 2,372 surveys were completed. The respondents were 55.6 percent male; their average age was 36, and on average they had spent 11 years in the government or CCP offices.[7] Since the focus of my study is business–state relations, I examine a subsample of these respondents comprised of bureaucrats and officials who "frequently" or "at times" interact with local businesses (55 percent of the sample).

The following question was asked in the *China Youth Survey*:

There are many reasons private entrepreneurs join the legislature. Which are the main reasons, do you think, they join the legislature?

Subjects chose from among multiple listed motivations,[8] and Table 4.2 presents a summary of their answers. Consistent with Table 4.1, the

---

[6] Other studies using this dataset include Meng, Pan, and Yang (2014).
[7] See Appendix B for additional details about the survey.
[8] My qualitative data provided the list of possible answers for the motivation question.

TABLE 4.2 *Motivations to secure a legislative seat: Chinese officials'*
perspectives

Motivation	N	Percentage
To help develop business	2,141	90
To build connections with local elites	1,530	65
To protect business from local predation	963	41
Total	2,372	

Data source. The 2013 *China Youth Survey.* Individuals sometimes discussed multiple
motivations to run for office, therefore the total percentage adds up to more than 100
percent.

majority of Chinese officials believe that entrepreneurs join the legislatures to develop their businesses, to build connections with local elites,
and to protect their business from local predation.[9]

This survey provides suggestive evidence that government officials are
aware that private entrepreneurs use legislative seats to help grow their
businesses and to defend their property rights. No officials in this sample
believe that entrepreneurs join legislatures in order to serve the public.
The strategy of using a legislative seat to deter expropriation would only
work if local bureaucrats see a legislator status as a deterrent, and the
survey findings suggest that bureaucrats indeed understand entrepreneurs'
motivations to compete for legislative seats.

4.4 POLICY PROPOSALS FOR PROPERTY SECURITY

If property security is a main concern for private entrepreneurs, do they
use formal channels to address their concerns once they become part of
the formal institutions? Do entrepreneur–legislators try to change local
legislation or policy to ensure stronger property protection? This section
focuses on entrepreneur–legislators' formal legislative behavior by surveying the legislative and policy proposals they submitted. I show that they
seldom discuss property security because it is a politically sensitive issue.
In very rare cases when they do discuss this topic, they use mild language
to avoid any potential political backlash.

[9] The option of "to protect business from local predation" might appear politically
undesirable for government officials to answer, and we embedded this option in a list
experiment (Blair and Imai 2012) for half of the subjects in our sample. Surprisingly, the
percentage of subjects who chose this option in the list experiment is similar to those
answering the question directly. This option turns out to not be too sensitive, at least for
the respondents in this study.

4.4.1 Legislative and Policy Proposals

Local legislators are invited to submit legislative and policy proposals to local governments. Legislative proposals must follow a strict format, while the process for policy proposals is much simpler. Once they receive a response from the local government, the case can be closed. Therefore, many legislators are encouraged to submit policy proposals rather than legislative proposals, and many legislative proposals are converted into policy proposals (Interview G136).

Similar to the NPC proposal process, the local legislative proposal process has three stages: submission, classification, and response (Truex 2016). Deputies are required to conduct research before drafting their proposals to ensure that their proposals represent local interests and convey local public opinion. Legislative proposals have to be collective, but policy proposals can be either individual or collective. In some cases, local congressional offices screen deputies' proposals before submission. For example, prefectural deputies are sometimes required to give their proposals to the congressional office of their county for a "check" to make sure they represent local interests (Interviews G122; G123). The majority of proposals are submitted at the annual plenum, but they can be submitted at any time.

After proposals are submitted, the local people's congress office classifies them as either legislative proposals (*motions*) or policy proposals (*opinions*). Policy proposals are then sent to the corresponding government bureaus. Local bureaus are required to respond to legislators within six months, and legislators rate the "quality" of the response (Interview G136). If a legislator is not "satisfied" with the response, the proposal will be sent back to the corresponding bureau for another round of feedback.

A large number of proposals are submitted to the NPC and the local congresses each year. NPC deputies propose more than 9,000 opinions and motions each year (Truex 2016). Many more are submitted to the provincial-, prefectural-, county-, and township-level congresses. In the following analysis, I focus on county-/district-level legislatures, given data availability. I sampled legislative and policy proposals from six local congresses in three provinces in China: two (I will call them "County A" and "County B") from a southeastern province, two (C, D) from a central province, and two (E, F) from a western province.[10] Most of these

---

[10] In five of the six cases, proposals are not public, and I acquired them through personal connections. Therefore, I do not disclose the name of the county or district.

TABLE 4.3 *Legislative and policy proposals from six counties*

County	Year	Proposals	PE Proposals	Annual #	Total Deputies	PE Deputies
A	2007–13(7)	743	301(40.5%)	106	257	92(35.8%)
B	2008–12(5)	799	141(17.6%)	160	388	80(20.6%)
C	2008–12(5)	310	46(14.8%)	62	301	51(16.9%)
D	2008–12(5)	1091	50(4.6%)	218	379	20(5.3%)
E	2011–13(3)	279	1(0.4%)	93	240	5(2.1%)
F	2014(1)	21	8(38.1%)	21	207	39(18.8%)

Note. The column *Year* denotes the years that I have collected proposals. The column *Proposals* counts the total number of proposals submitted by all deputies in all years for which I have collected proposals. The column *PE Proposals* counts the numbers of proposals from private entrepreneur deputies, and the number in the parentheses represents the percentage of proposals from private entrepreneurs. The column *Annual #* calculates proposals from all deputies per year in the years studied. The column *PE Deputies* counts the number of private entrepreneur deputies and calculates the percentage of private entrepreneurs in each county.

proposals are not public, and I did not have access to all proposals that are submitted in all years. For example, I had access to seven years of proposals from County A, but only one year of proposals from County F (see Table 4.3). If a year is included, it means that I was able to obtain all proposals submitted that year in that county.

Within the six cases, deputies are more active in some local congresses than others. For instance, deputies in County D submitted 218 proposals per year in the years studied, whereas deputies in County F only submited 21 proposals per year. The total number of deputies ranges from 200 to 400 in these local legislatures, and private entrepreneurs are more represented in some locations than others. In the southeastern province, private entrepreneurs hold more seats in the local legislatures compared to in the inland provinces, but they do not necessarily submit a higher proportion of proposals.

4.4.2 What Do Entrepreneur–Deputies Propose?

Chinese private entrepreneurs are concerned about a wide variety of issues. Across the six counties, the top issue areas private entrepreneurs care about include: business environment, regional economic development, public transportation, and other public goods-related topics. Entrepreneurs in the coastal province submitted a wider range of proposals compared to their inland counterparts. Nevertheless, entrepreneurs in

TABLE 4.4 *Proposals from private entrepreneurs: issue areas*

Issue Areas	A	B	C	D	E	F
Business Environment	14.3	15.6	16.7	14.0	100.0	12.5
Regional Economic Development	7.6	2.8	14.6	26.0	0	0
Social Insurance/Unemployment	2.7	2.1	2.1	0	0	0
Education	4.7	2.8	2.1	0	0	12.5
Environment	4.0	7.8	8.3	0	0	12.5
Crime, Order, and Stability	5.6	2.1	2.1	6.0	0	0
Healthcare,	2.7	5.7	0	2.0	0	0
Food Safety,	0.7	2.1	0	0	0	0
Cultural Protection	0	4.3	0	2.0	0	0
Housing	5.3	0	0	0	0	0
Political Openness, Gov't Performance	4.0	0	8.3	0	0	25.0
Property Rights	4.7	2.1	4.2	4.0	0	12.5
Disaster Prevention, Public Safety	0.3	4.3	0	0	0	0
Public Transportation	27.9	21.3	18.8	36.0	0	25.0
Agriculture and Irrigation	0.3	7.8	8.3	14.0	0	0
Other Public Goods	12.3	0.7	10.4	0	0	0
Other	1.3	20.6	4.2	0	0	0
Total number of proposals	301	141	46	50	1	8

Note. The table displays the percentage of proposals in each issue area in the six counties. Hand coded by author. The selection of these issue area categories follows Truex (2016), who also studies deputy proposals but at the national level.

inland provinces are as active as those in coastal provinces: in County F, 38.1 percent of all proposals came from private entrepreneurs, which is close to the highest rate, 40.5 percent in County A. Table 4.4 provides a summary of all proposals from private entrepreneurs collected from all six counties. Even though property rights and property security are a primary concern for entrepreneurs, they do not frequently write proposals asking for stronger property rights.

4.4.3 Proposals Regarding Property Security

Now I turn my focus to entrepreneurs' legislative and policy proposals that either directly mention property security or touch upon the issue indirectly. Table 4.5 shows that although property insecurity remains a main threat to their business, only a small percentage of private entrepreneurs' proposals deals with property security issues.

Of the 22 proposals regarding property security or violations, nine discuss problems of "arbitrary or excessive fees or taxes" that were (or are) imposed either in their industry or in the local economy. Six propos-

TABLE 4.5 *Proposals on property security*

	A	B	C	D	E	F	Total
Property Security	14	3	2	2	0	1	22
Percentage	4.7	2.1	4.2	4.0	0	12.5	4.02

Note. The table shows the numbers of proposals related to property security submitted by private entrepreneurs in my database. I also calculate the number of proposals as a percentage of total proposals submitted by private entrepreneurs in each location and in total.

als concern specific land disputes that might or might not be related to legislators' own businesses. Two proposals are about the city patrol team (*cheng guan*), either suggesting that the staff should "get more professional training" or carefully complaining (in their language, "suggesting") that the team sometimes oversteps in areas in which they do not have authority. The other proposals are general business environment proposals that touch on property security and expropriation. I randomly sampled seven proposals from these 22 proposals related to property security, two from A, two from B, and one each from C, D, and E, in order to better understand their contents. Table 4.6 provides brief summaries of the seven proposals.

Most proposals use a polite tone and implicit language when describing local predation conducted by bureaucrats. For example, Policy Proposal A625 – submitted by Deputy Huang, the vice president of an electronics company, entitled "On the Development of High-tech Small and Medium Enterprises (SMEs)" – is a well-crafted and well-argued six-page document that lists major problems in the high-tech industry and provides systematic suggestions on how to promote growth in this industry. The proposal identifies six main problems, including an overly simplified product structure, a decrease in exports due to Chinese yuan appreciation, lack of focus on research and development, and difficulties in fundraising/financing. The two remaining problems identified are related to property insecurity:

#4. Tax. More than 90% of firms believe that the tax rate is too high, that tax reduction policies are "empty" and hard to extend to individual firms. The main reason is that there are only a few tax reduction policies, and the procedure to apply for those is too complicated. It results in high costs in applying for those policy benefits. Also, we need to be more informed about tax policy. There are not enough pre-tax reduction items, and I believe the current tax and fee standard is too strict.

#6. Low levels of coordination in policy implementation. Different government bureaus do not work together at all, and they only care about the interests of their

TABLE 4.6 *Content of property security-related proposals*

Proposal	Industry	Proposal Title	Property Security Content
A625	Electronics	On the development of high-tech SMEs	Points out the costliness of applying for a tax break Tax standard is "too strict" Suggests reducing "unreasonable" fee Convert fees into tax; be transparent about what to collect
A39	Electronics	On the need to develop an official standard for house demolition compensation	Points out the lack of official standard and government misconduct Proposes a new compensation standard
B4067	Machinery	On helping SMEs to respond to the financial crisis	Proposes reduction of other fees
B6061	Bamboo Art	On restoring order to the bamboo art industry	Points out some businesses owe money to farmers/factories Suggests that the government standardize industry-wide practice
C01	Manufacturing	On reducing the business-related transportation fee for Area S	Points out that the road fee is too high in the area Proposes reducing the fee for business-related transportation
D24	Coal Mining	On suggesting not to collect "older" tax	Suggests that the previously owed tax/fee presents a burden Suggests that tax bureau not collect the old tax/fee
E16	Retail	On stopping residents dumping trash at a property	Reports residents dumping trash at a property (his firm) Suggests that relevant government offices take action

Note. Industry denotes the private entrepreneur's industry. *Property Security Content* summarizes the proposal's main points on property security. The letter in front of the proposal number denotes where the proposal comes from. For instance, A625 is proposal #625 from County A. The number is greater than 301 (number of proposals from private entrepreneurs) because there are also proposals from other, non-entrepreneur deputies.

own bureau. It hurts us businessmen in the sense that procedures to get anything done are too complicated. We need to get "certified" and "approved" by too many bureaus. Such inefficiency costs us business opportunities.

At first glance, these points do not seem like a discussion of property security. But the proposal goes on to mention that tax laws and policies are too complicated, and the implication is that bureaucrats can use these policies and procedures to collect extra taxes and fees. This implied message becomes clear when Huang provides five policy ideas on how to strengthen control over local predation, using very careful and polite language:

#3(3) I suggest that relevant taxation officials provide lectures, distribute documents, and set up banners in taxation bureaus to inform entrepreneurs on tax reduction policies and to illustrate for entrepreneurs how to apply for benefits. Officials should inform us about this information as timely as possible.

#3(4) The government should clean up unreasonable fees. Some fees should be converted to taxes. We want transparency in tax and fee rates.

Similar to Proposal A625, Proposals A39, C01, and D24 all use relatively neutral language to describe property infringement. Yet Proposal B4067, entitled "On Helping SMEs Respond to the Financial Crisis," directly calls for a halt to *tanpai*, which has a negative connotation that suggests illicit behavior on the part of government officials. Proposed by Deputy Lin, a private entrepreneur in the machinery industry, this document makes four suggestions on how local governments could help small and medium size companies cope with the 2009 financial crisis. One of the suggestions is specifically about local expropriation:

#3 The government should help local companies to ease their burden – to reduce fees, to reduce *tanpai*, and to eliminate unreasonable charges. In doing so, local enterprises can get rid of these senseless fees and get out of trouble.

This proposal has already received a reply from the district government office.[11] In response to the request to reduce local expropriation, the reply reads:

We have carefully implemented national and provincial policies regarding the elimination and reduction of fees, including the elimination of the individual business management fee (*getihu guanli fei*), the farmer's market management fee (*jimaoshichang guanli fei*), and 100 different administrative and institutional fees (*xingzheng shiyexing shoufei*). We have implemented tax and fee reform in

[11] See the proposal and response at http://jyta.jiangmen.gov.cn/ShowNews.aspx? guid=1160 (in Chinese). Last accessed November 8, 2017.

the refined oil industry and eliminated six fees. ... In sum, enterprises and society at large saved 0.67 billion yuan per year.

[...]

To make sure tax and fee reduction policies are implemented at each level of offices, we will start a new campaign that investigates the implementation of fee reduction programs. Between March and July, we will explicitly and implicitly monitor the fee collection procedure of the following local bureaus: environment protection, quality inspection, housing and urban–rural development, commerce, work safety and coal mine safety, and quality supervision, inspection, and quarantine. We will pay particular attention to and stop any incidence of excessive fee collection and repetitive fee collection. We stand firmly against illegal fee collection.

At the end of this response, there is the name of the corresponding government official along with his telephone number and e-mail address. This response received a "satisfactory" rating from Deputy Lin.

A final category of relevant proposals relates to property infringement imposed by non-government parties. Proposal B6061, for instance, was submitted by an entrepreneur in the bamboo art industry. This entrepreneur–legislator reports to governments that some businesses are engaging in illegal activities and owe money to local farmers and other suppliers. The proposal suggests that the relevant government bureau take actions to "standardize practices." Similarly, Proposal E16, submitted by a shopping mall owner, reports that local residents have been dumping trash on his property and asks the local government to take action to stop them. These proposals are more about personal business interests than property security more generally.

4.4.4 Responses to Proposals

It is difficult to obtain government responses to proposals. I was only able to collect a small subset of responses to the proposals regarding property security. Therefore, I supplement this limited information with evidence from interviews with bureaucrats to get a sense of how bureaucrats react to proposals from entrepreneur–deputies. My understanding is that bureaucrats do not generally treat proposals from private entrepreneurs seriously. The primary goal of lower-level bureaucrats who handle these proposals is to take the least action possible without making a mistake. Entrepreneurs do not expect to receive wholehearted responses, and thus easily rate bureaucrats' responses as "satisfactory," which further decreases incentives for bureaucrats to put in more effort when responding to proposals.

The response to Proposal B4067, for example, was sincere, comprehensive, and hopefully effective in addressing the issue presented. Yet this kind of response might simply be an exception, as government officials do not usually take proposals from entrepreneur–legislators too seriously. Mr. Zhang, a bureaucrat who works at a district-level congressional office in Guangdong Province, dismisses many entrepreneur-legislators as "zombie deputies," because they usually "sit in the plenum meetings and do nothing at all." His office sometimes engages in a screening process and makes sure that "not everybody writes about the same thing" (Interview G136). Mr. Yang, a bureaucrat who is in charge of replying to policy proposals at his bureau in Hunan, commented that "the average quality of policy proposals is quite low," and said that "many deputies write proposals simply for the reason of fulfilling their duties." When I asked Yang how he makes sure that deputies rate his responses as satisfactory, he confessed that getting satisfactory ratings from legislators is not a priority. "I usually use empty language: if the proposal requires a solution that is not feasible, I would usually reply that 'our bureau is under-staffed to fulfill the request.'" The ultimate goal for lower-level bureaucrats like him is to make sure that his superior believes his responses are appropriate to the institution (Interview G1217). Yang, of course, does not speak for all bureaucrats who deal with policy proposals submitted by entrepreneurs. Mr. Hu, a bureaucrat in Beijing, also responds to policy proposals from legislators in his district using the opposite approach to Yang. Hu believes entrepreneur–legislators write higher-quality policy proposals than government deputies, and that these proposals represent real interests and demands from the business class (Interview G1210). Hu therefore enjoys reading those proposals and takes them seriously.

4.5 DISCUSSION

Formally, legal developments to ensure greater property security for firms have progressed significantly in the past few decades in China, and the private sector has thrived. But private firms are still often expropriated, and property security remains a fundamental challenge for private entrepreneurs. Interview evidence suggests that entrepreneurs who run small businesses are much more vulnerable to local expropriation than those with bigger businesses and better government connections. Bureaucrats who engage in exploitative behavior try not to target entrepreneurs with legislator status in order to avoid negative consequences from their superiors.

Few entrepreneur–legislators submit policy proposals related to property security or property rights, but a few deputies have carefully raised the issue using politically correct language such as "easing the burden on business" and "helping enterprises grow." Entrepreneurs rarely use the word "extraction" in these formal proposals, even though more than half of them have experienced some level of extraction in their district of operation. Pessimistic entrepreneurs suggest that local governments never take their proposals seriously in any case, and some local bureaucrats have openly confirmed that this is the case.

Why, then, do some entrepreneur deputies still spend time researching and writing proposals that are unlikely to matter? "I don't know. It became a habit," says Mr. Qian, whose company now operates in Beijing, but who still flies back to his home district at least twice a year to attend meetings and to fulfill other deputy duties (Interview P124). There are also believers in the current legislative system who remain positive that their suggestions will be more likely to be taken into account by local governments as the system develops. Mr. Gao is one of those believers: he submitted a policy proposal requesting a new road in his county. Although aware that the road will be built regardless of his input, he believes his proposal has "pushed the project" to get started earlier. He adds, "more frequent interaction with local entrepreneurs will make government officials more sympathetic toward our problems and our needs" (Interview P139). Hopeful entrepreneurs like Gao and outspoken entrepreneurs like Lin have proved that they are participating in authoritarian politics in a somewhat meaningful way.

APPENDIX A: LIST OF INTERVIEWS

	Interview Number	Location	Industry/Bureau/Profession	Date
1	G1210	Beijing	Banking and Finance	June 2012
2	O1210	Beijing	Economics Professor	June 2012
3	O122	Beijing	Banking and Finance	June 2012
4	O123	Beijing	Economist	June 2012
5	O1214	Beijing	Economist	June 2012
6	O125	Beijing	Political Science Professor	June 2012
7	O126	Beijing	Business Researcher	June 2012
8	O121	Beijing	Political Science Scholar	June 2012
9	G121	Hunan1	Provincial People's Congress Office	June 2012
10	G1212	Hunan1	Provincial People's Congress Office	June 2012
11	G1213	Hunan1	Provincial People's Congress Office	June 2012
12	G122	Hunan1	County People's Congress Office	June 2012

(continued)

(continued)

	Interview Number	Location	Industry/Bureau/Profession	Date
13	G123	Hunan1	County People's Congress Office	June 2012
14	G124	Hunan1	Finance and Banking	June 2012
15	G126	Hunan2	County CPPCC Office	June 2012
16	G1262	Hunan2	Banking and Finance	June 2012
17	G127	Guangdong1	Banking and Finance	June 2012
18	G128	Guangdong1	Banking and Finance	June 2012
19	G129	Guangdong1	District CPPCC Office	June 2012
20	P122	Guangdong1	Manufacturing	June 2012
21	P123	Guangdong1	Manufacturing	June 2012
22	P1218	Hunan1	Dairy Production	July 2012
23	P1219	Hunan1	Architecture	July 2012
24	P1220	Hunan1	Online Commerce	July 2012
25	P12202	Hunan1	IT	July 2012
26	P124	Hunan1	Interior Design	July 2012
27	M121	Guangdong1	CPPCC Off-season Meeting	July 2012
28	O1211	Guangdong1	CPPCC Deputy	July 2012
29	O124	Hangzhou	Public Policy Professor	July 2012
30	G1211	Wenzhou	Business Association	July 2012
31	G12112	Wenzhou	Business Association	July 2012
32	G12113	Wenzhou	Business Association	July 2012
33	P125	Zhejiang1	Garment Manufacturing	July 2012
34	O1212	Zhejiang1	Political Commentator	July 2012
35	P1221	Zhejiang1	Electronics	July 2012
36	P1222	Zhejiang1	Trading	July 2012
37	P126	Guizhou1	Pharmaceutical	July 2012
38	P128	Guizhou1	Entertainment	July 2012
39	O1210	Guizhou1	Banking and Finance	July 2012
40	P1215	Guizhou1	IT	July 2012
41	P127	Guizhou1	Bookstore Owner	July 2012
42	P129	Guizhou1	Real Estate	July 2012
43	P1210	Guizhou1	Automobile Retail	July 2012
44	P1211	Guizhou1	Real Estate	July 2012
45	G1212	Hunan1	Provincial ACFIC Office	July 2012
46	G1213	Hunan1	Provincial ACFIC Office	July 2012
47	P1217	Hunan1	Manufacturing	July 2012
48	G1214	Hunan1	Taxation	August 2012
49	G1215	Hunan1	Taxation	August 2012
50	G12152	Hunan1	Taxation	August 2012
51	P1212	Hunan1	Food	August 2012
52	P12122	Hunan1	Communication	August 2012
53	O1213	Hunan1	Legal Scholar	August 2012
54	G1216	Hunan1	Finance and Banking	August 2012
55	O127	Hunan1	Finance and Banking	August 2012
56	G1218	Hunan1	Taxation	August 2012
57	G1219	Hunan1	Taxation	August 2012

	Interview Number	Location	Industry/Bureau/Profession	Date
58	G1220	Hunan1	Taxation	August 2012
59	P1213	Hunan1	Jewelry	August 2012
60	P1216	Hunan1	Real Estate and Construction	August 2012
61	P1214	Hunan1	Online Commerce	August 2012
62	G1217	Hunan1	Finance and Banking	August 2012
63	G132	Hunan1	Work Safety	January 2013
64	O131	Beijing	Political Science Professor	January 2013
65	G131	Hunan1	Taxation	January 2013
66	P132	Hunan1	Manufacturing	January 2013
67	P133	Hunan1	Online Travel Agency	January 2013
68	P134	Hunan1	Online Commerce	January 2013
69	P1342	Hunan1	Online Commerce	January 2013
70	G133	Hunan1	Taxation	January 2013
71	G134	Hunan2	Taxation	January 2013
72	P135	Hunan2	Manufacturing	January 2013
73	G137	Hunan2	Taxation	January 2013
74	P137	Hunan2	Firecracker Manufacturing	January 2013
75	P1372	Hunan2	Transportation	January 2013
76	P1373	Hunan2	Electronics	January 2013
77	P1374	Hunan2	Retail	January 2013
78	P1375	Hunan2	Pharmaceutical	January 2013
79	P1376	Hunan2	Retail	January 2013
80	P1377	Hunan2	Pharmaceutical	January 2013
81	P1378	Hunan2	Clothing Retail	January 2013
82	M131	Hunan2	Local ACFIC Office	January 2013
83	P136	Hunan1	Manufacturing	January 2013
84	P1311	Zhengzhou	Real Estate	January 2013
85	P138	Hunan1	IT	January 2013
86	P139	Hunan1	IT Retail	January 2013
87	P131	Hunan1	Interior Design Company	January 2013
88	P131f	Hunan1	Yoga Studio Owner	January 2013
89	G135	Hunan1	Finance and Banking	February 2013
90	P1310	Hunan1	Real Estate	February 2013
91	G136	Guangdong1	District People's Congress Office	July 2013
92	O141	Shanghai	Political Science Professor	May 2014
93	P1312	Hunan1	Manufacturing	August 2013
94	P151	Hunan1	Manufacturing	January 2015
95	P152	Hunan1	Tourism	January 2015
96	O151	Hunan1	Private Bank Manager	January 2015
97	P153	Hunan1	Interior Design (a second interview)	January 2015
98	O154	Hunan1	Interior Design	January 2015

(continued)

(continued)

Interview Number	Location	Industry/Bureau/Profession	Date
99	G151	Hunan1	Provincial PC Standing Commitee Official	January 2015
100	G152	Hunan3	County PC Standing Commitee Official	January 2015
101	G153	Hunan4	County PC Standing Commitee Official	January 2015
102	G153	Hunan4	County PC Standing Commitee Official	January 2015
103	P154	Hunan1	International Trade	January 2015
104	P155	Guizhou2	Agriculture	January 2015
105	P156	Beijing	Online Commerce	January 2015
106	P157	Shanghai	Construction	January 2015
107	G161	Hunan1	County PC Standing Commitee Official	December 2016
108	O161	Guangzhou	Political Science Professor	December 2016

Note. P denotes private entreprise owner or top management personnel of a private company; G denotes Government Official; O denotes Other; and M denotes Meeting. Location shows the location of the interview, either the name of the city or province.

APPENDIX B: THE CHINA YOUTH SURVEY

The China Youth Survey was conducted in August 2013. The sampling method divided China into an eastern region and a west-central region, and three provinces or provincial-level municipalities were selected from each region. Beijing, Shandong, and Zhejiang were selected to represent the eastern region, and Henan, Sichuan, and Guangxi were selected to represent the west-central region. Within each provincial unit, two or three prefectures were sampled. The sampled prefectures are representative of Chinese cities in terms of population size and level of economic development.

The surveys were distributed to officials in all prefectures based on a quota sampling method aimed at reaching a certain number of respondents by the type of state unit and the rank of the respondent. The local collaborators sampled officials and bureaucrats from the following categories, using the ratio of 6:2:2, respectively.

1. Government administrative units: office of the local government; development and reform commission; finance; education; human resources and social security; public security; health; taxation; state-owned asset supervision and administration;

2. CCP units: office of the party committee; organization department; propaganda department;
3. Other units: people's congress standing committee; people's political consultative conference standing committee; People's Court; People's Procuratorate; Communist Youth League; Federation of Trade Unions; Women's Federation; Federation of Industry and Commerce.

The surveys were printed out in Beijing and were distributed at the respondents' places of work. No personal identifiers were collected, and the surveys were supposed to be completed by respondents in private.

APPENDIX C

Below is an example of a legislator's policy proposal from Jiangmen Prefectural people's congress of Guangdong Province, and the government's reply:[12]

Proposal Number: Bi Zi (2007) #29 (Jiangmen Prefectural People's Congress, Guangdong Province)

Category: Urban Development

Title: On Reconstructing Shuzijie Road

Deputy: Wu Zhihong

Content:

In recent years, the city government has exerted good effort in road reconstruction near Shuinanshi District. Residents no longer have to paddle through flooded or bumpy streets. Now local businesses have thrived and residents have benefitted. All these efforts deserve praises. Jiangmen is a nationally-renowned tourism city, and Gangkou Road is located in the CDB district, and Shunanshi District is a district where local business vendors convene. Shuizijie Road connects Gangkou Road and Shuinanshi District, which is a crucial connection and should be at least orderly. Quite the opposite, at the entrance to this road, there is a huge wall sticking out of the road, which is about 100 meters long and is very ugly. It hurts the name of our city. Moreover, the wall has been in existence for a while and is old

---

[12] See the original document at http://jyta.jiangmen.gov.cn/ShowNews.aspx?guid=1852 (in Chinese). Last accessed October 14, 2017.

and poses safety concerns for passers-by. We do not know when it might collapse. Across the wall there is the Shuinan Kindergarten, Eryou School, and Shuinan Market. The traffic is heavy during off-school and rush hours. Traffic accidents happen quite often.

Thus, in order to eliminate accidents, to make sure roads are safe, and to make our city more beautiful, I suggest the city government and other relevant government offices conduct a field investigation and include the Shuizijie Road reconstruction project in official city planning. I suggest the government tear down the wall and widen the road, so that Shuzijie becomes a wide, orderly road with few traffic jams. This project improves traffic conditions, beautifies the city, benefits local residents, improves local businesses, and helps the city develop in a holistic way.

This proposal was forwarded to the district government office and received the following response within three months:

Pengjiang District Government Response #53(B)

Deputy Wu Zhihong,

We have received your proposal entitled "On Re-constructing Shuzijie Road." Below is our reply:

In December 2007, relevant bureaus in our district conducted field research in Shuzijie Road. This road is a standard urban road with the length of 462 meters, and the width of 14 meters (driving lane is 7-meter wide and 3.5-meter wide on each side). It is an important road connecting Gangkou Road and Qian Road. The parking lot (facing Jiuzhaigou Restaurant) takes too much space from the driving lane and one side of the pedestrian lane (about 100 meters), resulting in the narrowing of the end of the road and affecting traffic. According to the transportation bureau and bureau of land and resources, this area has 11 acres and was originally the office space for the transportation bureau. Jiangmen Infrastructure Company is allowed to use this space. After the transportation bureau was relocated in 1994, this space has been vacant and was lent to Jiangmengang Yinhang Station and four other government departments. In April 2007, Jiangmen Infrastructure Company used this piece of land as collateral to get a loan in the amount of 19,500,000 yuan, from the China Construction Bank Jiangmen Branch.

On March 5th, 2008, the municipal public utility administration bureau, transportation bureau, urban planning bureau, and the bureau of land and resources had a joint meeting on Shuizijie Road reconstruction, and we have decided on the following three options:

One. To include the road reconstruction in the city planning proposal. The prefectural government takes back the land use right and redevelops the district. This plan will avoid repetition in investment. But the implementation of this plan will take a long period of time, since there are many problems involved regarding reconstructing an old district.

Two. According to urban planning standards, we widen the road, and tear down the wall. But this "temporary" plan would not benefit the subsequent reconstruction of the old district and will result in repetitive investment and reconstruction. At the same time, according to the planning map, this plan requires additional care for two buildings close to the edge of the road. The costs are high.

#Three. As a most temporary solution, we tear down the 30-meter slope in Area A and 60-meter Slope in Area B (shown in the graph attached). Then according to Road A16-17, we reconstruct slope A and B and rebuild the surface of the road as well as the sewerage system. The total cost is 300,000 yuan (not including costs of house demolition). We suggest that we adopt Plan #3.

No matter which plan is finally implemented, we need to have the permission of the Jiangmen Infrastructure Company and China Construction Bank Jiangmen Branch.

In the end, thank you for your valuable proposal.

Jiangmen District Government
March 19, 2008
(Contact: Xu Chunhong, 8222370)

Most proposals posted on the Jiangmen Prefectural congress website received similarly thorough responses by relevant government agencies. In other cases discussed in this chapter, I was only able to collect legislators' proposals but did not have access to governments' responses.

5

Protection from Predation

There can be few, if any, parallels for this intense desire of the middle-class Frenchman to cut an official figure; no sooner did he find himself in possession of a small capital sum than he expended it on buying an official post ... (Tocqueville [1858]1955, 91)

"I became a deputy in the local congress because I wanted to help the local economy grow (by giving my input). But looking around, I think 80–90 percent of entrepreneur-deputies participate because they are seeking protection from local governmental predation."
An entrepreneur-legislator in Prefecture L (Interview P123)

Liaoning, one of the very first provinces in China to industrialize, was championed as "the eldest son of the People's Republic" because of its earlier economic importance to the new Republic. In the reform era, with the decline of heavy industry, this northeastern province has fallen largely out of sight. In the fall of 2016, Liaoning made national news again. On September 13 that year, the Chairman of the Standing Committee of the National People's Congress, Zhang Dejiang, convened an emergency meeting and decided to expel 45 legislators, all of whom came from Liaoning, in light of a serious vote-buying scandal they had allegedly been involved in.[1] The Chinese Communist Party leadership expressed unprecedented anger. Zhang commented that this scandal severely challenged both "the party's bottom line" and "the authority and dignity of

---

[1] Michael Forsythe, September 14, 2016. *The New York Times.* "An Unlikely Crime in One-Party China: Election Fraud." www.nytimes.com/2016/09/15/world/asia/china-npc-election-fraud-liaoning.html. Last accessed November 8, 2017.

the communist rule of law."[2] It turns out that 38 out of the 45 national legislators also served in the standing committee of Liaoning's provincial congress,[3] and the committee had to stop functioning because now it had lost more than half of its members. Liaoning produced yet another first – it was the first time in PRC's history that a provincial congress standing committee stopped working.

Besides two city-level government officials, the other 43 of the 45 legislators who bribed their way up to the national legislature are business owners of private firms or managers of large state-owned enterprises.[4] This event reminds us of a similar vote-buying scandal in early 2013 in the central province of Hunan, where 56 provincial legislators were removed from the provincial congress as a result of a vote-buying scandal – evidence surfaced that these candidates spent 110 million yuan in bribes to get themselves elected. Among these 56 provincial legislators, 32 were private entrepreneurs.[5] According to Minxin Pei's analysis, the buying and selling of public office spreads across many provinces, and the majority involves bribes from private businesses (Pei 2016, chapter 3).

Why do these individuals seek office in a people's congress which is so often dismissed as weak and ineffective in interest representation or policy influence? If the costs of getting into these institutions are so high, what are the benefits of holding a seat? Recall that my theory proposes that entrepreneurs use the status and connections associated with holding a legislative seat to protect their property. The second empirical implication of the theory is about the "effectiveness" of this strategy, that is, whether a legislator status indeed provides property protection for entrepreneur–legislators effectively. Entrepreneurs who are members of the congresses should experience less severe expropriation by local bureaucrats, compared with those without this political status. This chapter assesses this empirical prediction.

---

[2] Mo Bai, September 15, 2016. *BBC China*. "Focus: The Background Story of How the Niaoning Vote Buying Scandal Angers Zhognanhai" (*Jiaodian: Niaoling Huixuanan Zhennu Zhongnanhai de Beihou*). www.bbc.com/zhongwen/simp/china/2016/09/160915_ana_liaoning_renda_political_impact. Last accessed November 8, 2017.

[3] It is common for legislators to serve in different levels of congresses in China.

[4] According to the *Caixin people* profiles ("*Caixin Renwu Pu*"). This piece has been taken off the web.

[5] *Tencent News*, December 29, 2013. "Hunan Announces the Names and Occupations of the 56 Provincial Legislators Involved in Vote-Buying" (*Hunan Gongbu 56ming Huixuande Sheng Renda Daibiao Mingdan he Zhiwu*). www.360doc.com/content/13/1229/13/6791042_340982375.shtml. Last accessed November 8, 2017.

The first section situates this chapter in a broad body of literature on political connections and returns to office. Using a national survey of private entrepreneurs, I then evaluate the empirical implication that being a legislator protects a private entrepreneur from government expropriation. The analysis shows that entrepreneurs who serve in the local legislature spend 14.5 percent less on informal payments to local governments, on average. The next section explores variations among industries and probes two industry-level hypotheses. Both interview and survey evidence suggest that entrepreneurs from industries with heavy government intervention or whose companies are geographically immobile have more incentive to run for office, and enjoy greater protection from expropriation when they hold seats in local legislatures. The concluding section proposes an "insurance premium" framework to describe private entrepreneurs' decisions to enter a competitive and expensive local legislative race: the price these individuals pay to secure congressional seats buys them "insurance" against full-fledged expropriation.

5.1 POLITICAL CONNECTIONS AND RETURNS TO OFFICE

The analysis of this chapter is related to recent research on political connections, firm performance, and returns to office. Recent studies have provided causal estimates on returns to political office in many democratic contexts. For example, Eggers and Hainmueller (2009) show that serving in office almost doubled the wealth of Conservative Members of Parliament in postwar Britain. Querubin and Snyder (2013) identify significant returns to office among members of the US House of Representatives during the Civil War years. Lenz and Lim (2009), on the other hand, find that US representatives accumulate wealth at a rate consistent with similar non-representatives, suggesting that corruption in the US Congress is not widespread.

It is much more challenging to estimate returns to office in an authoritarian context with the absence of elections, but Truex (2014) has argued that a seat in the Chinese National People's Congress brings about real monetary payoff, that is, an NPC seat is worth an additional 1.5 percentage points in returns and a 3–4 percentage point boost in operating profit margin in a given year.

These new findings help us answer the old question of how political connections affect firm performance. In developing economies in which institutions are weak and politicians have much policy discretion, explicit corrupt exchanges can take place between politicians and firms, especially politically connected ones. Fisman's seminal 2001 study suggests that a large percentage of well-connected firms' values may be derived from their political connections in Indonesia; Khwaja and Mian (2005) find that lenders in Pakistan favor politically connected firms, who on average get 45 percent more loans, but have 50 percent higher default rates. In places where institutions are strong and explicit corruption is less likely, connections still matter. In Faccio's 2006 study of 20,202 firms across 47 countries, many of which are developed economies, she finds that stock prices of related firms increase when a businessperson enters politics.[6]

This book makes an important contribution to the political connection literature by providing a new estimate of "returns to office" in an authoritarian context. Returns to political office in the Chinese context are not only measured by a certain amount of monetary payoff; more fundamentally, the most valuable "return to office," I argue, is property security.

5.2 LEGISLATORS EXPERIENCE LESS EXPROPRIATION

Recall that 42 percent of entrepreneurs in my interview sample believe that legislator status helps "protect business from local predation" (Chapter 4), and recall the claim of the entrepreneur who stated that "80 percent to 90 percent of entrepreneur–deputies participate because they are seeking protection." Here, I use a national survey dataset to assess this proposition.

My primary quantitative data source is a national survey of Chinese private entrepreneurs from 2000 to 2012. It is by far the most commonly used Chinese private entrepreneur survey by scholars (e.g., Ang and Jia 2014; Li et al. 2006; Sun, Zhu, and Wu 2014). The survey was conducted every other year jointly by the ACFIC, the China Society of Private Economy at the Chinese Academy of Social Science, and the United Front Work Department of the Central Committee, the Communist Party of China (the ACFIC survey). The dataset does not have a panel structure: in each survey year, individual enterprises were drawn into the sample from 31 provinces. The sampling method was multi-stage stratified random sam-

---

[6] Also see Ferguson and Voth (2008); Goldman, Rocholl, and So (2006); Johnson and Mitton (2011); and Roberts (1990).

pling, with geographic location (province and prefecture) and industry as strata. Chinese native speakers conducted direct interviews with company owners or top executives using a questionnaire.[7]

The outcome variable of interest is the level of expropriation, which is measured as a percentage of a firm's total expenditure in a given year.[8] As discussed in Chapters 1 and 4, the variable expropriation differs from bribes, which are more likely to be captured by the category of "public relations spending;"[9] it is not a legitimate form of taxation, which should be captured by the categories of "taxes" and "fees."

People's congress membership (PC membership) is a binary variable on whether an entrepreneur is a local people's congress deputy in that year.[10] Most legislators in the sample are from the prefectural congresses or below. Firm- and individual-level characteristics are measured in the survey and are either used as covariates or matched on, depending on the specification. Firm-level variables include: how long the firm has been in operation, whether the firm was a state-owned enterprise (SOE) in the past, which industry the firm belongs to, and which province the firm operates in. Characteristics of firm owners include: age, gender, education level, whether the owner is a CCP member, and whether the owner worked for the government in the past (see Appendix for summary statistics of all variables).

A few caveats need to be made regarding the quality of this survey. First, the organizations conducting the survey did not report a response rate, and the entrepreneurs responding to the surveys could be qualitatively different from those who chose not to respond. Therefore, the inference I make only applies to those who chose to answer the survey. Second, it is a self-reported survey, and entrepreneurs could choose not

---

[7] An individual may own or have joint ownership in multiple firms, but since the survey is anonymized, I am unable to identify them. Because the unit of analysis is the firm, the possibility of multiple of ownership issue does not affect the inference.

[8] In some survey years, total expenditure was reported as a stand-alone value. In other years, the category did not exist. To be consistent across all years, I constructed a new variable – total expenditure – defined as the total amount a company spent on taxes, fees, expropriation payments and public relation in a given year.

[9] Choi (2011) suggests that some entrepreneurs "openly use their money to get appointed or elected." Those costs, clearly correlated with the variable PC membership, are more likely to be accounted for under the category of "public relation spending" instead of "extraction payment."

[10] Please see Appendix for the original wordings of these questions.

to answer some of the questions for reasons I cannot identify; thus this dataset suffers from a missing data problem. I approach the missing data problem by comparing results using datasets generated from multiple imputation (results presented in the Appendix).

Finally, the survey responses were all self-reported, and the data could suffer from non-negligible measurement error, especially with regard to the main dependent variable expropriation. For instance, entrepreneurs who are legislators might either be more honest about reporting their informal payments, because they are better protected by the government, or be more cautious about not reporting the expropriation of their profits out of political sensitivity or political correctness considerations. Ideally, I could use the actual level of extraction to benchmark the self-reported values of extraction, but there is no reliable data on this. Nevertheless, I am still confident about using this survey to estimate the effect of being a legislator on deterring expropriation. Over-reporting is less of an issue for the purpose of this study: even if all legislators over-reported the level of extraction they experienced, the estimated effect size would have become a lower bound and the true effect size would only have been more significant. Systematic under-reporting, however, could have been a more serious issue, but systematic under-reporting would only have happened if political sensitivity is a stronger concern for legislators than for the non-legislators. Based on my interviews, the entrepreneur–legislators did not appear to worry more than the non-legislator entrepreneurs about political sensitivity, although this might have been a concern for both groups.

The reported overall level of expropriation is 5.25 percent, which means that, on average, 5.25 percent of an entrepreneur's annual total expenditure goes to informal payments to local bureaucrats. On average, entrepreneur–legislators experience lower levels of expropriation than non-legislators: the mean value of expropriation level is 4.11 percent among legislators and 5.52 percent among non-legislators. The biggest threat to the inference of the effect of PC memberships on the level of extraction is that PC memberships are not randomly assigned. A brief look at the data shows that entrepreneurs who are members of people's congresses are different from those who are not. Consistent with interview evidence, entrepreneurs who are PC deputies have bigger and older firms. Most PC deputies are CCP members and male, and they are more likely than entrepreneurs who are not deputies to have worked in the government in the past. They are also slightly older and more educated than non-PC entrepreneurs (see Table 5.1).

TABLE 5.1 *Comparing PC entrepreneurs and others*

	PC Entrepreneurs	Non-PC Entrepreneurs	p-value
Firm level			
Extraction	4.111%	5.519%	0.000
	(0.162)	(0.105)	
	(0.043)	(0.022)	
Ex-SOE firm	0.337	0.189	0.000
	(0.010)	(0.004)	
Firm age	8.835	7.473	0.000
	(0.010)	(0.049)	
Individual level			
Ex-government official	0.216	0.181	0.000
	(0.009)	(0.004)	
CCP membership	0.542	0.296	0.000
	(0.010)	(0.005)	
Age	47.474	44.624	0.000
	(0.156)	(0.088)	
Education	3.554	3.443	0.000
	(0.018)	(0.009)	
Gender: Whether an	0.904	0.855	0.000
entrepreneur is a male	(0.006)	(0.004)	
Obs.	2,325	9,692	

Note. Summary statistics from ACFIC survey 2000–2012. Standard deviation in parentheses. Right-hand column reports *p*-values for two-sided *t*-test.

To address these concerns, I estimate the effect of PC membership on the level of expropriation using a variety of reweighing and matching methods. I first estimate a simple linear model controlling for firm- and individual-level covariates.[11] I always include industry, provincial, and year fixed effects. All individual level covariates are strictly pre-treatment. Both firm-level variables – the age of a firm and whether a firm was an SOE before – are also pre-treatment: an entrepreneur's legislator status would be obtained after his company was established; and it is a fair assumption that a company owner usually acquires his legislator status after his company has already converted from an SOE to a private firm. My fieldwork of investigating the deputy selection process suggests that these are the most relevant set of observables from the survey to be

[11] Firm-level covariates include: firm age and whether a firm was an SOE in the past. Individual-level covariates are: age, gender, CCP membership, and education.

included in the analysis. Note that firm sizes are always incorporated, because the level of extraction is normalized by total expenditure.

To ensure a better balance on covariate moments, I employ entropy balancing (Hainmueller 2009). This method gives weights to control units such that after weighting, the marginal distribution of covariates is the same for the treated and control groups in order to satisfy a set of moment conditions, while keeping the weights close to equality. I include the same covariates as those in the first OLS model. In this analysis, entropy balancing is successful at achieving full balance on the covariate distribution between those who are PC deputies and those who are not (the covariate balance is shown in the Appendix Table A5.3.). I then employ these weights in OLS regressions with year, province, and industry fixed effects to complete the required conditioning. Similar to the estimates from the OLS model, this model suggests that being a PC member saves an entrepreneur 0.761 percent of his total expenditures on forced unofficial payments to local governments. Thus, an entrepreneur with a PC membership would save 14.5 percent (= 0.761 percent/5.25 percent) of his expenditures on expropriation. Again, the level of the legislative body does not seem to affect the estimation. Estimates from Mahalanobis matching analyses are consistent with these regression estimates in both magnitude and significance. These results are summarized in Figure 5.1 and Appendix Tables A5.2 and A5.4.

To further ensure that the finding does not rely on a linear and additive parametric model, I conduct additional analysis to test the robustness of the findings. I use matching methods, and the idea is again to create a comparable portfolio of non-PC companies similar to those in the "PC treatment" group but without having any linear or other parametric assumptions of how the models might look like. In these specifications, each entrepreneur with a PC membership in the same province, industry, and year is matched to other entrepreneurs who are the most similar on the characteristics mentioned earlier. After entrepreneur–legislators are matched with other entrepreneurs, I then compare their levels of expropriation. Similarity is determined by a distance measure, the Mahalanobis distance, that calculates "nearness" in the multi-dimensional space.

Finally, I use quantile regressions to study the effect of PC membership on the levels of expropriation at different quantiles. Results show that the effect of PC membership is larger at higher quantiles: while on average being a PC delegate saves an entrepreneur 14.5 percent of his expenditures on forced unofficial payments to local governments, the effect size becomes 20.78 percent at the 80th percentile and 30.48 percent at the

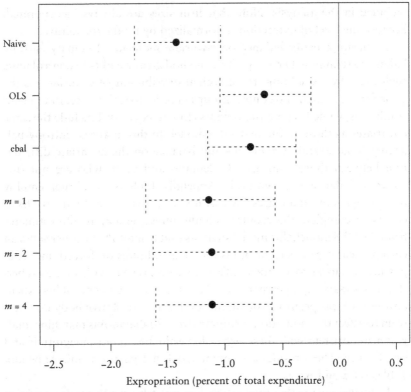

FIGURE 5.1 Effect of PC membership on the level of expropriation

Note. Summary of effect estimates of PC membership on expropriation under five models: OLS with covariates (OLS), entropy balancing followed by weighted OLS with covariates (ebal), and nearest neighbor matching: 1-to-1 ($m = 1$), 2-to-1 ($m = 2$), and 4-to-1 matching without replacement ($m = 4$). The top bar shows the naive difference in means between the two groups. These models find that having a PC membership reduces an entrepreneur's spending on expropriation by 0.641–1.126 percentage points. That is, regardless of the model used, being a legislator saves an entrepreneur about 12.21 percent to 21.45 percent in total expenditure.

90th percentile (see Table A5.9 for results). These findings suggest that the protective effect of political office is stronger when expropriation is more severe.

Besides informal payments to local governments, entrepreneurs make many other types of payments to local governments. One may suspect that perhaps legislators' savings on expropriation are insignificant compared with their extra spendings on other forms of payments to local governments, such as involuntary donations. Several scholars have argued exactly this point. Using a 1995 survey of private firms, Ma and

Parish (2006) find that political representation (measured by congress membership at various levels) is positively associated with charitable contributions. Sun, Zhu, and Wu (2014) discover a similar correlation between entrepreneurs' political positions and amount of donations. On the other hand, Zhang (2013) argues that forced donations should be negatively correlated with political connections.

My interviews also provide suggestive evidence about the positive relationship between donations and political status. Mr. Zhao, a prefectural legislator, did not hide his complaints that government-affiliated organizations come to his office excessively to seek donations, and he finds them "deeply annoying." He believes that, as a legislator, he (and his company) bears heavier "involuntary social responsibility" compared to other, lower-profile companies (Interview P126).

A problem with using the ACFIC survey to systematically understand whether legislators donate more is that in the survey the "donation" category does not distinguish between voluntary and involuntary donations. Therefore, it is difficult to move beyond anecdotes and to systematically assess whether entrepreneur–legislators are more likely to be forced by local governments to make involuntary donations to local public goods projects, or whether entrepreneur–legislators are simply more altruistic and voluntarily donate more to government and social organizations compared to their peers without the political status. Bruce Dickson's 1999 survey of Chinese private entrepreneurs did ask whether a company's donation is voluntary or pressed by governments, but the survey did not ask for the specific amount of the donation. With this distinction in mind, Dickson does not find a correlation between charitable giving and congress membership (Dickson 2008, chapter 7).

5.3 EXPLORING VARIATIONS AMONG INDUSTRIES

Every company wants protection from expropriation, but I do not wish to argue that a legislator's seat has equal importance to all candidates interested in the position. What types of companies need greater protection from expropriation?

First, companies that are part of an industry where governments intervene heavily are more likely to be expropriated – these industries usually have more stringent regulations, many of which can be interpreted in different ways by bureaucrats. Officials and bureaucrats have more opportunities to seek rents given frequent interactions between business and state. Therefore, entrepreneurs located in these industries should have stronger incentives to compete for office, and a seat brings a higher return (e.g., savings from expropriation) compared with entrepreneurs in a low-intervention industry. Second, companies that are difficult to move are more likely to be expropriated – because of their geographic immobility and lack of exit options. Changdong Zhang makes a similar observation, arguing that as companies become more mobile, they acquire more de facto power over local governments and force them to become more investment-friendly (Zhang 2010, chapter 2). Thus, entrepreneurs whose assets are immobile should have stronger incentives to seek a legislative seat and would benefit more from securing office.

Two observable implications are derived from the industry-level argument. First, entrepreneurs in different industries should exert different levels of effort in competing for seats. Entrepreneurs in industries that experience higher levels of expropriation and in immobile industries are more likely to exert higher effort; second, returns to office are different for entrepreneurs located in different industries. Entrepreneurs located in high-intervention industries or immobile industries should experience greater reduction in government expropriation. I assess both implications using interview evidence, and I test the second implication using the ACFIC survey data. The first implication is not empirically testable using quantitative data at hand, because given data limitations we cannot observe all entrepreneurs who have competed for seats.

Interview evidence suggests that entrepreneurs in different industries indeed experience varying types and levels of interaction with local governments. Local bureaucrats have more opportunities to expropriate when they have more frequent interactions with local businesses. During our conversations, many entrepreneurs mentioned that "the frequency of interaction with government" is a strong predictor for competition to join the legislatures.

Interviewer: Why was the Hengyang people's congress deputy willing to pay three million yuan to secure a seat? Is a seat worth that much?

Lang: It really depends on the industry. Businesses in the real estate industry, for example, have to interact with the government at every step of the way when they develop a new property. Starting from purchasing land, to getting permission to sell their property ... They really need to know people [in the government] and have good connections. (Interview P154)

Entrepreneurs from some industries express less concern about expropriation. Gao, a private entrepreneur in the IT industry, has been content that his industry "is highly marketized and experiences very little government intervention," and therefore he does not worry much about expropriation (Interview P139). Some other entrepreneurs, although agreeing that some industries experience more expropriation than others, say there are universal problems plaguing all industries.

I spend a quarter of my time socializing [with the government] and it is exhausting. But I know other industries, such as real estate and alcohol production, have much more frequent interaction with the government. We all hope that government gives us less trouble and we know that it is very easy for them to "finish" (*shou shi*) us. (Interview P127)

Whether a company is geographically mobile also seems to matter. If a company belongs to an industry that makes it difficult to relocate, local governments might expropriate the company more often, knowing that the company has no exit strategy. In this situation, an entrepreneur might have even more incentives to secure a seat in the local legislature to protect his property, and a seat matters much more to this entrepreneur. Let us take a look again at Mr. Zhao, an entrepreneur–legislator who runs a pharmaceutical firm in Guizhou Province. Although he is not always bothered by local governments and remains on "good terms" with many local bureaus, he still thinks that private entrepreneurs are located at the bottom of the "social ladder." Because the materials used in the drugs his company produces are locally sourced, he is hesitant to move to other areas where "governments might be friendlier to private businesses," yet he concludes that companies have taken on "too much social responsibility," forced upon them by other government actors (Interview P126). On the other hand, entrepreneurs like Mr. Tan, who owns companies that are easily moveable, do not worry much at all about expropriation. In fact, when rumor had it that Mr. Tan's company planned to relocate to another province, the local government tried very hard to entice Tan to stay by offering beneficial policies such as a major tax reduction (Interview P1217).

These interviews further motivate two hypotheses regarding industry variations in terms of "return to office:"

H1 (The Intervention Hypothesis): The protective effect of a people's congress membership is stronger when the entrepreneur–legislator is in an industry with heavy government intervention.

H2 (The Immobility Hypothesis): The protective effect of a people's congress membership is stronger when the company of an entrepreneur–legislator is immobile.

The ACFIC survey data allows me to test both hypotheses. I created two binary variables: *Intervention* and *Immobile*. *Intervention* takes the value of 1 if the subject comes from a company in an industry heavily intervened in by governments, namely the real estate, mining, and construction industries, and 0 otherwise. *Immobile* takes the value of 1 if the subject comes from a company in an immobile industry, namely the agriculture and mining industries. Among all subjects, 7.75 percent are in immobile industries, and 10.49 percent are in industries with heavy government intervention. To test the two hypotheses, I look at the following specifications:

$$Expropriation_i = \alpha_1 + \beta_1 PC_i + \beta_2 Intervention_i$$
$$+ \beta_3 PC_i \cdot Intervention_i + \beta_{x1} X_i + \eta_t + \varepsilon_{i1}$$
$$Expropriation_i = \alpha_2 + \beta_4 PC_i + \beta_5 Immobile_i$$
$$+ \beta_6 PC_i \cdot Immobile_i + \beta_{x2} X_i + \eta_t + \varepsilon_{i2}$$

In these two specifications, i indexes each individual and t indexes year. *Expropriation$_i$* is defined as expropriation payment paid as a percentage of total expenditure by individual i PC_i denotes whether an individual i was a PC deputy *Intervention$_i$* and *Immobile$_i$* are dummy variables which take the value of 1 if the company of i's was in a high intervention or an immobile industry; X_i is a vector of company- and individual-level covariates; η_t are year fixed effects; and ε_i is the error term. Results are presented in Table 5.2.

Surprisingly, the coefficient of *Intervention* is negative, suggesting that private companies located in the mining, real estate, and construction industries experience lower levels of expropriation compared to companies in other industries in the survey. There are two possible explanations for this counter-intuitive result. First, private companies in these industries in fact experience less severe expropriation, against what China scholars and my interviewees suggested; second, the ACFIC survey might have sampled companies in these industries in a different manner from how it had sampled companies in other industries, and it happens to have selected companies which experience lower expropriation in these heavily intervened industries. Given my fieldwork and conversations with scholars who are familiar with the ACFIC data, the latter is more likely to be the case.

The ACFIC sample, although frequently used by scholars, is not a representative sample of private entrepreneurs, and it over-samples large enterprises. Certain details about their sampling strategy are missing

TABLE 5.2 *Heterogeneous effects across different industries*

	(1)	(2)	(3)	(4)
PC membership	−0.747%	−0.707%	−0.909%	−0.837%
	(0.218)	(0.211)	(0.198)	(0.195)
Intervention	−1.772%	−2.236%		
	(0.692)	(0.772)		
PC · *Intervention*	−0.455%	−0.439%		
	(0.558)	(0.566)		
Immobile			0.717%	1.856%
			(0.643)	(0.797)
PC · *Immobile*			0.946%	0.694%
			(0.866)	(0.892)
Other Covars	✓	✓	✓	✓
Year Dummy	✓	✓	✓	✓
Province Dummy	✓	✓	✓	✓
N	10,921	10,921	10,921	10,921

Note. Immobile is a binary variable which takes the value of 1 if the subject comes from a company in an immobile industry (i.e., agriculture and mining), and 0 otherwise. The variable *Intervention* is a binary variable which takes the value of 1 if the subject comes from a company in an industry heavily intervened in by governments (i.e., mining, real estate, and construction). Robust standard errors are shown in parentheses. Models (1) and (3) are OLS regressions; (2) and (4) are OLS models using weights generated by entropy balancing. Data: ACFIC 2000–2012.

for researchers. The industry category is very coarse: around 40 percent of the surveyed entrepreneurs come from the "manufacturing industry." A company in the manufacturing industry could range from a large heavy machinery manufacturer to a small electronics manufacturer. These two manufacturing firms certainly have different levels of asset mobility and types of interactions with local governments, yet the ACFIC data does not allow me to analyze any of these differences. Given these limitations, although I can still make macro-level (e.g., industry- or provincial-level) inferences, I feel more confident in making individual-level inferences within industry and province.

More fine-grained data is needed to further analyze the effect of legislative membership on different types of industries, but the current result is more supportive of the *Intervention* hypothesis than the *Immobility* one. If the company of an entrepreneur–legislator comes from an industry in which the government heavily intervenes, he would save 1.146 percent (0.707 percent + 0.439 percent, estimated in model 2) to 1.202 percent

(0.747 percent + 0.455 percent, estimated in model 1) more of his total expenditures on expropriation payment compared with an entrepreneur in the same industry but without the political title. The protective effect for companies in *Immobile* industries are statistically indistinguishable from those in industries in which companies are mobile.

This industry-level analysis provides suggestive evidence to my theoretical prediction that the protective effect of local legislatures is highly industry specific. In industries in which expropriation is higher, the return to office also appears higher.

5.4 ALTERNATIVE FRAMEWORKS

How would state-centric theories explain entrepreneurs' participation in legislatures and their privileged position in regard to property security? One possible explanation could be that the "entrepreneurs in the legislature" phenomenon is simply a state-engineered process. The state co-opts business elites by both giving them political status and extracting less from them. "Savings from extraction payment" is a type of rents individuals receive in return. Firms have little autonomy in deciding whether they get a seat or not, as well as whether they experience predation or not.

Although such a state-engineering explanation would predict an empirical association between entrepreneurs with legislator status and the severity of property extraction similar to what I establish in this chapter, qualitative evidence suggests that such a state-engineering theory might not fully explain Chinese entrepreneurs' political participation. If these entrepreneur–deputies were successfully co-opted, we would not have observed them behaving against state interests. Truex (2016) suggests that NPC deputies exhibit a behavior pattern of "representation with bounds," reflecting the interests of their constituents on non-sensitive issues but not on sensitive ones. Politically sensitive topics include freedom of speech, association, and the press; political rights; multi-party competition; and high-level corruption, among others. At the local level, I observe cases where deputies are active and outspoken on issues that are politically sensitive. For instance, in a district-level congress located in a coastal province, among the 301 policy proposals from private entrepreneurs between 2007 and 2013, 37 were sensitive or contentious proposals.[12] One proposal asked the local government to "resolve land

---

[12] Similar to King et al. (2013) and Truex (2014), I define issues related to democratic reform, threatening the legitimacy of the central or local governments, and collective actions as sensitive issues.

disputes now" and "give back land to rural residents" (Proposal S119-2012), while another entrepreneur proposed that "better compensation policy" is needed for relocated residents "whose houses are torn down for development projects" (Proposal S39-2012). Another provocative entrepreneur demanded "real district-level self governance" (Proposal S35-2013). These cases show that entrepreneurs who are part of the local legislatures sometimes pose potentially genuine opposition and propose progressive reforms. Perhaps it was in the state's interest to co-opt these successful businessmen and women by offering them legislative seats and rents, but based on the evidence, the strategy is not working very well. Not everyone of them appears to acquiesce to the state and the party's demands.

A second state-centric argument could be a "state capacity" one. A local government expropriates from businesses more heavily when local revenue is low or when expenditure is high, and less heavily when local revenue is abundant or when spending is low. Consequently, a local government decides on the numbers of entrepreneurs to include in the legislature, reflecting either strong or weak reliance of the local government on entrepreneurs. Similarly, a revised version of local state corporatism theory argues for a fiscal dependency theory: local governments increase their credibility of property security in the eyes of investors by raising taxes, so that the government is more dependent on the revenue these local businesses provide (Lewis 1997). These state-capacity hypotheses are theoretically plausible, but they are not supported by any macro-level evidence in the Chinese case. Figure 5.2 plots the prefectural-level expropriation rate against local government revenues (left) and against local government expenditure (right). The fitted flat lines suggest that there is essentially no correlation between government revenue (or expenditure) and how much a local government extracts from local businesses in a given year. Local governments' financial capacities do not determine their propensity to predate.

A third explanation is that legislative institutions reduce the cost of collective action among the entrepreneur–legislators, thus enhancing these individuals' de facto power vis-à-vis the government (Gehlbach and Keefer 2011; 2012).[13] In this account, an institutionalized ruling party allows rulers to "make credible commitments by designating a party elite who are expected to invest, and by facilitating collective action

---

[13] Also see Jensen, Malesky, and Weymouth (2013) for a counter-argument.

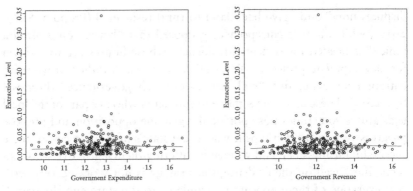

FIGURE 5.2 Local extraction vs. government revenue and expenditure

Note. The first graph plots the bivariate correlation between prefectural-level government revenue (logged) and average local extraction level. The local extraction level is calculated as the average of extractive payments of all surveyed local private entrepreneurs in a given prefecture and a given year. Similarly, the second graph shows the bivariate relationship between prefectural-level government expenditure and local extraction level. The flat lines suggest that there is no correlation between government revenue (or government expenditure) and local extraction level. Expropriation data is from ACFIC surveys 2002–2006. Government revenue and expenditure data is from *China Statistical Yearbook.*

by that elite in the event of their expropriation." More specifically, in the case of China, Gehlbach and Keefer argue that in the Deng era, the introduction of a transparent cadre evaluation system increased "information among party cadres about their collective treatment by the party leadership," which is a "prerequisite for collective action." In the meantime, "investment and growth" are explicitly evaluated according to the benchmarks set in the evaluation system. This claim is interesting in theory, but in practice it is difficult to think of a scenario in which discontent elites in the system used or will use the cadre evaluation platform or other formal institutional settings to initiate any kind of meaningful collective action.

Chinese congresses, on the other hand, are even further away from serving as a platform for collective action in the event of wealth holders becoming dissatisfied with the autocrats in Beijing. First, while prior research finds limited representation (Manion 2016; Truex 2016), entrepreneur–legislators have not yet been true representatives of their business interests. Local legislators represent local interests, but rarely sectoral interests (Manion 2016, chapter 3). Second, entrepreneur–

legislators are constantly watched by the party: the majority of local legislators come from the party, the government, and the military offices, rendering any intention of collective action almost immediately impossible because these deputies are chosen by the party. Therefore, it is difficult to argue that the CCP sets up local congresses to attract investment while allowing the possibility of collective action among the local business leaders in China.

5.5 DISCUSSION

Chapter 4 showed that entrepreneur–legislators think they pay less "expropriation" to local governments and, in this chapter, I show that they in fact do pay significantly less. The analysis suggests entrepreneurs who serve in the local legislature spend 14.5 percent less on informal payments to local governments. This difference between legislator and non-legislator entrepreneurs holds after taking into account of individual- and firm-level characteristics. Moreover, the protective effect of holding an office is highly industry specific.

Is 14.5 percent a significant amount? According to the ACFIC survey, the 14.5 percent savings or 0.763 of a percentage point of total expenditure, translates to a monetary value of 1,290 yuan per year. Many would think that such a figure is negligible, especially considering the cost of competing for a legislative seat, which, as some extreme-case anecdotes suggest, could be as high as millions of yuan.

There are two reasons why this type of cost-benefit analysis does not reflect entrepreneurs' calculations. First, as shown in this chapter, there exists heterogeneity of the "protective effect" of a congressional seat, and the 14.5 percent only presents an average value. Quantile regression analysis reveals that the effect of legislative membership is stronger when expropriation is more severe: the effect size is 20.78 percent at the 80th percentile and 30.48 percent at the 90th percentile. In localities where government agents are less predatory, entrepreneurs with or without a legislator status are likely to experience similar levels of expropriation. If I had only studied regions with predatory governments, I would have observed a much stronger effect. More nuanced data is needed to further understand industry and regional heterogeneity, and whether and how such heterogeneity might be related to other formal legislative behavior. We also need to remember that subjects in the ACFIC survey are entrepreneurs with operating firms, but entrepreneurs shaken down by local governments to the extent that their enterprises no longer function are automatically dropped from the dataset. It is unlikely that many of those entrepreneurs were people's congress deputies, but they might have constituted a comparable counterfactual to some of the entrepreneur–legislators in the dataset. If these owners of closed businesses had been included in the survey, the treatment effect of people's congress membership would have been much larger. Instead of seeing informal payment saved as a return on the investment in getting a legislative membership, it might be more accurate to see a legislative membership as an insurance policy against expropriation, and different individuals are willing to pay different premiums to get that insurance. In this case, an insurance premium is higher than the average amount of expropriation.

Second, I do not wish to argue that "property protection" is the only form of benefit that entrepreneur–legislators enjoy. For instance, for many established entrepreneurs who no longer worry about expropriation, joining the legislature is about understanding the business environment and macro-economic policies (Interview P1217). For entrepreneurs who think *tanpai* is tolerable, having a seat in the legislature might provide important connections for their family members (Interview P1222). For some, a seat does not mean much at all (Interview P1216); for others, a seat might be valuable as an indicator of social status (Interview P134). Again, instead of arguing for one single cause of participation, I am bringing a much-neglected motivation into the theoretical and empirical debate about political participation in authoritarian contexts.

The analysis thus far has touched upon whether a seat in the people's congress protects an entrepreneur from government expropriation, but we still do not know how exactly entrepreneur–legislators gain such protection. Do entrepreneur–legislators have any formal policy influence that grants greater property security to them as a class? Are there any positive external perceptions, as proposed by Truex (2016) in his explanations of returns to office at the NPC? Or is the "political capital" mechanism, proposed in the introduction and Chapter 2, really at work? The next chapter answers these questions by probing these possible channels systematically.

APPENDIX

TABLE A5.1 *Summary statistics: the ACFIC survey*

Variable	Obs.	Mean	Std. Dev.	Min	Max
Firm level					
PC membership	12,017	0.193	0.395	0	1
Expropriation	12,017	0.0525	0.099	0	1
Ex-SOE firm	12,017	0.218	0.413	0	1
Firm age	11,554	7.736	4.776	0	28
Individual level					
Ex-government official	12,017	0.188	0.391	0	1
CCP membership	12,017	0.343	0.475	0	1
Age	11,951	45.18	8.49	16	84
Gender	11,993	0.865	0.342	0	1
Education level					
1	183			0	1
2	1,407			0	1
3	3,877			0	1
4	5,578			0	1
5	866			0	1

Note. ACFIC Surveys 2000, 2002, 2004, 2006, 2008, 2010, and 2012. The unit for total expenditure, extraction expenditure, and public relation expenditure is 10,000 yuan (1 US dollar = 8.11 Chinese yuan, average exchange rate in 2000–2012). Expropriation is calculated as forced unofficial payment to governments as a percentage of a firm's total expenditure. Education is a categorical variable: 1 denotes primary school education, 2 denotes middle school education, 3 denotes high school or vocational education, 4 denotes college education, and 5 denotes above college education. This sample only includes entrepreneurs who responded to the *tanpai* question. Whether or not one is a PC deputy does not predict the *tanpai* missingness.

TABLE A5.2 *Main results: PC membership on level of expropriation*

	OLS (no weights)	OLS (entropy bal weights)	Matches = 1	Matches = 2	Matches = 4
PC membership	−0.641 (0.202)	−0.762 (0.195)	−1.126 (0.288)	−1.101 (0.267)	−1.098 (0.258)
Obs.	10,921	10,921	10,921	10,921	10,921

Note. The table only presents the coefficient and standard error of the treatment (of being a PC member) effect under each specification. Robust standard errors are in parentheses. The dependent variable level of expropriation is defined as a percentage of the firm's total expenditures in a given year. All firm- and individual-level variables are either matched or included as covariates in the models.

TABLE A5.3 *Entropy balancing: covariates balance*

	Treatment		Control (before)		Control (after)	
	Mean	Variance	Mean	Variance	Mean	Variance
Firm age	8.83	22.07	7.469	22.62	8.829	22.07
Ex-SOE firm	0.3373	0.2236	0.2084	0.165	0.3373	0.2235
Ex-government official	0.22	0.172	0.185	0.151	0.22	0.172
Individual age	47.30	55.70	44.55	73.06	47.30	55.70
CCP membership	0.547	0.248	0.295	0.208	0.547	0.248
Education	3.564	0.714	3.454	0.715	3.564	0.714
Gender	0.905	0.0866	0.856	0.124	0.905	0.086

Note. Results of entropy balancing across the treatment group (entrepreneurs with a PC status, $N = 2,209$) and the control group (other entrepreneurs, $N = 9,176$).

TABLE A5.4 *OLS and fixed effects models with and without entropy balancing weights*

	OLS	FE	OLS with ebal weights	FE with ebal weights
PC membership	−0.977	−0.641	−0.938	−0.762
	(0.203)	(0.202)	(0.201)	(0.195)
Ex-SOE firm	−0.824	0.228	−0.700	−0.265
	(0.185)	(0.200)	(0.204)	(0.212)
Firm age	0.036	0.029	0.036	0.040
	(0.021)	(0.022)	(0.024)	(0.024)
Ex-government official	0.689	0.298	0.529	0.186
	(0.233)	(0.268)	(0.246)	(0.284)
CCP membership	−0.463	−0.244	−0.233	0.012
	(0.193)	(0.200)	(0.210)	(0.216)
Age	−0.086	−0.072	−0.104	−0.089
	(0.012)	(0.013)	(0.013)	(0.013)
Gender	−1.110	−0.954	−1.378	−1.311
	(0.313)	(0.324)	(0.430)	(0.456)
Education FE		✓		✓
Province FE		✓		✓
Year FE		✓		✓
Constant	✓	✓	✓	✓
Observations	11,385	10,921	11,385	10,921
R-squared	0.0142	0.0575	0.0185	0.0670

Note. The table presents the full sets of coefficients and robust standard errors from four specifications: OLS, Fixed Effects, OLS and Fixed Effects with ebal weights.

Missingness

The following variables suffer from a small degree of missingness: firm age, firm's main industry; entrepreneur's age, gender, education.

There are several ways to deal with missingness besides listwise deletion, which results in loss of valuable information and potential selection bias. One could substitute the mean values into the missingness (Schafer and Graham 2002). A more commonly used method is multiple imputation (King et al. 2001; Rubin 1977; Schafer and Graham 2002). Under the assumption of missingness at random (MAR), the method of multiple imputation imputes *m* values for each missing item and creates *m* complete data sets. Assumptions also need to be made on the distribution of the variables, and a jointly multivariate normal model usually works well in a wide variety of cases (King et al. 2001).

Using both methods of mean substitutions and multiple imputation, results are consistent with the main findings.

TABLE A5.5 *Summary: missing values*

	Obsevations Missing	% Missing
Firm age	463	3.85
Main industry	501	4.17
Entrepreneur age	66	0.55
Gender	24	0.20
Education	106	0.88

Note. Total $N = 12,017$.

TABLE A5.6 *Results from multiple imputation: full dataset*

	OLS (no weights)	OLS (entropy bal weights)	Matches=1	Matches=2	Matches=4
PC membership	−0.604 (0.193)	−0.711 (0.186)	−1.167 (0.278)	−1.150 (0.257)	−1.103 (0.246)
Obs.	12,017	12,017	12,017	12,017	12,017

Note. Five multiply imputed datasets generated using Amelia II package. Table shows results using the same specifications as those in the main results section. Standard errors are adjusted following King et al. (2001).

TABLE A5.7 *Main results: PC membership on expropriation, 2012*

	OLS (no weights)	OLS (entropy bal weights)	Matches=1	Matches=2	Matches=4
PC membership	−0.964 (0.570)	−1.174 (0.521)	−1.373 (0.863)	−1.398 (0.503)	−1.752 (0.713)
Obs.	2,718	2,718	2,760	2,760	2,760

Note. The table only presents the coefficient and standard errors of the treatment effect under each specification. Robust standard errors are in parentheses. The dependent variable extraction is defined as extraction value as a percentage of the firm's total expenditures in a given year. All firm- and individual-level variables are either matched or included as covariates in the models.

Only Looking at Year 2012

One commentator suggests I conduct a robustness check only looking at years in which my fieldwork overlaps with the survey years. Table A5.7 reflects such an analysis. In year 2012, having a PC membership protects an entrepreneur from government expropriation. The effect size is similar to those estimated in the main specifications.

CPPCC Membership

I also investigated whether a CPPCC membership is really a "weaker treatment" of a PC membership. That is, does being in a local CPPCC also bring about political capital, which in turns deters expropriation? Because local CPPCCs have lower political status than congresses, and there are more seats available for private entrepreneurs, I argue that the protective effect of a CPPCC is smaller and more insignificant compared to that of a seat in the local congress. Table A5.8 reports the average effect of having a local CPPCC seat on levels of extraction, using the same specifications as the ones reported in Table A5.2. Effect sizes are at least twice as small, and statistically indistinguishable from zero.

Quantile Regressions

We can also identify the effect of PC memberships on the level of expropriation at different quantiles, using quantile regression analysis. Quantile regression helps identify the effect on the distribution, not on specific individual units. Table A5.9 presents the results from quantile regression at the quantiles 0.4, 0.5, 0.6, 0.7, 0.8, and 0.9.

TABLE A5.8 *Main results: CPPCC membership on expropriation*

	OLS (no weights)	OLS (entropy bal weights)	Matches=1	Matches=2	Matches=4
CPPCC membership	−0.348 (0.198)	−0.315 (0.204)	−0.456 (0.250)	−0.543 (0.269)	−0.533 (0.229)
Obs.	10,921	10,921	10,921	11,010	11,010

Note. The table only presents the coefficient and standard errors of CPPCC membership under each specification. Robust standard errors are in parentheses. The dependent variable is expropriation. All firm-level and individual-level variables are either matched or included as covariates in the models.

TABLE A5.9 *Quantile regression estimates of PC membership on expropriation*

Quantile	Coefficient of PC membership	Standard error	Percent reduction in expropriation(%)
0.4	0.000	(0.000)	0
0.5	0.003	(0.028)	0
0.6	−0.158	(0.102)	3.01
0.7	−0.581	(0.209)	11.07
0.8	−1.091	(0.286)	20.78
0.9	−1.600	(0.867)	30.48

Note. All quantile regressions contain the same controls included in the main OLS regression. Standard errors are bootstrapped; replications = 100. I do not report results below the 40th percentile, because the level of expropriation equals 0. I calculate "percent reduction in expropriation" by dividing the estimated coefficients of PC membership by 5.25 percent, the average firm percentage point expenditure on involuntary payment.

Original Wording of the Survey Questions

(in Chinese, translated into English by author)

- Tax: How much tax did your company pay last year?
- Fee: How much fee did your company pay last year?
- Expropriation: How much forced payment did the local government extract from your company last year?
- Public Relation Spending: How much did your company spend on PR last year?

Total Expenditure = A + B + C + D; Expropriation (percent) = C/Total
Expenditure

- Treatment Variable: Are you currently a people's congress deputy?

If so, at which level of the people's congress are you serving?

6

Legislator Status and Political Capital

Liang Guangzheng, a private entrepreneur and the CEO of a billion-dollar conglomerate called Guanglong, was a three-term Yunfu prefectural congress deputy in Guangdong Province and a Baise prefectural congress deputy in Guangxi Province in 2007. Earlier that year, Liang was found to have been involved in a public fund embezzlement case in Yunfu prefecture ten years earlier, and other accomplices had recently been convicted. Because Liang was a congressional deputy, he enjoyed immunity from prosecution, unless the corresponding congressional standing committee granted a waiver. The Yunfu procuratorate submitted an application to waive Liang's immunity, which the local congressional standing committee immediately granted. The investigation was about to move forward in Yunfu, but the congressional standing committee in Baise prefecture, where Liang also served as a local legislator, put a stop to proceedings by insisting that it would be "a serious violation of the law" to prosecute Liang without its permission, and that the prosecution had to be (and was indeed) delayed. A month later, journalists who went to Liang's company to interview him were told that he was "already on his way to the United States for a month-long business trip."[1] He has not been seen since.

In some countries, parliamentary immunity protects legislators from arrest, detention, and criminal charges. In Egypt, for instance, immunity essentially excuses businessmen from corruption charges (Blaydes 2011).

[1] *The Procuratorial Daily*. "The two-city dilemma" behind the "Liang Guangzheng phenomenon" (*"Liang guanzhen xianxiang" Beihou de Shuangcheng Kunju*). June 2, 2008. www.jcrb.com/n1/jcrb1657/ca715890.htm. Last accessed April 8, 2015.

In China, congressional status protects legislators from being immediately investigated and prosecuted by the procuratorate, unless the corresponding congressional standing committee waives the immunity, as it did in the Liang case described here. This chapter shows that the formal powers associated with holding a legislative seat, including parliamentary immunity, are insufficient to explain a legislator's ability to deter predation by local bureaucrats.

I argue that the key mechanism is the political capital associated with their office: the political status of a people's congress deputy sends a credible signal of strong political connections to low-level bureaucrats, which deters expropriations. To illustrate this, I first show that the alternative mechanism of "legislative supervision" is unlikely to explain the property-protection effect of being a legislator. Even though legislators can exercise supervisory power, they rarely supervise government activities, and supervision itself cannot deter expropriation.

I then propose the "political capital" mechanism and argue that the political capital associated with being a legislator deters bureaucrats from expropriation. As discussed in earlier chapters, becoming a legislator requires significant political capital, which only increases during an official's tenure through interacting with other legislators, many of whom are party and local government officials. Since low-level bureaucrats do not have complete information on local business–government connections, they rely on signals such as holding a legislative seat: entrepreneurs who serve as legislators are likely to have more political capital than those who do not. Some of this political capital might be observable. For example, all lower-level tax collectors in the same bureau may know that a particular entrepreneur is the golf buddy of a local taxation bureau head. But some political capital might not be observable: an entrepreneur may have become friends with a local taxation bureau head serving in the same congress (e.g., after the 18th party congress in 2012, they would not be allowed to play golf together because officials are banned from playing golf), but this information sometimes can only be inferred by lower-level tax collectors. How an entrepreneur musters sufficient political capital to get elected in the first place is also unobservable, because it takes place privately between entrepreneurs and high-level officials. Therefore low-level bureaucrats must make assumptions about the strength of the connections, if any, between an entrepreneur and low-level bureaucrats' superiors (as well as the larger political network associated with the seat) and try to extract only from those who have low political capital.

The mechanism of political capital as a deterrent is supported by interview evidence, a case study, and two national audit experiments on Chinese local government officials. I directly contacted prefectural tax officials and examined their responses to information requests about how they respond to requests from private entrepreneurs with and without political connections to local congresses. Using an experimental manipulation, I show that Chinese bureaucrats are much more likely to respond to entrepreneurs with connections to the local people's congress, while being a CCP member does not trigger any preferential behavior of bureaucrats towards entrepreneurs.

6.1 SUPERVISORY POWER

Chinese legislatures perform four main functions: legislation, supervision, representation, and regime-maintenance or support (Cho 2009). In China, systematic rule of law and enforcement of property rights can only be pushed forward through legislation,[2] and I showed in Chapter 5 that entrepreneurs have not been collectively pushing for property rights legislation. The most relevant legislative function in the context of individualistic property protection is supervision.

Chinese people's congresses were invited to oversee policy implementation in the 1980s (O'Brien 1994b). As alternatives to agents of the state and the CCP, congressional deputies in the 1990s slowly gained a reputation as "remonstrators" who had the capacity to channel social demands and to link constituents to the government (O'Brien 1994a). Over time, the party came to view legislative supervision as "a useful means of checking and preventing corruption in governments" (Cho 2009, 47). Legislative supervision has since been playing an increasingly important role in local politics.

Deputies supervise governments through two methods: examination of law enforcement and appraisal of government officials. There are two types of appraisals: self-reporting of performance appraisal and deputies' appraisal (see Chapter 3 for a more detailed description). On paper, these formal powers make entrepreneur–legislators quite influential – they decide who gets promoted or demoted. But Wu Hai, the entrepreneur (who wrote an open letter to the Chinese premier) mentioned at the

---

[2] Liu and Weingast (2018) argue that the Chinese state can effectively transfer a part of the development of rule of law to private actors.

beginning of this book, gives an interesting analogy when he describes the low social status of private entrepreneurs in China:

In terms of social status, government officials are like the children of the wife in a big family, state-owned enterprises are the children of the concubines, but private entrepreneurs like us, we are the children of prostitutes. We all share one father, but we [the private entrepreneurs] are constantly bullied by children of the wife and the concubines.[3]

Do all private entrepreneurs feel the same way? How about the entrepreneur–legislators who have the powers to remove government officials? Do they have higher social status? Do congressional deputies actually exercise their power to dismiss government officials? How much say do they have in appointing new officials?

Legislators admit that they are usually not influential in appointing new officials. Local party committees usually nominate the candidates; deputies only have access to the files of each candidate right before the voting process. They usually vote yes, since they believe the nomination is already "set in stone" and that their votes are not likely to matter (Interview M131).

More congressional deputies have recently used their dismissal power to make sure that officials and bureaucrats are doing their jobs. After receiving complaints from his constituents regarding garbage pick-up, Deputy Huang Ye from Yulin Prefecture informed the prefectural health commission head about the situation. Huang pointed out that a "people's congress deputy (like myself) can impeach you if you do not perform your duty as a public servant and a government official." As a result, the street was cleaned within three days.[4]

Congressional deputies are sometimes assigned to an appraisal or supervisory group that corresponds to a specific government agency. In theory, a group should conduct investigations for several months by visiting relevant officials and interviewing residents (Cho 2009, 59); in fact, these supervisory groups usually visit the assigned agency only once

---

[3] *Forbes China*, March 24, 2015. "Wu Hai, the CEO of Crystal Orange, Complains to the Premier: I Am too Frustrated for Many Years" (*Juzi Shuijing CEO Wu Hai Xiang Zongli Jiaoqu: Chuangye Zheme Duonian, Wo Tai Biequ Le*). www.forbeschina.com/news/news.php?id=41541&page=2&lan=zh. Last accessed November 8, 2017.

[4] *Jinchu Network*, August 27, 2014. "Liu Lifeng: When Is It Not News When People's Congress Deputies Criticize Government Officials?" (*Liu Lifeng: Renda Daibiao Chize Guanyuan Heshi Buzai Shi Xinwen?*). http://focus.cnhubei.com/original/201408/t3027081.shtml. Last accessed November 8, 2017.

a year, when the agency hosts a focus-group meeting (*zuotan hui*) and discusses its work. A supervisory group then evaluates the work quality of the agency's work and submits an appraisal report to the people's congress standing committee. The report is then delivered to the party committee and, if a majority of members of the supervisory group do not approve the officials or agencies supervised, the official faces punishment, including a dismissal. This supervisory system gives the congressional deputies another "check" on local government agencies, but in reality, government agencies and the congress deputies usually operate under the implicit agreement that this type of supervision does not and should not mean much. Mr. Lang, a prefectural legislator, commented on this point:

Lang: I was once chairing a supervisory group to the prefectural bureau of land and resources. When we (the supervisory group) visited their office, the bureaucrats and leaders were very polite to us, because they knew that we needed to sign forms [to let them pass the supervision/examination].

Interviewer: How worried do you think they were that you might not give them a good rating?

Lang: We were being very understanding. We told them up front that we would not do what we should not do [fail the appraisal]. And they understood.

Interviewer: What is the point of going there then, if you know that you are not going to give them a hard time?

Lang: It is still a good opportunity to get to know people from the agency and make some friends.

(Interview P154)

Furthermore, there is limited evidence that deputies have much agency in appointing and dismissing government officials after the appraisal process. It is clear that supervisory groups that conduct deputies' appraisals are just a formality. As Lang suggested, membership in a supervisory group provides welcome networking opportunities between government officials, entrepreneurs, and other deputies. Several entrepreneurs and bureaucrats pointed out that "knowing that the supervisory power exists" could affect how bureaucrats treat entrepreneur-legislators (Interview P154). Although deputies rarely exercise their appraisal power, it could give entrepreneur–deputies a more advantageous bargaining position when dealing with local officials. Although I do not completely rule out this possibility, the fact that deputies and government officials seldom mention these formal powers suggests that they are not the main mechanisms to explain why officials treat legislator–entrepreneurs preferentially.

6.2 USING POLITICAL CAPITAL TO DETER EXPROPRIATIONS

I argue that the political capital associated with being a legislator explains why low-level government officials are deterred from expropriating from entrepreneur–legislators. Both qualitative and experimental evidence suggests that the "political capital" mechanism is more plausible than the alternatives.

The size of political capital of an entrepreneur–legislator is mostly private information. Some of those political connections might be observable to low-level bureaucrats. For instance, a low-level tax collector might be aware that an entrepreneur–legislator went to college with his superior, or notice that this entrepreneur is in his boss's office quite often, or that the son of a bureau chief recently married the daughter of a local entrepreneur.

But most of these political connections are invisible to low-level bureaucrats, such as an entrepreneur sponsoring the son of a bureau head's college education abroad, or a superior is playing *mahjong* with a few entrepreneurs on the weekends. How a private entrepreneur was initially nominated and then elected is a largely unobservable process involving a large amount of political capital.

Therefore when a low-level bureaucrat is deciding whether to expropriate from an entrepreneur who is a local legislator, the bureaucrat makes inferences about the entrepreneur's political connectedness. Given his status as a legislator, the safe strategy is to not expropriate from him. Next, I provide an example of the process of "inferring political capital."

District 51 is one of the four main districts in a prefecture located in Hunan Province. The district covers a large portion of the prefecture's commercial areas, and its local taxation bureau usually has a sustainable stream of tax revenue. In addition to retail businesses, the bureau also collects taxes from jewelry importing, textile, and light manufacturing firms. A few local business owners are district- or prefectural-level congressional deputies. When I asked a tax collector, Li, whether it would be possible to collect one million yuan in extra tax in the current fiscal year, he answered, "One million is too easy! We could easily collect 10 million extra."

I then presented him with a hypothetical scenario in which he had the opportunity to extract additional revenue from one of two companies in the district. The two hypothetical companies are identical in all dimensions, and the only difference is that the owner of one company is a district-level congressional deputy. Without hesitation, the tax collector chose to extract rent from the company without the congressional affiliation. He explained that he "would definitely avoid people's congress deputies to avoid trouble," because they "could easily phone my bosses." His use of the word "could" suggests that Mr. Li thinks that legislators might have political capital that he does not necessarily observe.

He further referred to congressional deputies as "the privileged class" (*tequan jieji*) and noted that they were "difficult to deal with." When I asked him to describe their privileges, he brought up a recent encounter with Company X in his jurisdiction, which owed the district taxation bureau a significant amount of back taxes. Li thus requested that Company X pay the "missing" taxes. A few days later he received a call from his boss, asking him not to collect these taxes, but to make sure that in the future Company X does not owe taxes. Li later realized that the company's owner is a district-level congressional deputy and knew Li's boss personally. Collecting additional taxes might be important, but obviously listening to his superior is more important for Li and other low-level civil servants.

After this incident, Li decided to avoid all companies owned by congressional deputies – not because his boss phones him every time he goes to check their books, but because their status signals that they likely have good political connections (Interview G133). Mr. Li's case demonstrates what happens when private information about political capital becomes visible, and how he uses past experience to infer unobserved political capital that other entrepreneurs might have.

In Zhang Changdong's study of private entrepreneurs, one of his entrepreneur interviewees told a similar story:

A political title is very helpful [for entrepreneurs]. A CPPCC title is useful already, and a PC title has even higher value. For instance, a private entrepreneur who was a CPPCC member was in trouble – the local taxation bureau found a serious tax evasion problem. The business owner sought help from the local CPPCC chair, and the chair made a call to the local taxation bureau head, blaming the bureau for collecting excessive tax and driving enterprises away. As a result, the taxation bureau head stopped the investigation. (Zhang 2014)

In both Li's case and the one depicted in Zhang (2014), low-level agents from a tax bureau took actions to expropriate from a highly connected local business, and the owners of the business used their political capital to protect the business. During the process, private information about entrepreneurs' political connections was made public to future expropriators. Yet other strategies and types of political capital could also deter expropriation.

First, companies hire retired politicians to strengthen their image and market power. Politicians and bureaucrats frequently enter government from industry jobs and return to industry jobs all the time, and such shuffling has profound consequences for business and politics (Gormley 1979; Makkai and Braithwaite 1992). In the United States, almost half of former senators and governors serve on at least one board after leaving office, and the average compensation may reach a lucrative $251,000 per year for "relatively little work" (Palmer and Schneer 2015). In Britain, Members of Parliament (MPs) have the right to work as consultants and directors while in office, and many MPs take directorships after they retire from politics (Eggers and Hainmueller 2009). This "revolving door" phenomenon is also widely observed in many other economies, ranging from Japan (the phenomenon of *amakudari,* see Colignon and Usui 2003) to Thailand (Laothamatas 1988) and Libya (Confessore and Schmidt 2015).

What makes former government officials an attractive addition to a company? The firm that hired retired British MP Reginald Maudling explained that "it was very useful indeed to have on tap the knowledge and contacts made by a former Cabinet Minister who had been Chancellor of the Exchequer and President of the Board of Trade" (Eggers and Hainmueller 2009).

Former officeholders can provide specialized knowledge of policymaking and lawmaking,[5] as well as access to the connections they established while in office. They also serve a public relations purpose, which strengthens a company's status and reputation: hiring a high-profile former government official serves as a strong signal of a company's resources and political connectedness.[6]

In China, countless individuals quit their government or party jobs to enter the business world (in Chinese, *xia hai),* and they bring their resources (e.g., knowledge and networks) with them. Many big companies also hire retired high-level government officials as "independent directors," including the former governors of Guizhou Province and Shandong Province, and the former deputy commissioner of the State

---

[5] On the other hand, James Wilson argues that professional civil servants do not necessarily desire private sector employment, because "the kind of work that will impress a potential private employer is not necessarily that which favors industry but that which conveys evidence of talent and energy" (Wilson 1989, 86).

[6] During one interview, an entrepreneur told me that he heard one company recently hired the son of a state-level bureau head. "The kid got paid 200,000 yuan per year and he does not need to do anything," suggesting that it was not the person himself but rather the connections he brings to the company that matter (Interview O132).

Taxation Bureau (Wu 2013). A recent regulation issued by the organization department of the Central Committee made it more difficult for former government and party officials to enter business immediately after retirement (Central Committee 2013), but there is leniency in interpretation and enforcement. In these cases, although it is possible that retired officials claim to have more political capital than they actually do, companies that spend the money and effort to hire them have likely done their due diligence and have observed some real political capital that would help the company.

The second alternative strategy for deterring expropriation relies on *relatives in politics* as a powerful source of political connections. In Mara Faccio's work on "politically connected firms," in which she surveys firms in 47 countries, about a quarter of the countries have firms with political connections "through close relationships" (Faccio 2006).

In China, it is often said that the best business partner one can have is a spouse in politics. Another new term, *ping die* (literally "daddy competition") points to the importance of having a powerful parent (or other close relative), usually in politics or in business. Having a close relative in politics not only generates tangible connections and resources, it also serves as a visible deterrent to potential predators. Clearly, the more powerful, the higher up, and the more relevant the relative is, the more effective the deterrence will be. The high-profile "Sons and Daughters" programs of JP Morgan Chase, under which many candidates with elite pedigrees were hired on a separate track, illustrates the lucrative effect of "relatives in politics" (Silver-Greenberg and Protess 2013). There are many more lower-profile cases in businesses throughout China.

Information on relatives in politics travels quickly within local business–politics circles. Mr. Sun, one of my interviewees, was a very modest and successful private entrepreneur serving in the local prefectural legislature (Interview P136). Coincidentally, during a conversation with another local entrepreneur, Mr. Qian, Qian mentioned Sun and told me that Sun is the son of a deputy governor in the same province. When I asked how Qian knew about this, he said, "everyone knows about it" and added "it is probably very easy for him [Sun] to do business here [in this province]" (Interview P124).

Third, firms can "flex their muscles" through *corporate political expenditures*. In the United States, a firm "may never need to fight an agency politically if it can credibly signal its willingness to do so," and political expenditures serve as such a visible means (Gordon and Hafer 2005). Gordon and Hafer (2005) find that firms that make more donations are monitored less by the US bureaucracy. In Ukraine, oligarchic financing of parties proves to be an effective strategy for wealth defense (Markus and Charnysh 2017).

In China, business lobbying generally happens collectively through business associations. Membership in such associations is usually not very competitive or expensive, but entrepreneurs can "upgrade" their membership with a large donation. Scott Kennedy shows that in certain industries and regions, business associations might influence policy (Kennedy 2005; 2009; see also Dong 2005), but they remain a weak player. Membership in a business association thus only allows a company to "flex its muscles" to a limited extent.

Can Chinese business people contribute financially to individual legislators? The large majority of legislators are either government, CCP, military officials, or business elites. Government, party, or military affiliated legislators are prohibited from accepting business money, and it makes little sense to contribute money to another entrepreneur–legislator in exchange for policy changes. Without the option to invest in corporate political expenditures, entrepreneurs run for legislative seats directly.

Fourth, many entrepreneurs acquire *Chinese Communist Party membership.* More companies are setting up party units.[7] The literature on political capital and business in China primarily focuses on CCP membership and the benefits it brings to Chinese business elites. The concept of "making money and getting rich" seems to be at odds with the concept of "communism," yet many entrepreneurs have been eager to pursue a party membership.

Many scholars argue that "wearing a red hat" has been a successful strategy for Chinese entrepreneurs to demonstrate their political loyalty and political connections to the government. For example, Victor Nee and Sonja Opper argue that "party membership signals to government officials and bureaucrats commitment to the established political order" (Nee and Opper 2012, 237). Bruce Dickson (2008) discusses the many benefits for entrepreneurs of CCP membership, and their strong desire

---

[7] Some private entrepreneurs have expressed concern that by requiring private companies to establish a party unit, the party would interfere with company decisions on a daily basis. Xi's announcement in 2017 that "the party exercises overall leadership over all areas of endeavor in every part of the country" has increased anxiety and worry. See *Bloomberg News* "How to Succeed in China? Communist Party Groups in Your Company." October 19, 2017. www.bloomberg.com/news/articles/2017-10-19/how-to-succeed-in-china-communist-party-groups-in-your-company. Last accessed January 21, 2018.

to be seen as operating "within the system" (95). "Wearing a red hat" has also become a non-market strategy in other countries. In Vietnam, an increasing number of entrepreneurs have joined the Vietnamese Communist Party (VCP), and they welcome the new VCP policy of formally allowing private business owners to join the party (Rupasingha 2011).

More recently, established entrepreneurs in China have begun trying to enter the prestigious National Party Congress. Liang Wengen, the founder and chairman of a heavy machinery company, Sany Heavy Industry, and the richest man in mainland China in 2011, became the first private entrepreneur in the Central Party Congress as an alternate member (Mo 2011). Although party membership might be associated with some level of political capital, since the party has grown to nearly 90 million members,[8] it has become less of an exclusive club in which insiders know and trust each other. Thus, the political capital associated with being a party member is arguably less significant today than in the past.

6.3 USING LEGISLATOR STATUS TO SIGNAL POLITICAL CAPITAL

In Truex's (2016) study of National People's Congress deputies, he suggested that "positive external perceptions" might help explain why the businesses of national entrepreneur–legislators enjoy higher profits. Li et al. (2006) make a similar point that "PC/CPPCC members can effectively shield themselves against state encroachment when local governments act as a 'grabbing hand'," but they have not explored this mechanism in depth.

I argue that *local people's congress membership* is a strong signal of one's connections to local political elites. First, an entrepreneur–legislator needs a high level of political capital to get nominated and elected. After one is elected, through attending required plenums, collaborating in working groups, and participating in congress related events, an entrepreneur–deputy expands his personal network to incorporate political elites who are also local legislators.

---

[8] *Xinhua News*, June 30, 2016. "China Focus: CPC Has nearly 89 Million Members." http://news.xinhuanet.com/english/2016-06/30/c_135478976.htm. Last accessed August 27, 2016. Beginning in 2000, Bruce Dickson documented that a large number of party members started to abandon "their party responsibilities to pursue economic opportunities" (Dickson 2000), a trend that we continue to witness.

A low-level bureaucrat – who is well aware that entrepreneur–deputies are elected by mobilizing their political capital, and that after being elected they gain access to an extensive network of political elites (potentially including the bureaucrat's own superior) – will be particularly careful when deciding whether to extract or not, especially when he does not have the information about the entrepreneur's political connectedness. If he decides to extract from an entrepreneur who is a legislator, the entrepreneur may contact relevant higher-level officials in his network to report the extractive behavior. Such a report could be detrimental to a local bureaucrat's career.

Interview evidence suggests that bureaucrats indeed use entrepreneurs' political status to infer the strength of their political connections. When I asked a prefectural-level tax collector whether he would collect extra tax from a firm headed by a local legislator, he gave a quick and certain "no," because "membership in the congresses means good connection with superiors," and he does not want to "receive a call from his superior" and "get in trouble" (Interview G133).

For entrepreneurs who serve as legislators, showing their political status is a common practice and rational strategy. They will prominently display the title of "people's congress deputy" on their business cards, sometimes even before their titles of "CEO" or "General Manager." In China, websites such as LinkedIn, which host resumés and individual profiles, are not yet prevalent; thus trading business cards remains an important way to exchange contact information and to make connections. At a provincial ACFIC banquet following a regular meeting, I observed that entrepreneurs were so busy exchanging business cards with each other and with government officials, and drinking and socializing, that they hardly had time to eat during a two-hour lunch event (Interview/Observation O132).

Entrepreneur–legislators believe that their political status helps deter expropriation: when they are in trouble, they can call friends in their political networks. If predatory bureaucrats do not take this signal of "political connectedness" seriously, there are potential consequences. Mr. Xu, a fourth-term prefectural people's congress deputy, recalled that things like "investigations, requests to join government-affiliated organizations" happened in the past to his company but not anymore.

Interviewer: So a prefectural people's congress deputy has a lot of power?

Xu: The seat is pretty useful. There was this one time when a bureaucrat from the Commerce Bureau came to my firm and fined us for something unreasonable.

I became angry and wrote down her name. At that time, I already had been in the local people's congress for a few years and knew many people. I called the head of the Commerce Bureau and filed a complaint against the bureaucrat for conducting an informal/illegal investigation. The bureaucrat came to my firm to apologize in the same week. And it never happened again to me. (Interview P134)

Yet signaling political capital to deter expropriation does not always work. Mr. Deng, a one-term legislator, still encountered informal and ad hoc investigations from the taxation investigation bureau even after he became a legislator. Unlike Xu, although Deng considered the investigation to be illegal, he did not mobilize his political capital and just paid the amount requested, perhaps to save his political capital for future use (Interview P1218).

Does it matter how many terms one has served? Is Deng, a single-term legislator, much less politically connected than Xu, a four-term legislator, and does that explain the differences in their political efficacy? Such a proposition seems likely, mostly because Xu has had more time to accumulate more political capital, and he might have felt safer than Deng in voicing discontent. It could also be that, having been in the legislature for longer, Xu has more insider information regarding which government leader is more likely to be responsive to his complaint. Personality differences might also explain the varying levels of efficacy between deputies.

During my conversations with entrepreneurs, the phrase "selective enforcement of rules and laws" (*xuanzexing zhifa*) came up quite often.[9] Entrepreneur–legislators such as provincial legislator Luo admitted that his firm is usually a beneficiary of the "selective enforcement" in the sense that local bureaucrats more loosely enforce laws and regulations on the company (Interview P1312). However, entrepreneurs with smaller businesses who do not have a political title or political connections believe they are frequently the targets of selective enforcement (Interview P135).

The fact that entrepreneur–legislators still experience some expropriations means that the strategy does not always work. Low-level bureaucrats usually do not fear that legislators will use their formal power to sanction illicit behavior; they worry that an entrepreneur is friendly with their superior(s), who will in turn punish them. By expropriating from their boss's friend, a low-level bureaucrat risks getting on the wrong side of the boss. A low-level bureaucrat does not fear an

---

[9] The term also appeared in Wu Hai's open letter to Premier Li Keqiang, referred to at the beginning of this book.

entrepreneur–legislator if he or she believes there is little chance that the legislator knows his boss. For example, if an entrepreneur serves as a local legislator in a district congress, and a local tax officer knows that his superior holds a seat in the prefectural congress, he might conclude that there is little likelihood that they have met and therefore chooses to expropriate from this entrepreneur.

6.4 TWO EXPERIMENTS ON LOCAL BUREAUCRATS

To further test whether legislator status is a strong signal of political capital and to compare different types of political capital signals, I conducted two national audit experiments on local officials in China. In these experiments, I requested business-related policy information from local mayors' offices and randomly manipulated the identity of the requesters – a local private entrepreneur (control), a local private entrepreneur who signals his political connections in the local legislature (the PC Experiment), or an entrepreneur who reveals his CCP membership (the CCP Experiment). I then compared whether entrepreneurs with a PC connection or a CCP membership received preferential treatment compared to those without such affiliations. In other words, in these experiments I am comparing the effectiveness of wearing new types of a "red hat."

The purpose of these two experiments was not to assess the effect of having either a connection in a local legislature or CCP membership on the likelihood of experiencing expropriation. Rather, these experiments were designed to test whether a connection in the local legislature causes local officials to treat entrepreneurs preferentially, and whether CCP membership would trigger a similar effect. Below, I further justify my choice of experimental outcome – the government's provision of information – by arguing that it provides important insights to help us understand how bureaucrats make decisions when faced with limited information.

Most Chinese local governments have established websites to facilitate interactions between citizens and public officials. Among many services these websites provide, one called "Mayor's Mailbox" provides a channel for citizens to directly address the mayor (*shizhang*) with their queries, and the mayor's office replies via the website, e-mails, or phone calls. Previous studies have shown that contacting government agencies is a common form of citizen political participation in China (Michelson 2007; Shi 1997), and online mailboxes have been quite responsive to Chinese citizens' requests (Chen, Pan, and Xu 2015; Distelhorst and Hou 2014; 2017).

Private entrepreneurs have a variety of channels through which they can address their concerns to the government, including through directly contacting government agencies. According to Kellee Tsai's 2002 survey, 67.7 percent of private entrepreneurs reported that they have written letters to relevant government agencies (Tsai 2007, 120).

I designed two audit experiments to identify the effect of having certain types of political capital on government responsiveness, and to compare the effect of indicating a congressional connection versus indicating party membership. In the first experiment – the PC Experiment – the entrepreneur, who is an established firm owner in the IT service industry, requested information about a new tax reform policy. In the treatment condition, the entrepreneur wrote that he had a connection in the local congress. In the control condition, he did not reveal any political connections.

Informed by prior literature on the effect of CCP membership on firm performances (Dickson 2003; Morduch and Sicular 2000; Walder 1995), I designed a second experiment – the CCP Experiment – to explore the effect of having a party membership on firms. The CCP Experiment addresses the following questions: do bureaucrats treat entrepreneurs

FIGURE 6.1 "Mayor's mailbox: the city of Nanjing"

Note. A prefectual mayor's mailbox website. http://szxx.nanjing.gov.cn/. Last accessed and captured April 22, 2015.

with a CCP membership preferentially, as the literature suggests? If so, what is the magnitude and how does the effect compare to that of indicating a people's congress connection? The CCP Experiment has the exact same setting as the PC Experiment; the only difference is that in the treatment condition, the entrepreneur indicated his Chinese Communist Party membership, instead of a connection in the local legislature.

The PC Experiment was implemented in the summer of 2013, and the CCP Experiment was implemented in the spring of 2014. The context of each experiment is described below. The PC Experiment requested information on a new tax policy – converting business tax to value-added tax (*"ying gai zeng"*). The new tax policy was first announced by the State Administration of Taxation at the end of 2011 and was implemented in selected prefectures and industries starting in the beginning of 2012. The policy rolled out nationally in August 2013. I submitted the requests at the end of July 2013, right before the policy's nationwide implementation.[10]

Although this tax reform has affected different industries differently, firms in many industries expected to experience a tax cut under the new tax regime, since the pre-existing method of calculating business tax had already included the value-added tax and thus sometimes resulted in double counting.[11] I chose to have the requester come from the IT service industry, because this industry was one that qualified for the tax reform.

It is important to note that, although most entrepreneurs had heard about the tax reform at the time of the experiment, many were not sure when it would be effectively implemented and what procedure they would need to follow in order to be qualified. Thus, the reform required sufficient and private knowledge of the conditions of eligibility (e.g., whether a certain industry or locale was covered, when it would roll out) and which government agencies to contact. The information demand on individual entrepreneurs was thus relatively high.

Local mayors' offices received the following electronic message:

Dear Leader:
I am a local private entrepreneur in the IT service industry. I heard that the business tax to value-added tax reform is going to roll out in selected cities nationwide. My firm will be directly affected by this policy.

---

[10] The official policy documents are available in Chinese at www.chinatax.gov.cn. Last accessed February 21, 2016.
[11] *NetEase News*, May 29, 2013. "Business Tax to Value-Added Tax Reform Starts August 1st" (*Bayue Yiri Qi Yingyeshui Gai Zengzhishui*). http://money.163.com/13/0529/10/901MCVNJ00253BoH.html. Last accessed November 8, 2017.

{I contacted a local people's congress deputy, and he suggested I write to you.}

[I am a CCP member, and I am loyal to the party.]

When will my firm be affected by this policy?

Thank you,

Name

The one-line "treatment" in the curly brackets only appeared in the treatment letter in the PC Experiment, indicating that the requester either had a personal connection with a local people's congress deputy or contacted one directly. The former is much more likely, because local deputies' contact information is rarely public. When local legislators' contact information is made public, such information is usually not credible. For instance, two Chinese political scientists have sent survey questionnaires to all prefectural legislators in Xiamen, where legislators' personal e-mail addresses were posted online. They received zero response (Interview O141).

The ideal treatment here would be "being a legislator" instead of "contacting a legislator." However, because the letters were signed with a pseudonym, it would be easy for the receiving bureaus to figure out that the pseudo legislator did not exist, rendering the experiment invalid. Nor could I use real legislators' names, because (i) I did not have the contact information for one legislator in each prefecture from the same industry and (ii) I would not be able to record the responses unless I had their consent to work with each one of them. Therefore, I chose to use the experimental condition of "contacting a legislator" to proxy for the effect of being a legislator. If contacting a legislator prompted preferential treatment from the bureaucrats in the experiment, then *being a legislator* would only have elicited a stronger effect. Thus, what I observed in the PC Experiment represents a lower bound of what the real treatment would elicit.

The one-line "treatment" in the square brackets only appeared in the treatment letter in the CCP Experiment, indicating that the entrepreneur is a loyal communist party member.

In both experiments, I attempted to submit information requests to 336 prefectural governments in China, 265 of which did not require a national identification card number and had a valid website. I then randomized treatment assignment[12] within each province and tried to

---

[12] The government issues the national ID number – the Chinese equivalent of the US Social Security Number.

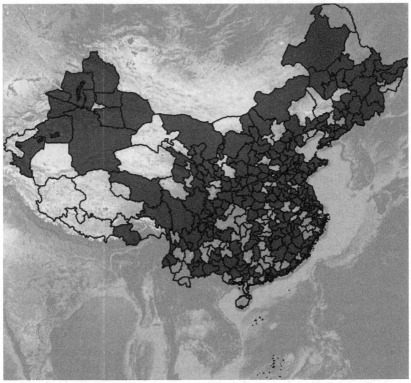

FIGURE 6.2 Chinese prefectures contacted in the experiments

Note. All Chinese prefectures I tried to contact in the PC Experiment and the CCP Experiment are highlighted on the map. Satellite imagery © 2014 NASA, Terrametrics, accessed using Google Maps API.

submit the requests. Of these 265 prefectures, 23 did not accept the requests in the PC Experiment and 27 did not accept the requests in the CCP Experiment. In these failed-to-submit cases, either e-mail servers bounced the messages back right away, or their online forums did not allow me to submit the message. I successfully submitted my requests to 242 localities in the PC Experiment and 238 in the CCP Experiment. In both experiments, prefectures that did not accept my requests are not statistically different from those that did; thus the internal validity of the experiment is not threatened by these attritions (see Table A6.1 for a comparison between prefectures that did and did not accept the requests).[13] All the Chinese names used in the experiments are considered male names.

6.4.1 Experimental Results

The key outcome of interest is whether the contacted government agency disclosed any information regarding the requested policy. In the PC Experiment, 40.91 percent of all prefectual governments replied to the request for tax reform information. In the CCP Experiment, 43.28 percent did so. The difference in these two response rates is not statistically significant. These response rates are comparable to other studies on government responsiveness in China, which again suggests that local governments treated these inquiries as real letters from citizens.

The PC Experiment revealed a large magnitude of official preference for entrepreneurs with a political connection in the local legislature. Officials' response rate increased by 12.09 percentage points when the requester signaled that he had contacted a local legislator prior to writing to the office. As the disclosure rate for entrepreneurs with no connection was 34.96 percent, this effect represents an increase in the probability of disclosure by 35 percent (12.09 percent/34.96 percent = 35 percent).

Party membership, however, elicited no preferential treatment in official behavior. In the CCP Experiment, entrepreneurs with no party or political affiliation were equally likely to receive a response from the local government compared with those who were CCP members: 42.50 percent vs. 43.22 percent, respectively.[14] The difference is indistinguishable from 0. In this context, having a contact in the people's congress seems much more helpful than being a party member.

---

[13] Pre-treatment covariates across the treatment and control groups are well balanced in both experiments (see Table A6.2). Although there are differences between the two groups in each experiment, these differences are not statistically significant.

[14] If we compare the two control conditions across these two experiments, we see that the response rate was 34.96 percent in the PC Experiment, and a much higher 42.50 percent in the CCP Experiment. Because these two rounds of experiments were conducted in two different years, this 7.54 percent difference in the baseline conditions might be attributed to factors that are different in 2013 and 2014. There could have been some central policy change or mandate that drove up government response rates to citizen requests in 2014. Therefore, it is more meaningful to compare response rates within each experiment but not across these experiments.

TABLE 6.1 *Outcome: Whether a government replied*

	The PC Experiment			The CCP Experiment		
	Treated	Control	Difference	Treated	Control	Difference
Disclosure	47.05	34.96	12.09*	44.07	42.50	1.57
Rate (%)	(4.59)	(4.32)	(6.30)	(4.59)	(4.53)	(6.45)
Obs.	119	123		118	120	

Note. Disclosure was measured 30 days after requesting information from China's prefectural governments. *p = 0.028 (one-tailed); p = 0.056 (two-tailed).

6.4.2 Bureaucrats' Decisions: Provision of Information versus Expropriation

Elsewhere in the book I study how entrepreneurs use legislator status to protect their property, but the outcome in these experiments is whether (and how) bureaucrats provide business information to entrepreneurs. Officials' decisions to provide information are different from their decisions not to extract from a local business. Given the constraints of field experiments, it is impossible to directly study decisions to extract in this context. Nevertheless, the information provision outcome helps us understand local governments' decisions about whether to predate.

First, the bureaucrats in the experiments are the "likely candidates" who conduct certain types of expropriation in the local economy. In the experiments I asked for tax-related information, and those queries were usually directed to local taxation bureaus, which then decided to either answer or ignore my requests; if they decided to answer, they provided relevant information regarding the new tax reform. Importantly, local tax officers have frequent interactions with local firms, and these bureaucrats are the usual suspects of "predators" seeking opportunities to expropriate. Therefore, studying tax bureaus' preferences towards various entrepreneurs in these experiments reveals how they interact with entrepreneurs and whether they "play favorites."

Second, even though there is much more to gain by expropriating from businesses than from failing to provide information to an entrepreneur, the costs of "not expropriating" and "providing information" are similar in the following way. Providing information here is a low-cost activity, taking at most ten minutes of a bureaucrat's time if he decides to respond. "Not expropriating" is also a low-cost activity – although one might lose the opportunity to extract rents from a specific company, there remain thousands of other companies to profit from. On the flip side, if a bureaucrat extracts from an entrepreneur who has high political capital, or fails to provide cheap information to an entrepreneur with good connections, this bureaucrat might irritate the entrepreneur, who might use his political capital to retaliate. Although I was not able to directly study bureaucrats' extractive behaviors, examining how they decide whether to provide information to entrepreneurs contributes to our understanding of their general decision-making process.

6.4.3 Alternative Interpretations of the Treatment

Could the treatment of contacting a local legislator signal something other than political connections? Here I discuss two possible alternative explanations.

First, contacting a legislator is a treatment that signals effort. The treatment letters are longer than the control letters, and having contacted a congressional deputy could be interpreted by government officials who received this letter as a request from someone who exerts more effort in demanding information, which could indicate a citizen's likelihood of being a troublemaker. And the local government may be more likely to respond to potential troublemakers to maintain regime stability. This is a plausible alternative explanation. However, as discussed earlier, local legislators' contact information is usually private, and extremely difficult for a private citizen to find, even if they exert a good amount of effort.[15]

To further rule out the effort hypothesis, I conducted a very similar experiment (the College Student Experiment), where I sent out information request letters to local governments, in which the treatment group also indicated the effort of having contacted a local legislator. In this experiment, however, the entrepreneur was a young college graduate who had not started his business yet. Thus, the treatment of having contacted a local legislator is mostly a treatment of effort, and represents a much less credible signal of any established political connections to the local legislature. Below is the content of the letter:

[15] For a recent news report on the difficulty Chinese citizens face in trying to locate their deputies, see a Chinese video, "Finding Legislators Near Us" (*Xunzhao Shenbian de Renda Daibiao*), available at http://video.sina.com.cn/p/news/c/v/2014-03-05/163963585239.html. Last accessed November 8, 2017.

Dear Leader:

I am a college graduate who graduated last year. Now I am thinking about starting my own business. I am wondering whether our local government has any policies that support new businesses started by university graduates?

{I contacted a local people's congress deputy, and he suggested I write to you.}

Thank you,

Name

Since the PC Experiment and the College Student Experiment have exactly the same treatment, if effort were the true underlying mechanism, "additional effort" should have elicited higher response rates in both the PC and the College Student Experiments. However, in the College Student Experiment, the treatment did not trigger a higher response rate from local governments. This null effect suggests that Chinese local governments do not simply respond more often to those who exert greater efforts in making demands.

A second alternative explanation is that the treatment indicates not merely political connections, but more generally, *a high socio-economic status*. The alternative hypothesis then is that local officials are more likely to share information with individuals with higher socio-economic status, but not necessarily with those who have political connections.

This hypothesis can be tested by comparing the experiments in this chapter with similar experiments in the same context, in which putative citizens requested other information via the same government websites.

TABLE 6.2 *Response rates by citizens' socio-economic status*

Wave	Citizen identity	Socio-economic status	N	Service provided(%)
1	Unemployed	Low	258	43.0
2	Unemployed	Low	235	41.3
3	Migrant worker	Low	260	45.0
4	Recent college graduate	Medium	230	45.2
5	Entrepreneur (the PC Experiment)	High	242	40.9
6	Entrepreneur (the CCP Experiment)	High	238	41.6

Note. The first five rows of the table are from Distelhorst and Hou (2017): response rates of the five waves of the field audit reported in the article. The last row reflects results from the CCP Experiment.

In Distelhorst and Hou (2017), we experimented with citizen identities from a wide range of socio-economic backgrounds, from migrant workers to recent university graduates, and private entrepreneurs (in this chapter) in five rounds of audit studies. If socio-economic status drives government responsiveness and elite bias, we should find variations in response rates towards individuals with different levels of socio-economic status. However, entrepreneurs and recent graduates (*high* socio-economic status) were not more likely to receive a response from government than unemployed citizens and migrant workers (*low* socio-economic status). Thus, it is unlikely that socio-economic status, instead of political connections, explains the difference in the response rates in the PC Experiment.

There are, nevertheless, limitations to this experimental research design in understanding the effect of political capital associated with people's congress deputies. One major concern is that the political connection treatment is fabricated and might not represent real business–state interactions. Again, private entrepreneurs in reality do consider directly contacting government officials when they have questions or concerns, but those with good political connections would probably do so by calling their friends in the government instead of writing to the Mayor's Mailbox. This is a valid concern, but I argue that the estimate obtained in the PC Experiment can at least serve as a lower bound of the "true" treatment effect of having a legislative seat on preferential treatment by local bureaucrats. If a letter mentioning an anonymous congressional connection triggers a significant difference in response rates, an actual connection could only cause a larger effect.

A second concern is that the treatment of a congressional connection or being a party member could have indicated other firm characteristics that might affect how bureaucrats treat these entrepreneurs. For instance, having a congressional connection might suggest that the firm is large and thus a major taxpayer in the local economy, and local officials might be more likely to share information with important tax contributors. Or entrepreneurs with CCP memberships are more likely to have political connections and therefore local officials are more responsive to them. Theoretically, experiments should be able to solve problems of possible confounders and generate clean causal estimates. But in my experiments, the nature of the treatment of "contacting a congressional deputy" or "being a CCP member" could have suggested a bundle of other characteristics that might have affected the outcome.

6.5 DISCUSSION

This chapter assesses possible mechanisms that explain how legislative membership protects property security in China. Using interview evidence and case studies, the chapter shows that the formal powers associated with holding a legislative seat are insufficient to explain a legislator's ability to deter expropriation. The key mechanism is the political capital associated with their position as people's congress deputies: legislative membership signals high political connectedness to low-level bureaucrats, which deters them from expropriation.

Do entrepreneur–legislators abuse their political capital for offensive purposes? I have not observed direct evidence, but theoretically, they can engage in proactive or offensive deployment of political capital to hurt rival firms. We also know that these entrepreneur–legislators take advantage of their political connections to cut deals with the government, to obtain cheaper land and capital, and to further enhance their political networks, all of which help their own business and hurt their rivals. Political capital associated with public office can certainly be used for offensive as well as defensive purposes.

The political capital, sociopolitical networks, and other characteristics associated with a political title seem more important than the title itself. If what I study in this book is just about political connections, readers may ask why we need another study on the topic of political connections in China?

Immediately after President Xi Jinping took power at the 18th Party Congress in late 2012, China launched a far-reaching anti-corruption campaign.[16] The campaign has been voraciously welcomed by Chinese citizens, yet from the perspective of more than 11 million government officials, this campaign means fewer opportunities to access "grey income" (e.g., bribes and perks), which some estimated to have accounted for 12 percent of China's GDP.[17] By the end of 2014, some 180,000 officials

---

[16] *The People's Daily*, January 14, 2015. "Anti-corruption Campaign–Xi Jinping's Plan for this Year" (*Fan Fubai, Xi Jinping Jinnian Zhunbei Zhemegan*). http://politics.people .com.cn/n/2015/0114/c1001-26381980.html. Last accessed April 27, 2015; "Anti-corruption Is a War We Cannot Lose," by Wang Qishan, the then secretary of the central commission for discipline inspection, *People's Daily*, November 3, 2014. http://news .xinhuanet.com/politics/2014-11/03/c_127169976.htm. Last accessed April 27, 2015. (No longer available).

[17] *The Diplomat*, April 25, 2015. "The Anti-corruption Drive and Risk of Policy Paralysis in China." http://thediplomat.com/2015/04/the-anti-corruption-drive-and-risk-of-policy-paralysis-in-china. Last accessed April 27, 2015.

had already been "disciplined," and the campaign has been successful in forcing many officials to pull back from "past practices of collecting bribes," according to Li Yongzhong, the vice-director of a government institute that trains anti-graft investigators in Beijing.[18] Since the campaign has taken huge profits out of the public service sector, Li observes that "[t]here are also many problematic and corrupt officials who are passively or actively resisting."[19]

The campaign has impacted many of the entrepreneurs and officials that I interviewed. Many bureaucrats believe their gross income has gone down, which has made their jobs as civil servants less appealing (Interviews G1214; G1218; G153). A tax collector told me that it used to be the case that the period before the Chinese New year was the "busiest" time, but has now become the least busy time of the year because bureaucrats are "no longer allowed to conduct end-of-year visits to companies and stay for dinner" (Interview G133). An entrepreneur told me that now is an extremely "dangerous" time to socialize with government officials, and government officials are particularly careful when interacting with entrepreneurs, for fear of being investigated. In light of this campaign, my interviewees revealed that the legislator title appears more valuable and useful, because interactions between government officials and entrepreneur–deputies can be justified as purely related to legislative business and are less likely to trigger investigations (Interview P154).

The Chinese government continues to be heavily involved in the economy, and the anti-corruption campaign cannot transform the political economy into a rent-free one overnight. In sensitive times, legislator status brings legitimacy and convenience to business–government interactions and transactions. Businesses and governments still interact frequently and informal transactions continue to be made on a daily basis, further increasing entrepreneurs' investments in political instead of economic activities and therefore increasing inefficiency. This is an unintended consequence of the ongoing anti-corruption campaign, which is at odds with its objective; I return to this issue in the concluding chapter.

---

[18] "China's Fierce Anti-corruption Crackdown: An Insider's View," NPR, December 24, 2014. www.npr.org/blogs/parallels/2014/12/24/372903025/chinas-fierce-anti-corruption-crackdown-an-insiders-view. Last accessed April 27, 2015.
[19] Ibid.

APPENDIX A: ADDITIONAL RESULTS FROM THE EXPERIMENTS

TABLE A6.1 *Contacted and unreachable prefectures*

	The PC Experiment			The CCP Experiment		
	Contacted	Unreachable	t-statistic	Contacted	Unreachable	t-statistic
Area (sq km)	24818	29371	0.4664	24731	15583	−1.134
Population (million)	391.7	528.4	2.0621	2197	1111	0.4594
GDP (billion RMB)	1137.8	1307.2	0.5215	1049.7	1253.1	0.8272
GDP per capita	30455	25455	−0.7088	27966.9	28340.3	0.0613
Primary GDP (%)	0.1525	0.1408	−0.5876	0.1506	0.1411	−0.5787
Secondary GDP (%)	0.4863	0.4608	−1.0241	0.4606	0.4738	0.5106
Tertiary GDP (%)	0.3613	0.3983	2.0997	0.3713	0.3735	0.1303
Gov't Revenue (billion)	81.3419	99.1068	0.4835	68.06	93.92	1.16
Gov't Spending (billion)	145.109	189.853	1.049	141.1	164.4	0.6784
Trade Volume (% GDP)	0.2669	0.2207	−0.4799			
Posted Replies in 2012						
No replies posted	56	7		55	9	
1–10 replies posted	23	1		25	3	
>10 replies posted	163	16		149	23	
Obs.	242	24		228	34	

Note. Covariate means for prefectures contacted compared with prefectures I was not able to contact in both experiments. Posted replies in the Mayor's Mailbox are from Distelhorst and Hou (2014).

TABLE A6.2 *Balance table for submitted requests*

	The PC Experiment			The CCP Experiment		
	Contacted	Unreachable	t statistics	Contacted	Unreachable	t statistics
Area (sq km)	20,620.8	24,955.2	0.75	27,042.8	22,517.6	−0.72
Population (million)	27,60.9	15,63.4	−0.69	1,149.4	1,563.8	0.79
GDP (billion RMB)	1741.8	1,103.0	−0.89	1,099.0	1,020.2	−0.46
GDP per capita	27,136	29,717	0.58	27,974	26,232	−0.48
Primary GDP (%)	14.71	15.19	0.41	14.99	14.90	−0.07
Secondary GDP (%)	45.3	47.6	1.26	46.16	46.22	0.03
Tertiary GDP (%)	37.6	36.0	−1.40	37.62	36.72	−0.79
Gov't Revenue (billion)	64.11	75.25	−0.72	75.21	64.06	−0.74
Gov't Spending (billion)	139.8	139.2	−0.02	141.38	141.60	0.01
Trade Volume (% GDP)	48.87	35.81	−0.5	57.63	28.57	−1.05
Posted Replies in 2012						
No replies posted	35	27		31	34	
1–10 replies posted	10	14		15	13	
>10 replies posted	88	91		87	85	
Obs.	119	123		118	120	

Note. Means of pre-treatment covariates for prefectures in the treatment and control group. This includes only prefectures where requests were successfully submitted. T All the economic and demographic data come from the 2010 statistical yearbook. Trade data is missing for four prefectures: Haibei, Hainan, and Yushu Prefectures in Qinghai Province and Shannan Prefecture in Tibet Province. Trade volumes in these prefectures are coded as 0.

TABLE A6.3 *OLS estimates: treatment effects in the PC and CCP experiments*

	The PC Experiment			The CCP Experiment		
Treatment	12.10	14.20	14.96	3.22	3.11	1.46
	(6.30)	(6.21)	(6.19)	(6.41)	(6.62)	(6.16)
General Covars		✓	✓		✓	✓
Province FE			✓			✓
Obs.	243	243	243	220	220	220

Note. OLS estimates for the treatment effects on government disclosure in the PC experiment and the CCP experiment. Robust standard errors are in parentheses. The dependent variable is government disclosure.

TABLE A6.4 *How long does it take to reply*

	The PC Experiment			The CCP Experiment		
	Treated	Control	Difference	Treated	Control	Difference
Days to Reply	7.0	8.7	1.7	7.4	6.1	−1.3
	(1.1)	(2.0)	(2.3)	(0.8)	(0.7)	(1.1)
Obs.	52	39		46	44	

Note. The dependent variable: number of days the government takes to reply. It is measured by calculating the number of days between the date when the letter was replied to and the date when the letter was submitted. This sample only includes those who replied to the letters. Letters that do not indicate a reply date are dropped from the analysis. Robust standard errors are is in the parentheses. In both experiments, the difference is statistically insignificant.

Response Speed and Quality

I also compare how fast local governments respond as well as the quality of responses between different groups. In the PC Experiment, officials reply to entrepreneurs with a congress connection in a more timely fashion: on average it takes a local official 8.7 days to reply to an entrepreneur with no political connection, and 7 days to reply to an entrepreneur with a connection. The difference is, however, imprecisely estimated. Similarly, in the CCP Experiment, it takes local officials on average a week to reply to the requests.

The differences in terms of the quality of replies between the groups are also small. In the PC Experiment, I analyze the quality of replies using the following five criteria: whether the reply indicates (i) if the IT service industry qualifies for the tax reform; (ii) when the tax reform policy becomes effective; (iii) the name of the bureau to contact; (iv) the contact information of the relevant bureau; and (v) whether relevant governmental documents are cited.

TABLE A6.5 *The PC experiment: qualities of replies*

	Entrepreneurs with PC Connection	Entrepreneurs No Connection	Difference
Qualify	80.4%	76.7%	3.6%
	(5.4)	(6.5)	(8.4)
Starting Date	75.0%	83.7%	−8.7%
	(5.8)	(5.7)	(8.2)
Bureau Name	73.2%	72.1%	−1.1%
	(6.0)	(6.9)	(9.1)
Contact Info	42.9%	32.6%	10.3%
	(6.7)	(7.2)	(9.9)
Documents	48.8%	42.9%	−5.9%
	(7.7)	(6.7)	(10.2)
Obs.	56	43	

Note. The dependent variables are five dummy variables, and they are explained as follows. The variable *Qualify* denotes whether the reply indicates if the requester's industry qualifies for the new tax policy. The variable *Starting Date* is coded as 1 if the reply indicates when the tax policy becomes effective in the locale. The variable *Bureau Name* is coded as 1 if the reply discloses the relevant bureau to contact. The variable *Contact Info* is coded as 1 if the specific contact information of the relevant bureau is given. The variable *Documents* is coded as 1 if the reply discloses a specific document number or context. This sample only includes those who replied to the letters. Robust standard errors are in the parentheses. None of the differences reaches 0.05 significance level.

A possible explanation for these null effects is that officials who handle these requests have pre-processed replies to frequently asked questions, and all they need to do is to copy and paste these replies. Thus, preferential effect is only identified in terms of the response rates, but not in terms of response quality.

APPENDIX B: ETHICAL CONSIDERATION

I took careful consideration in seeking institutional waivers of informed consent for the experimental subjects (local officials) and the use of deception when designing this experiment. The request for information came from fictitious citizens, and officials were not notified that they were participating in a study. The manipulation of connection with a local congress while holding all other characteristics constant is only possible through the use of fictitious aliases or a similar form of deception. The use of deception has been crucial to the study of discrimination in politics (Butler and Broockman 2011; McClendon 2016), in employment (Bertrand and

Mullainaithan 2004), and in the housing market (Yinger 1995). Since discriminatory behavior is generally socially undesirable and officially forbidden, informing officials of their participation in my study would cause results to suffer from social desirability bias.

I also designed the requests to be as simple and minimally burdensome to the officials as possible. Each office received at most three messages, and the requested policy information was straightforward. Since the new tax reform and policy regarding starting up new businesses will affect business across industries in the majority of provinces, disclosing relevant policy information might help other entrepreneurs who are also looking for this information.

7

Conclusion

In 1973, political scientist Jean Blondel wrote that "[l]egislatures (or assemblies, or parliaments) pose perhaps the most fascinating problem of all structures of government, for they have been and continue to be both the most decried and the most revered, the most hoped for and often the least successful institution in contemporary governments" (Blondel 1973, 2). More than four decades have passed, and scholars still find legislatures to be playing a key part in the "development of political societies" (Blondel 1973, 142) around the world. A question unaddressed by Blondel, however – or his contemporaries interested in the development of Western politics – was how and why these institutions might function in authoritarian contexts in which they do not develop through bargaining with a national class of wealth-holders, but are created by governing parties or bodies. In such a context, even though individuals appear to have little to gain by taking part in such formalistic, meaningless institutions, why do they choose to participate?

I examine the experiences of private entrepreneurs in China to provide some new answers to the question of why individuals participate in legislative institutions in authoritarian systems. I argue that Chinese entrepreneurs seek office mainly to protect their property from government expropriation. By holding seats in local legislatures, entrepreneurs use their political capital to deter local bureaucrats from demanding bribes, ad hoc taxes, and other forms of informal payments.

7.1 FINDINGS

As in other developing economies in Latin America, the former Soviet Union, Africa, and many parts of Asia, in China, property protection remains weak, the rule of law is poorly enforced or nonexistent, and government expropriation poses an endemic problem to the private sector as a whole. As Stanislav Markus describes it:

> Predation in modern developing states is often conducted by high-powered mini-beasts: policemen, party functionalities, local administrators, directors of state-owned enterprises, tax collectors, or the agents at any of the myriad of departments with the power to halt productive activity ... (Markus 2015, 11)

Chinese entrepreneurs, especially those with few or no political connections, have struggled to make their property secure. From the Mao era to the reform period, private entrepreneurs have relied on an innovative set of strategies to protect their property from expropriation when formal rule of law was or is lacking. This book has argued that joining local legislatures constitutes one such strategy, which has become more effective in deterring expropriation than other traditional strategies such as obtaining a Chinese Communist Party membership.

Interview evidence presented in Chapter 4 indicates that one of the main motivations for private entrepreneurs to seek seats in local legislatures is to secure property. Findings from surveys and interviews presented in Chapter 5 show that legislator–entrepreneurs are protected from local expropriation. Entrepreneurs who have seats in the local legislatures on average spend 14.5 percent less on informal payments to local officials than those who do not.

Legislative membership signals an entrepreneur's level of political capital, which triggers preferential treatment and deters expropriation. Qualitative data rules out the alternative mechanism that legislative membership might indicate "supervisory power," which results in lower levels of expropriation. Original audit experiments, which involved directly contacting officials to examine how they respond to realistic messages from citizens, show how local government bureaucracies respond to constituents with connections to legislatures. Using an experimental manipulation, I demonstrate that Chinese bureaucrats are 35 percent more likely to respond to a constituent with a connection to the local legislature. A simple signaling game further demonstrates how entrepreneurs use their political titles to indicate that they have strong political capital and thus receive preferential treatment.

In short, if we only looked at the formal functions of institutions and legislative outcomes, it would be difficult to explain why individuals participate in Chinese local legislatures at all: legislators do not make laws, and they have little influence over local policies. Moreover, obtaining a seat is becoming increasingly competitive and costly, and serving in a legislature entails a considerable time commitment. Paying more attention to the previously unobserved benefits of membership in these political institutions, in this case property protection, helps explain private entrepreneurs' choice to participate in seemingly weak and ineffective authoritarian political institutions.

7.2 UNDERSTANDING AUTHORITARIAN LEGISLATURES

In 1990, Kevin O'Brien commented on the main approaches to studying Chinese legislatures at the time and suggested that those approaches were functionalist in the sense that they "look for functions performed by institutions" and were not well suited "to identify institutional and systemic change" (O'Brien 1990, 8). More than 20 years later, Tom Pepinsky provides a similar critique regarding contemporary authoritarianism research:

In contemporary authoritarianism research, though, institutions do exactly what their creators want them to do, and leaders adjust institutional forms when doing so is in their interest. Because the new literature holds that institutions are created to solve concrete political problems, and that successfully do this, scholars have not sought evidence that history has "locked in" the crafters of institutions to a trajectory that they would not have otherwise chosen. This leaves their analyses vulnerable to the institutional critiques ... (Pepinsky 2014, 637)

Following these critiques to the existing works on authoritarian institutions, I move beyond state-centric accounts of authoritarian legislatures as a source of legitimacy, a channel of rent distribution, a tool of elite co-optation and power sharing, a method of information collection, or a combination of the above (for example, among others, Blaydes 2011; Brownlee 2007; Gandhi 2008; Magaloni 2006; Malesky and Schuler 2010; Noble 2018; Svolik 2012; Truex 2014). Instead of focusing on the functions the Chinese legislature was designed to do, this book highlights the unplanned functions that authoritarian institutions can perform.

Instead of showing that institutions do exactly what their creators want them to do, this book shows that institutions can serve a purpose that their creators did not foresee. Specifically, instead of being passive rule takers, individuals actively seek membership in the legislature to ensure property security. While the ruling elites did not plan for this to happen, it has been compatible with the CCP's interests. The party's legitimacy is largely based on delivering economic growth, and this selective property rights system, to some extent, has encouraged competition and private sector development.

Another important issue in the political institution literature regards the cognitive limits of rule makers, as pointed out by Streeck and Thelen in their conceptualization of *institutions as regimes*. They argue that "regimes capable of survival in a complex environment are likely to have built-in feedbacks that inform rule makers how their rules are working out in practice," and that rule takers can influence rules and rule makers through such feedbacks (Streeck and Thelen 2005, 15).

Even in strong states like China, individuals might not just be passive rule takers of existing institutions designed by powerful actors within the CCP and authoritarian leaders. The formal functions of the Chinese legislatures are still weak, and legislators are relatively powerless to influence law and policy. Nevertheless, private entrepreneurs have worked within the institutional arrangements to create new ways to protect their interests.

7.3 ECONOMIC GROWTH

The findings of this book have implications for long-term growth. My research suggests that China's current selective property rights system seems to choose and reward successful businesses (e.g., the ones headed by legislators), and to allow low-level bureaucrats to extract rents from smaller and less connected businesses. Such a system has worked so far for two reasons. First, it selects winners and discards losers in a Darwinian sense: less competitive and competent companies are more likely to be weeded out. Second, it allows petty corruption to keep bureaucrats motivated, but only to a level that does not hurt private sector growth too much. An important question remains: can this system remain sustainable and conducive to growth in the long run? Next, I briefly discuss three topics that are usually associated with studying economic growth in a developing economy: innovation, corruption, and property security.

First, development scholars have argued that innovation might be less important (or in other words, generates fewer opportunities) for late developers because they first take shortcuts through emulation (Gerschenkron 1962; Hirschman 1968). But in the long term, there is nearly universal agreement that innovation is crucial for growth. As Acemoglu et al. (2013) show, subsidizing incumbent firms reduces growth and welfare, because it deters the entry of new, potentially more innovative, firms. I find that newer and smaller firms are less likely to have a representative in local legislatures, and are more likely to be expropriated in China. It will be even more concerning if, instead of investing in innovation, firms devote resources to cultivating political connections because they see a higher return from the latter type of investment. Such a system, one might worry, will indeed hurt firm-level innovation and productivity growth in the long run.

Second, despite the fact that tournament-like regional competition provides incentives for sub-national officials to curb corruption, China remains one of the most corrupt countries in the world (Pei 2016). Earlier scholarly works have shown that a certain level of corruption could "grease the wheels," remove government-imposed rigidities, and allocate capital to the most efficient sectors (see Tanzi 1998 for a review), yet Paolo Mauro's seminal work shows that corruption lowers private investment and therefore reduces growth even in places where bureaucratic regulations are cumbersome (Mauro 1995; see also Tanzi and Davoodi 2001). One study, for instance, finds that spending on entertainment and travel costs – their measure of corruption – hurts firm productivity in China (Cai, Fang, and Xu 2011).

The Xi Administration's ongoing anti-corruption campaign sends a clear signal to national and sub-national officials that corruption is less likely to be tolerated, and the campaign has already had a profound effect on reducing bribes and extravagant consumption by government officials (Ding et al. 2017; Qian and Wen 2015; Truex 2016, chapter 8). As a result, many public servants have complained that their salaries are way too low in the absence of any "gray-area income."[1] Although a government job is still the top choice among Chinese college graduates (Jia and Li 2016; Liu forthcoming), fewer graduating students are choosing to enter public

---

[1] "Bi-weekly Discussion" (*Ban Yue Tan*), January 22, 2015. "Gray-Area Income Supports Public Servants' High Consumption in Spite of Low Salary" (*Huise shouru zhicheng yixie gongwuyuan zai di gongzi shidai de gao xiaofei*). www.chinanews.com/sh/2015/01-22/6993291.shtml. Last accessed July 16, 2015.

service.[2] If the anti-corruption campaign is successful in cleaning up the government in the long term, it should be welcome news for the millions of private entrepreneurs who can then use their money to develop their business instead of giving to "the grabbing hand." The anti-corruption campaign alone, however, cannot fundamentally change business–state relations if the government is still heavily involved in the economy. We will have to wait and see whether the Chinese leadership will meet its commitment to further liberalizing its state-dominated industries and to ensuring the market a stronger role in resource allocation. If these reforms were to continue and to eventually succeed, the government will be more likely to become "the helping hand" rather than "the grabbing hand." By then, entrepreneurs' motivation to participate in legislatures and other political institutions should also change: legislators might start to actually legislate.

Finally, I return to the topic of property rights and growth. Douglass North and Robert Thomas famously argue that efficient organization, which entails "the establishment of institutional arrangements and property rights," is the key to economic growth (North and Thomas 1973, 1). This view has been supported by numerous scholars in economics and political science: property security encourages individuals' investment incentives, enhances their access to credit and other resources, and generates efficiency gains by freeing up producers' time.

Accepting these premises, development economists such as Dani Rodrik argue against the simplistic "best-practice" approach to development and propose that developing countries might instead need "second-best" institutions that take into account "context specific market and government failures that cannot be removed in short order" (Rodrik 2008, 2). To cope with the absence of property rights, entrepreneurs in Russia and Ukraine make alliances with various stakeholders connected to their firms (Markus 2015) and/or have frequent contacts with private protection rackets (Frye and Zhuravskaya 2000). In Peru, property is "protected by all sorts of extralegal arrangements firmly rooted in informal consensus dispersed through large areas." In countries like Ghana and Vietnam, where legal recourse is lacking, firms rely on relational contracting to build long-term and personalized relationships and sustain cooperation through repeated interactions (Rodrik 2008).

---

[2] *The People's Daily*, April 26, 2014. http://politics.people.com.cn/n/2014/0426/c1001-24945133.html. Last accessed July 16, 2015.

In China, despite the underdevelopment of secure property rights and the rule of law, the economy has still managed to grow quickly.[3] Yingyi Qian reasons that China's "transitional institutions" have been able to "improve economic efficiency by unleashing the standard force of incentives" (Qian 2002).[4] Complementing Qian's analysis of "transitional institutions," in this book, I show that such a transitional institution can also be generated through a bottom-up process: Chinese private entrepreneurs create selective and individualized property security by seeking legislative office.

Competition for legislative seats in China is stiff, and those who secure seats are more likely to reap the benefits of a system of individualized property security. Even though the state did not initiate this selective property rights system, it understands that the system is conducive to short-term growth. This individualized and selective property protection system is therefore compatible with the CCP's incentives, since the legitimacy of the party is largely based on delivering growth.

I further argue that, rather than a "second-best" solution, the selective and predictable property rights system described in the book could be a first-best institution for the autocrats and a select group of property holders. This selective property rights system supplies the government with a steady stream of income from the protected businesses, as well as rents extracted from unprotected ones. A select group of entrepreneurs enjoys property rights security, and if this group represents the most productive sector of the economy, this selective and partial property rights system could be relatively efficient in the short or even medium run.

Nevertheless, we still need to think about long-term growth. Although transitional institutions, such as a selective property rights system, "do not necessarily lead to a partial reform trap" (Qian 2002, 42–43), it is safe to assume that at some point transitional institutions will run into problems. Hence, many scholars advocate that these transitional institutions should "eventually be replaced by the more conventional, best practice institutions when the underlying environment improves" (Qian 2002; Xu 2015), in this case, a fully fledged system of property rights. And this leads to a discussion of systematic institutional change.

---

3 Yuhua Wang (2015), on the other hand, argues that China has "partial form of the rule of law," and such a system is better enforced in some regions than others.

4 Yasheng Huang provides a different perspective: he suggests that China's growth experience is more conventional than others have argued. In the 1980s, even if there was little protection of property security, there was "security of the proprietor" (Huang 2008, especially chapter 2).

7.4 ENTREPRENEURIAL SOURCE OF DEMOCRATIZATION?

Douglass North and Barry Weingast's (1989) seminal work on the institutional development of seventeenth-century England documents how the wealth-holders gradually gained their decision-making power through their parliamentary representatives, which formed the basis of the government's commitment to honoring its agreement and the promise not to expropriate wealth.

Are China's wealth holders likely to follow a similar path? Various scholars of democracy and democratization have made predictions about China's trajectory. By analyzing GDP per capita and Freedom House rankings, Henry Rowen put a time stamp on China's democratization – 2015 – which he later revised upwards to 2025 (Rowen 2007). Larry Diamond predicts that China's middle class would be behind such a process: "[to] the extent that the CCP succeeds, however, it generates the very forces – an educated, demanding middle class and a stubbornly independent civil society – that will one day decisively mobilize to raise up a democracy and end CCP rule for good" (Diamond 2012, 12). Further complicating such analysis is the prediction that China will enter a new era of much more moderate economic growth in the years to come. In one study, for instance, Hongbin Li and colleagues predict a growth rate of an alarmingly modest 3 percent over the next two decades (Li et al. 2017).

Many China scholars, however, do not think the Chinese business elite will be a driving force behind any political change. Kellee Tsai contends that "... even if China eventually were to develop a capitalist class (a class for itself), there is no reason to expect that it would lead or ally with other classes in pushing for political change" (Tsai 2007, 220; see also Tsai 2005). In the same vein, Bruce Dickson concludes that, instead of pressing for political change, Chinese private entrepreneurs have turned out to be partners with the Communist Party to promote economic growth while supporting the status quo (Dickson 2008, chapter 8). Similarly, Margaret Pearson argues that the state initiated its strategy for organizing the business class and pre-empted any independent societal pressure (Pearson 1997). John Osburg also suggests that the majority of Chinese entrepreneurs are "far from being a class spawned by an unruly, latently democratic market that potentially poses a threat to Communist Party rule" (Osburg 2013, 9). Speaking in more general terms, Andrew Nathan argues that China's particular authoritarian system "has proven resilient" (Nathan 2003, 6) to challenges to the CCP's rule.

Chinese private entrepreneurs in the new century are different from what Dickson, Pearson, and Tsai observed in the 1990s and the early and mid-2000s. They still pose no immediate threat to the CCP, but it is doubtful that they are still "among the party's most important bases of support" (Dickson 2008, 3). While private business owners might still appear "diverse" and do not "fall into the (same) income and lifestyle strata" (Tsai 2007, 4), I argue that the common interest of property rights protection is strong enough to provide a sufficient condition for a unified class and to initiate institutional change when opportunity arises.

Institutions are sticky, but even relatively powerless players within authoritarian institutions might have started to use whatever little power they have to reshape institutions from within. In China, some private entrepreneurs are included in the people's congress system while the rest are more exposed to "the grabbing hand." It is possible that a benevolent cycle will be created in which private entrepreneurs start to use formal means to secure property by pushing for deeper legal and policy reform, and that formal institutions will eventually start to change in order to reflect and respond to these demands. Yasheng Huang believes that private entrepreneurs like Nian Guangjiu and Sun Dawu "created the true China miracle" (Huang 2008). There is no reason to believe they cannot create another.

Bibliography

Acemoglu, Daron, Simon Johnson, and James A. Robinson. 2001. "The Colonial Origins of Comparative Development: An Empirical Investigation." *American Economic Review* 91(5):1369–1401.

Acemoglu, Daron, Ufuk Akcigit, Nicholas Bloom, and William Kerr. 2013. "Innovation, Reallocation and Growth." MIT Department of Economics Working Paper No. 13–10.

Almén, Oscar. 2005. "Authoritarianism Constrained: The Role of Local People's Congresses in China." PhD. Dissertation in Peace and Development Studies, Goteborg University.

Ang, Yuen Yuen. 2009. "State, Market, and Bureau-Contracting in Reform China." Unpublished Doctoral Dissertation.

Ang, Yuen Yuen. 2012. "Counting Cadres: A Comparative View of the Size of China's Public Employment." *The China Quarterly* 211:676–696.

Ang, Yuen Yuen and Nan Jia. 2014. "Perverse Complementarity: Political Connections and the Use of Courts Among Private Firms in China." *Journal of Politics* 76(2):318–332.

Ansell, Ben W. and David J. Samuels. 2014. *Inequality and Democratization: An Elite-Competition Approach*. Cambridge University Press.

Barzel, Yoram. 1989. *Economic Analysis of Property Rights, Second Edition*. Cambridge University Press.

Bertrand, Marianne and Sendhil Mullainaithan. 2004. "Are Emily and Greg More Employable than Lakisha and Jamal? A Field Experiment on Labor Market Discrimination." *The American Economic Review* 94(4):991–1013.

Besley, Tim. 1995. "Property Rights and Investment Incentives: Theory and Evidence from Ghana." *Journal of Political Economy* 103(5):903–937.

Besley, Tim. 2004. "Paying Politicians." *Journal of the European Economic Association* 2(2–3) (1 May):193–215.

Birney, Mayling. 2007. "Can Local Elections Contribute to Democratic Progress in Authoritarian Regime? Exploring the Political Ramifications of China's Village Elections." PhD Thesis, Yale University.

Blair, Graeme and Kosuke Imai. 2012. "Statistical Analysis of List Experiments." *Political Analysis* 20(1):47–77.

Blaydes, Lisa. 2011. *Elections and Distributive Politics in Mubarak's Egypt.* Cambridge University Press.

Blondel, Jean. 1973. *Comparative Legislatures.* Prentice-Hall, Inc.

Boix, Carles and Milan W. Svolik. 2013. "The Foundations of Limited Authoritarian Government: Institutions, Commitment, and Power-Sharing in Dictatorships." *The Journal of Politics* 75(2):300–16.

Brandt, Loren and Thomas G. Rawski. 2008. "China's Great Economic Transformation." In *China's Great Economic Transformation*, ed. Loren Brandt and Thomas G. Rawski. Cambridge University Press, pp. 1–26.

Brownlee, Jason. 2007. *Authoritarianism in an Age of Democratization.* Cambridge University Press.

Butler, Daniel and David Broockman. 2011. "Do Politicians Racially Discriminate Against Constituents? A Field Experiment on State Legislators." *American Journal of Political Science* 55(3):463–477.

Cai, Dingjian. 1992. *China's People's Congress System.* Social Science Literature Press.

Cai, Dingjian. 2006. *Constitutions: An Intesntive Reading.* Falü Press.

Cai, Dingjian. 2007. "People's Congress System and Constitutional Reform." Love Thinking Blog. www.aisixiang.com/data/31725.html. Last accessed June 22, 2015.

Cai, Dingjian. 2011. "The History and Current Situation of Political Reform." *Yan Huang Chun Qiu (China Through the Ages).*

Cai, Hongbin, Hanming Fang, and Colin Lixin Xu. 2011. "Eat, Drink, Firms, Government: An Investigation of Corruption from the Entertainment and Travel Costs of Chinese Firms." *Journal of Law and Economics* 54(1): 55–78.

Callander, Steven. 2008. "Political Motivations." *Review of Economic Studies* 75(3):671–697.

Calvert, Randall L. 1985. "Robustness of the Multidimensional Voting Model: Candidate Motivations, Uncertainty, and Convergence." *American Journal of Political Science* 29(1):69–95.

Central Committee. 2013. "Central Committee Organization Department Note on Regulating Government and Party Officials Taking Position in Firms." pkulaw.cn/. Last accessed June 22, 2015.

Chan, Hon S. and Jun Ma. 2011. "How Are They Paid? A Study of Civil Service Pay in China." *International Review of Administrative Sciences* 77(2): 294–321.

Chang, C.M. 1951. "Mao's Stratagem of Land Reform." *Foreign Affairs.* www.foreignaffairs.com/articles/china/1951-07-01/maos-stratagem-land-reform. Last accessed March 16, 2019.

Che, Jiahua and Yingyi Qian. 1998. "Insecure Property Rights and Government Ownership of Firms." *Quarterly Journal of Economics* 113(2):467–496.

Chen, An. 1999. *Restructuring Political Power in China: Alliances and Opposition 1978–1998.* Lynne Rienner Publishers.

Chen, Jidong, Jennifer Pan, and Yiqing Xu. 2015. "Sources of Authoritarian Responsiveness: A Field Experiment in China." *American Journal of Political Science* 60(2):383–400.

Chen, Ling. 2018. *Manipulating Globalization: The Influence of Bureaucrats on Business in China*. Stanford University Press.

Cho, Young Nam. 2009. *Local People's Congresses in China: Development and Transition*. Cambridge University Press.

Clarke, Donald, Peter Murrell, and Susan Whiting. 2008. "The Role of Law in China's Economic Development." In *China's Great Economic Transformation*, ed. Loren Brandt and Thomas G. Rawski. Cambridge University Press, pp. 375–428.

Colignon, Richard A. and Chikako Usui. 2003. *Amakudari: The Hidden Fabric' of Japan's Economy*. Cornell University Press.

Confessore, Nicholas and Michael S. Schmidt. 2015. "Clinton Friend's Memos on Libya Draw Scrutiny to Politics and Business." *The New York Times*, May 18, 2015.

Cooper, Richard N. 2014. "China's Growing Private Sector." Caixin Online. english.caixin.com/2014-10-30/100744910.html. Last accessed June 1, 2018.

Cull, Robert and Lixin Colin Xu. 2005. "Institutions, Ownership, and Finance: The Determinants of Profit Reinvestment among Chinese Firms." *Journal of Financial Economics* (77):117–146.

Dai, Zhiyong. 2008. "Selective Enforcement of Law." *Chinese Journal of Law* (4).

De Soto, Hernando. 1990. *The Other Path*. Harper and Row Publishers.

De Soto, Hernando. 2000. *The Mystery of Capital: Why Capitalism Triumphs in the West and Fails Everywhere Else*. Basic Books.

Demsetz, Harold. 1967. "Toward a Theory of Property Rights." *The American Economic Review Papers and Proceedings* 57(2):347–359.

Diamond, Larry. 2012. "China and East Asian Democracy: The Coming Wave." *Journal of Democracy* 23(1):5–13.

Dickson, Bruce J. 2000. "Cooptation and Corporatism in China: The Logic of Party Adaptation." *Political Science Quarterly* 115(4):517–540.

Dickson, Bruce J. 2003. "Whom Does the Party Represent? From 'Three Revolutionary Classes' to 'Three Represents'." *American Asian Review* 21(1):1–24.

Dickson, Bruce J. 2007. "Integrating Wealth and Power in China: The Communist Party's Embrace of the Private Sector." *The China Quarterly* 192:827–854.

Dickson, Bruce J. 2008. *Wealth into Power: The Communist Party's Embrace of China's Private Sector*. Cambridge University Press.

Dickson, Bruce J. 2016. *The Dictators Dilemma: The Chinese Communist Party's Strategy for Survival*. Oxford University Press.

Ding, Haoyuan, Hanming Fang, Shu Lin, and Kang Shi. 2017. "Equilibrium Consequences of Corruption on Firms: Evidence from China's Anti-corruption Campaign." Working paper.

Distelhorst, Greg. 2013. "Publicity-Driven Accountability in China." Doctoral Dissertation, MIT Department of Political Science.

Distelhorst, Greg and Yue Hou. 2014. "Ingroup Bias in Official Behavior: A National Field Experiment in China." *Quarterly Journal of Political Science* 9(2):203–230.

Distelhorst, Greg and Yue Hou. 2017. "Constituency Service under Nondemocratic Rule: Evidence from China." *Journal of Politics* 79(3):1024–1040.

Dong, Ming. 2005. "On the Political Participation of Contemporary Chinese Private Entrepreneurs." *Journal of Ningbo Municipal Party School* (1).

Edin, Maria. 2003. "State Capacity and Local Agent Control in China: CCP Cadre Management from a Township Perspective." *The China Quarterly* 173: 35–52.

Eggers, Andrew C. and Jens Hainmueller. 2009. "MPs for Sale? Returns to Office in Postwar British Politics." *American Political Science Review* 103(4): 513–533.

Egorov, Georgy, Sergei Guriev, and Konstantin Sonin. 2009. "Why Resource-Poor Dictators Allow Freer Media: A Theory and Evidence from Panel Data." *American Political Science Review* 103(4):645–668.

Faccio, Mara. 2006. "Politically Connected Firms." *American Economic Review* 96(1):369–386.

Falleti, Tulia. 2011. "Varieties of Authoritarianism: The Organization of the Military State and Its Effects on Federalism in Argentina and Brazil." *Studies in Comparative International Development* 46(2):137–62.

Fan, Gang. 1995. "On New Norms on Public Revenue and Expenditure: Research and Thinking about A Few Cases of Township Income" *Economic Research Journal* (6).

Ferguson, Thomas and Hans-Joachim Voth. 2008. "Betting on Hitler – The Value of Political Connections in Nazi Germany." *The Quarterly Journal of Economics* 1(1):101–137.

Field, Erica. 2007. "Urban Property Rights and Labor Supply in Peru." *The Quarterly Journal of Economics* 122(4):1561–1602.

Fisman, Raymond. 2001. "Estimating the Value of Political Connections." *American Economic Review* 91(4):1095–1102.

Friedman, Eric, Simon Johnson, Daniel Kaufmann, and Pablo Zoido-Lobaton. 2000. "Dodging the Grabbing Hand: The Determinants of Unofficial Activity in 69 Countries." *Journal of Public Economics* 76(3):459–493.

Frye, Timothy. 2004. "Credible Commitment and Property Rights: Evidence from Russia." *American Political Science Review* 98(3):453–466.

Frye, Timothy and Andrei Shleifer. 1997. "The Invisible Hand and the Grabbing Hand." *American Economic Review* 87(2):354–358.

Frye, Timothy and Ekaterina Zhuravskaya. 2000. "Rackets, Regulation, and the Rule of Law." *Journal of Law, Economics and Organization* 16(2):478–502.

Gandhi, Jennifer. 2008. *Political Institutions under Dictatorship*. Cambridge University Press.

Gandhi, Jennifer and Adam Przeworski. 2006. "Cooperation, Cooptation, and Rebellion under Dictatorship." *Economics and Politics* 18(1):1–26.

Gandhi, Jennifer and Adam Przeworski. 2007. "Authoritarian Institutions and the Survival of Autocrats." *Comparative Political Studies* 40(11):1279–1301.

Gans-Morse, Jordan. 2017a. "Demand for Law and the Security of Property Rights: The Case of Post-Soviet Russia." *American Political Science Review* 111(2):338–359.

Gans-Morse, Jordan. 2017b. *Property Rights in Post-Soviet Russia: Violence, Corruption, and the demand for Law*. Cambridge University Press.

Geddes, Barbara. 2008. "Party Creation as An Autocratic Survival Strategy." Working Paper.

Gehlbach, Scott and Philip Keefer. 2011. "Investment without Democracy: Ruling-Party Institutionalization and Credible Commitment in Autocracies." *Journal of Comparative Economics* 39(2):123–139.

Gehlbach, Scott and Philip Keefer. 2012. "Private Investment and the Instituional-ization of Collective Action in Autocracies: Ruling Parties and Legislatures." *Journal of Politics* 74(2):621–635.

Gerschenkron, Alexander. 1962. *Economic Backwardness in Historical Perspective*. Harvard University Press.

Goldman, Eitan, Jorg Rocholl, and Jongil So. 2006. "Does Political Connected-ness Affect Firm Value?" *Review of Financial Studies* 22:2333–2360.

Gordon, Sanford C. and Catherine Hafer. 2005. "Flexing Muscle: Corporate Political Expenditures as Signals to the Bureaucracy." *American Political Science Review* 99(2):245–261.

Gormley, William T. Jr. 1979. "A Test of the Revolving Door Hypothesis at the FCC." *American Journal of Political Science* 23(4):665–683.

Greif, Avner, Paul Milgrom, and Barry R. Weingast. 1994. "Coordination, Com-mitment, and Enforcement: The Case of the Merchant Guild." *Journal of Political Economy* 102(4):745–776.

Guo, Di, Kun Jiang, Byung-Yeon Kim, and Chenggang Xu. 2014. "Political Economy of Private Firms in China." *Journal of Comparative Economics* 42(2):286–303.

Haber, Stephen. 2008. "Authoritarian Governments." In *The Oxford Handbook of Political Economy*, ed. Donald A. Wittman and Barry R. Weingast. Oxford University Press, pp. 693–707.

Haber, Stephen, Armando Razo, and Noel Maurer. 2003. *The Politics of Property Rights: Political Instability, Credible Commitments, and Economic Growth in Mexico, 1876–1929*. Cambridge University Press.

Haggard, Stephan and Yasheng Huang. 2008. "The Political Economy of Private Sector Development in China." In *China's Great Economic Transformation*, ed. Loren Brandt and Thomas G. Rawski. Cambridge University Press, pp. 337–374.

Hainmueller, Jens. 2009. "Entropy Balancing for Causal Effects: A Multivariate Reweighting Method to Produce Balanced Samples in Observational Stud-ies." *Political Analysis* 20(1):25–46.

Hall, Peter and Kathleen Thelen. 2009. "Institutional Change in Varieties of Capitalism." *Socio-Economic Review* 7(1):7–34.

He, Baogang and Stig Thogersen. 2010. "Giving the People a Voice? Experiments with Consultative Authoritarian Institutions in China." *Journal of Contem-porary China* 19(66):675–692.

He, Junzhi and Leming Liu. 2012. "The New Features of Independent Candidates in China's Local People's Congress Election." *Journal of Shanghai Administration Institute.*

Henn, Matt. 1998. "Opinion Polling in Central and Eastern Europe under Communism." *Journal of Contemporary History* 33(2):229–240.

Hirschman, Albert. 1968. "The Political Economy of Import-Substituting Industrialization in Latin America." *Quarterly Journal of Economics* 82(1):1–32.

Hou, Yue. 2019. "The Private Sector: Challenges and Opportunities during Xi's Second Term." *China Leadership Monitor* 59 (Spring 2019). https://www.prcleader.org/hou. Last accessed June 1, 2019.

Hou, Yue, Tianguang Meng, and Ping Yang. 2014. "Exploring the Political Values of Public Servants in China." Author's survey.

Huang, Yasheng. 2005. *Selling China: Foreign Direct Investment during the Reform Era.* Cambridge University Press.

Huang, Yasheng. 2008. *Capitalism with Chinese Characteristics: Entrepreneurship and the State.* Cambridge University Press.

Jensen, Nathan M., Edmund Malesky, and Stephen Weymouth. 2013. "Unbundling the Relationship between Authoritarian Legislatures and Political Risk." *British Journal of Political Science* 44(3):655–684.

Jia, Nan and Kyle Mayer. 2016. "Complementariy in Firm's Market and Political Capabilities: An Integrated Theoretical Perspective." *Advances in Strategic Management* 34:435–468.

Jia, Ruixue and Hongbin Li. 2016. "Access to Elite Education, Wage Premium, and Social Mobility: The Truth and Illusion of China's College Entrance Exam." Working paper.

Jiang, Jinsong. 2009. "The Development of People's Congress System after the Reform and Open-Up." *Hunan Social Sciences (2).*

Johns, Leslie and Rachel L. Wellhausen. 2016. "Under One Roof: Supply Chains and the Protection of Foreign Investment." *American Political Science Review* 110(1):31–51.

Johnson, Simon, John McMillan, and Christopher Woodruff. 2002. "Property Rights and Finance." National Bureau of Economic Research Working Paper 8852.

Johnson, Simon and Todd Mitton. 2011. "Cronyism and Capital Control: Evidence from Malaysia." NBER Working Paper No. 8521.

Kennedy, Scott. 2005. *The Business of Lobbying in China.* Harvard University Press.

Kennedy, Scott. 2009. "Comparing Formal and Informal Lobbying Practices in China." *China Information* 23(2):195–222.

Key, V.O. 1956. *American State Politics: An Introduction.* Alfred A. Knopf.

Khwaja, Asim Ijaz and Atif Mian. 2005. "Do Lenders Favor Politically Connected Firms? Rent Provision in An Emeriging Financial Market." *Quarterly Journal of Economics* 120(4):1371–1411.

King, Gary, James Honaker, Anne Joseph, and Kenneth Scheve. 2001. "Analyzing Incomplete Political Science Data: An Alternative Algorithm for Multiple Imputation." *American Political Science Review* 95(1):49–69.

King, Gary, Jennifer Pan, and Margaret Roberts. 2013. "How Censorship in China Allows Government Criticism but Silences Collective Expression." *American Political Science Review* 107(2):326–343.

Kroeber, Arthur R. 2016. *China's Economy: What Everyone Needs to Know.* Oxford University Press.

Krueger, Anne O. 1974. "The Political Economy of the Rent-Seeking Society." *American Economic Review* 64(3):291–303.

Landry, Pierre F. 2008. *Decentralized Authoritariaism in China.* Cambridge University Press.

Laothamatas, Anek. 1988. "Business and Politics in Thailand: New Patterns of Influence." *Asian Survey* 28(4):451–470.

Lardy, Nicholas R. 2014. *Markets over Mao: The Rise of Private Business in China.* Peterson Institute for International Economics.

Lazear, Edward and Sherwin Rosen. 1980. "The Economics of Compensation of Government Officials." In *The Rewards of Public Service: Compensating Top Federal Officials*, ed. Robert W. Hartman and Arnold Weber. Brookings.

Lenz, Gabriel S. and Kevin Lim. 2009. "Getting Rich(er) in Office? Corruption and Wealth Accumulation in Congress." APSA 2009 Toronto Meeting Paper. www.researchgate.net/publication/228277073. Last accessed September 27, 2018.

Levi, Margaret. 1981. "The Predatory Theory of Rule." *Politics and Society* 10(4):431–465.

Lewis, Steven. 1997. "Marketization and Government Credibility in Shanghai." In *The Political Economy of Property Rights: Institutional Changes and Credibility in the Reform of Centrally Planned Economies*, ed. David L. Weimer. Cambridge University Press, pp. 20–42.

Li, David D. 1996. "A Theory of Ambiguous Property Rights in Transition Economies: The Case of the Chinese Non-State Sector." *Journal of Comparative Economics* 23(1):1–19.

Li, Hong and Enhua Gong. 2013. "Tax, Fee Burden and Development of Small and Medium Enterprises: The Case of Changzhou SMEs." *Development Research* (2).

Li, Hongbin and Li-An Zhou. 2005. "Political Turnover and Economic Performance: The Incentive Role of Personnel Control in China." *Journal of Public Economics* 89(9–10):1743–1762.

Li, Hongbin, Lingsheng Meng, and Junsen Zhang. 2006. "Why Do Entrepreneurs Enter Politics? Evidence from China." *Economic Inquiry* 44(3):559–578.

Li, Hongbin, Prashant Loyalka, Scott Rozelle, and Binzhen Wu. 2017. "Human Capital and China's Future Growth." *Journal of Economic Perspectives* 31(1):25–48.

Lieberthal, Kenneth. 2004. *Governing China: From Revolution through Reform, Second Edition.* W.W. Norton and Company.

Lin, Yi-Min and Zhanxin Zhang. 1999. "Backyard Profit Centers: The Private Assets of Public Agencies." In *Property Rights and Economic Reform in China*, ed. Jean C. Oi and Andrew G. Walder. Cambridge University Press, pp. 248–274.

Liu, Hanzhang. Forthcoming. "The Logic of Authoritarian Political Selection: Evidence from a Conjoint Experiment in China." *Political Science Research and Methods*.

Liu, Lizhi and Barry R. Weingast. 2018. "Taobao, Federalism, and the Emergence of Law, Chinese Style." *Minnesota Law Review* 102(4):1563–1590.

Liu, Zheng. 2004. "The Debate and Practice on Unicameralism versus Bicameralism in Chinese History." *Chinese Legislature*. www.people.com.cn/GB/14576/28320/35193/35204/2674556.html. Last accessed October 7, 2018.

Lorentzen, Peter L. 2013. "Regularizing Rioting: Permitting Protest in an Authoritarian Regime Regularizing Rioting." *Quarterly Journal of Political Science* 8(2):127–158.

Lorentzen, Peter L. 2014. "China's Strategic Censorship." *American Journal of Political Science* 58(2):402–414.

Lu, Xiaobo. 2000. "Booty Socialism, Bureau-Preneurs, and the State in Transition: Organizational Corruption in China." *Comparative Politics* 32(3):273–294.

Lü, Xiaobo and Pierre F. Landry. 2014. "Show Me the Money: Interjurisdiction Political Competition and Fiscal Extraction in China." *American Political Science Review* 108(3):706–722.

Lust-Okar, Ellen. 2006. "Elections under Authoritarianism: Preliminary Lessons from Jordan." *Democratization* 13(3):456–471.

Ma, Dali and William L. Parish. 2006. "Tocquevillian Moments: Charitable Contributions by Chinese Private Entrepreneurs." *Social Forces* 85(2):943–964.

MacFarquhar, Roderick. 1998. "Reports from the Field Provincial People's Congresses." *The China Quarterly* 155:656–667.

MacFarquhar, Roderick and Michael Schoenhals. 2006. *Mao's Last Revolution*. The Belknap Press of Harvard University Press.

Magaloni, Beatriz. 2006. *Vote for Autocracy: The Politics of Party Hegemony and Its Demise*. Cambridge University Press.

Magaloni, Beatriz. 2008. "Credible Power-Sharing and the Longevity of Authoritarian Rule." *Comparative Political Studies* 41(4–5):715–741.

Mahdavi, Paasha. 2015. "Explaining the Oil Advantage: Effects of Natural Resource Wealth on Incumbent Reelection in Iran." *World Politics* 67(2):226–267.

Makkai, Toni and John Braithwaite. 1992. "In and Out of the Revolving Door: Making Sense of Regulatory Capture." *Journal of Public Policy* 12(1):61–78.

Malesky, Edmund and Paul Schuler. 2010. "Nodding or Needling: Analyzing Delegate Responsiveness in an Authoritarian Parliament." *American Political Science Review* 104(3):482–502.

Manion, Melanie. 2016. *Information for Autocrats: Representation in Chinese Local Congresses*. Cambridge University Press.

Manion, Melanie. 2017. "'Good Types' in Authoritarian Elections: The Selectoral Connection in Chinese Local Congresses." *Comparative Political Studies* 50(3):362–394.

Markus, Stanislav. 2012. "Secure Property as a Bottom-Up Process: Firms, Stakeholders, and Predators in Weak States." *World Politics* 64(2):242–277.

Markus, Stanislav. 2015. *Property, Predation, and Protection: Piranha Capitalism in Russia and Ukraine*. Cambridge University Press.

Markus, Stanislav and Volha Charnysh. 2017. "The Flexible Few: Oligarchs and Wealth Defense in Developing Democracies." *Comparative Political Studies* 50(12):1632–1665.

Martina, Michael. 2017. "In China: the Party's Push for Influence Inside Foreign Firms Stirs Fears." *Reuters News*. goo.gl/2BuxzN. Last a January 19, 2018.

Matthews, Donald R. 1985. "Legislative Recruitment and Legislative Careers." In *Handbook of Legislative Research*, ed. Gerhard Loewenberg, Samuel C. Patterson, and Malcolm E. Jewell. Harvard University Press, pp. 17–56.

Mattingly, Daniel C. 2016. "Elite Capture." *World Politics* 68(3):383–412.

Mauro, Paolo. 1995. "Corruption and Growth." *The Quarterly Journal of Economics* 110(3):681–712.

McClendon, Gwyneth H. 2016. "Race and Responsiveness: An Experiment with South African Politicians." *Journal of Experimental Political Science*. 3(1):60–74.

Meng, Tianguang, Jennifer Pan, and Ping Yang. 2014. "Conditional Receptivity to Citizen Participation: Evidence from a Survey Experiment in China." *Comparative Political Studies* 50(4):399–433.

Michelson, Ethan. 2007. "Climbing the Dispute Pagoda: Grievances and Appeals to the Official Justice System in Rural China." *American Sociological Review* 72(1996):459–485.

Mo, Fengqi. 2011. "The Richest Man: Liang Wengen." *Jinghua Weekly*. paper .people.com.cn/jhzk/html/2011-10/01/content_957818.htm. Last accessed October 7, 2018.

Morduch, Jonathan and Terry Sicular. 2000. "Politics, Growth, and Inequality in Rural China: Does it Pay to Join the Party." *Journal of Public Economics* 77(3):331–356.

Morozov, Evgeny. 2012. *The Net Delusion: The Dark Side of Internet Freedom*. Public Affairs.

Nathan, Andrew J. 2003. "Authoritarian Resilience." *Journal of Democracy* 14(1):6–17.

Nee, Victor and Sonja Opper. 2012. *Capitalism from Below: Markets and Institutional Change in China*. Harvard University Press.

Nickerson, R.S. 1998. "Confirmation Bias: A Ubiquitous Phenomenon in Many Guises." *Review of General Psychology* 2(2):175–220.

Noble, Ben. 2018. "Authoritarian Amendments: Legislative Institutions as Intraexecutive Constraints in Post-Soviet Russia." *Comparative Political Studies* :1–38.

North, Douglass. 1973. *The Rise of the Western World: A New Economic History*. Cambridge University Press.

North, Douglass. 1981. *Structure and Change in Economic History*. Norton.

North, Douglass and Barry R. Weingast. 1989. "Constitutions and Commitment: The Evolution of Institutional Governing Public Choice in Seventeenth-Century England." *The Journal of Economic History* 49(4):803–832.

North, Douglass, John Wallis, Steven Webb, and Barry Weingast. 2013. *In the Shadow of Violence: The Problem of Development.* Cambridge University Press.

North, Douglass and Paul Thomas. 1973. *The Rise of the Western World.* Cambridge University Press.

O'Brien, Kevin J. 1990. *Reform without Liberalization: China's National People's Congress and the Politics of Institutional Change.* Cambridge University Press.

O'Brien, Kevin J. 1994a. "Agents and Remonstrators: Role Accumulation by Chinese People's Congress Deputies." *The China Quarterly* 138:359–380.

O'Brien, Kevin J. 1994b. "Chinese People's Congresses and Legislative Embeddedness: Understanding Early Organizational Development." *Comparative Political Studies* 27(1):80–109.

O'Brien, Kevin J. and Lianjiang Li. 1993. "Chinese Political Reform and the Question of 'Deputy Quality'." *China Information* 8(3):20–31.

Oi, Jean C. 1992. "Fiscal Reform and the Economic Foundation of Local State Corporatism in China." *World Politics* 45(1):99–126.

Oi, Jean C. 1999. *Rural China Takes Off: Institutional Foundations of Economic Reform.* University of California Press.

Oi, Jean C. and Scott Rozelle. 2000. "Elections and Power: The Locus of Decision-Making in Chinese Villages." *The China Quarterly* 162:513–539.

Olson, Mancur. 1965. *The Logic of Collective Action.* Harvard University Press.

Olson, Mancur. 1993. "Dictatorship, Democracy, and Development." *American Political Science Review* 87(3):567–576.

Osburg, John. 2013. *Anxious Wealth: Money and Morality among China's New Rich.* Stanford University Press.

Palmer, Maxwell and Benjamin Schneer. 2015. "Capitol Gains: The Returns to Elected Office from Corporate Board Directorships." maxwellpalmer.com/files/capitol_gains.pdf. Last accessed January 8, 2018.

Pearson, Margaret M. 1997. *China's New Business Elite: The Political Consequences of Economic Reform.* University of California Press.

Pei, Minxin. 2016. *China's Crony Capitalism: The Dynamics of Regime Decay.* Harvard University Press.

Pepinsky, Thomas. 2014. "The Institutional Turn in Comparative Authoritarianism." *British Journal of Political Science* 44(3):631–653.

Qian, Nancy and Jaya Wen. 2015. "The Impact of Xi Jinping's Anti-corruption Campaign on Luxury Imports in China." Working paper.

Qian, Yingyi. 2002. "How Reform Worked in China." William Davidson Working Paper No. 473.

Querubin, Pablo and James Snyder. 2013. "The Control of Politicians in Normal Times and Times of Crisis: Wealth Accumulation by U.S. Congressmen, 1850–1880." *Quarterly Journal of Political Science* 8(4):409–450.

Rithmire, Meg E. 2015. *Land Bargains and Chinese Capitalism: The Politics of Property Rights under Reform.* Cambridge University Press.

Roberts, Brian E. 1990. "A Dead Senator Tells No Lies: Seniority and the Distribution of Federal Benefits." *American Journal of Political Science* 34(1):31–58.

Rodrik, Dani. 2008. "Second-Best Institutions." NBER Working Paper, pp. 1–12.

Rowen, Henry S. 2007. "When Will the Chinese People Be Free." *Journal of Democracy* 18(3):38–52.

Rubin, Donald. 1977. "Formalizing Subjective Notions about the Effect of Nonrespondents in Sample Surveys." *Journal of the American Statistical Association* 72:538–543.

Ruf, Gregory A. 1999. "Collective Enterprise and Property Rights in a Sichuan Village: The Rise and Decline of Managerial Corporatism." In *Property Rights and Economic Reform in China*, ed. Jean C. Oi and Andrew G. Walder. Cambridge University Press pp. 27–48.

Rupasingha, Wasantha. 2011. "Vietnamese Communist Party Opens Its Arms to the Capitalist Elite." World Socialist Website. www.wsws.org/en/articles/2011/02/cpvc-f10.html. Last accessed March 16, 2019.

Rustow, Dankwart A. 1985. "Elections and Legitimacy in the Middle East." *Annals of the American Academy of Political and Social Science* 482:122–146.

Schafer, Joseph L. and John W. Graham. 2002. "Missing Data: Our View of the State of the Art." *Psychological Methods* 7(2):147–177.

Shen, Yan, Minggao Shen, Zhong Xu, and Ying Bai. 2009. "Bank Size and Small- and Medium-sized Enterprise (SME) Lending: Evidence from China." *World Development* 37(4):800–11.

Shi, Tianjian. 1997. *Political Participation in Beijing*. Harvard University Press.

Shih, Victor, Christopher Adolph, and Mingxing Liu. 2012. "Getting Ahead in the Communist Party: Explaining the Advancement of Central Committee Members in China." *American Political Science Review* 106(1):166–187.

Shleifer, Andrei and Robert W. Vishny. 2002. *The Grabbing Hand: Government Pathologies and Their Cures*. Harvard University Press.

Silver-Greenberg, Jessica and Ben Protess. 2013. "JP Morgan Hiring Put China's Elite on an Easy Track." *The New York Times*. dealbook.nytimes.com/2013/08/29/jpmorgan-hiring-put-chinas-elite-on-an-easy-track/. Last accessed March 16, 2019.

Solinger, Dorothy J. 1984. *Chinese Business under Socialism*. University of California Press.

Stasavage, David. 2002. "Private Investment and Political Institutions." *Economics and Politics* 14(1):41–63.

Stockmann, Daniela. 2013. *Media Commercialization and Authoritarian Rule in China*. Cambridge University Press.

Streeck, Wolfgang and Kathleen Thelen, eds. 2005. *Beyond Continuity: Institutional Change in Advanced Political Economies*. Oxford University Press.

Stuart, Toby and Yanbo Wang. 2014. "Who Cooks the Books in China, and Does it Pay?" Working paper.

Sun, Xin, Jiangnan Zhu and Yiping Wu. 2014. "Organizational Clientelism: An Analysis of Private Entrepreneurs in Chinese Local Legislatures." *Journal of East Asian Studies* 14:1–29.

Svolik, Milan W. 2009. "Power Sharing and Leadership Dynamics in Authoritarian Regime." *American Journal of Political Science* 53(2):477–494.

Svolik, Milan W. 2012. *The Politics of Authoritarian Rule.* Cambridge University Press.

Tanner, Murray Scot. 1999. *The Politics of Lawmaking in Post-Mao China.* Clarendon Press.

Tanzi, Vito. 1998. "Corruption around the World: Causes, Consequences, Scope and Cures." IMF Staff Papers. www.imf.org/external/pubs/ft/wp/wp9863.pdf, pp. 559–594. Last accessed March 16, 2019.

Tanzi, Vito and Hamid Davoodi. 2001. "Corruption, Growth, and Public Finances." In *The Political Economy of Corruption,* ed. Arvind K. Jain. Routledge, pp. 89–110.

Thomas, Jonathan and Tim Worrall. 1994. "Foreign Direct Investment and the Risk of Expropriation." *The Review of Economic Studies* 61(1):81–108.

Tilly, Charles. 1985. "War Making and State Making as Organized Crime." In *Bringing the State Back In,* ed. Peter Evans, Dietrich Rueschemeyer, and Theda Skocpol. Cambridge University Press, pp. 170–187.

Tocqueville, Alexis de. 1858. *The Old Regime and the French Revolution.* Doubleday.

Trebilcock, Michael and Paul-Erik Veel. 2008. "Property Rights and Development: The Contingent Case for Formalization." *University of Pennsylvania Journal of International Law* 30(2):397–482.

Truex, Rory. 2014. "The Returns to Office in a 'Rubber Stamp' Parliament." *American Political Science Review* 108(2):235–251.

Truex, Rory. 2016. *Making Autocracy Work: Representation and Responsiveness in Modern China.* Cambridge University Press.

Tsai, Kellee S. 2004. "Off Balance: The Unintended Consequences of Fiscal Federalism in China." *Journal of Chinese Political Science* 9(2):1–26.

Tsai, Kellee S. 2005. "Capitalists without a Class: Political Diversity among Private Entrepreneurs in China." *Comparative Political Studies* 38(9):1130–1158.

Tsai, Kellee S. 2006. "Adaptive Informal Institutions and Endogenous Institutional Change in China." *World Politics* 59(1):116–141.

Tsai, Kellee S. 2007. *Capitalism without Democracy: The Private Sector in Contemporary China.* Cornell University Press.

Walder, Andrew. 1995. "Career Mobility and the Communist Political Order." *American Journal of Sociology* 101:1060–1073.

Wang, Yuhua. 2015. *Tying the Autocrat's Hands: The Rise of the Rule of Law in China.* Cambridge University Press.

Wank, David L. 1996. "The Institutional Process of Market Clientelism: Guanxi and Private Business in a South China City." *The China Quarterly* 147:820.

Wank, David L. 1999. "Producing Property Rights: Strategies, Networks, and Efficiency in Urban China's Nonstate Firms." In *Property Rights and Economic Reform in China,* ed. Jean C. Oi and Andrew G. Walder. Stanford University Press, pp. 248–274.

Weingast, Barry R. 1993. "Constitutions as Governance Structures: The Political Foundations of Secure Markets." *Journal of Institutional and Theoretical Economics* 149(1):286–311.

Whiting, Susan H. 2001. *Power and Wealth in Rural China: The Politcal Economy of Institutional Change.* Cambridge University Press.

Whiting, Susan H. 2004. "The Cadre Evaluation System at the Grassroot: The Paradox of Party Rule." In *Holding China Together: Diversity and National Integration in the Post-Deng Era,* ed. Barry J. Naughton and Dali Yang. Cambridge University Press, PP. 101–119.

Wibbels, Erik, Anirudh Krishna, and M.S. Sriram. 2016. "Satellites, Slums and Social Networks: Evidence on the Origins and Consequences of Property Rights from 157 Slums in Bangalore." Working paper.

Wilson, James Q. 1989. *Bureaucracy: What Government Agencies Do and Why They Do It.* Basic Books.

Wu, Gufeng. 2013. "Retired High-Level Officials Taking Position in Business and Getting Attention." *The People's Daily,* August 12. finance.people.com. cn/n/2013/0812/c1004-22523681.html. Last accessed January 8, 2018.

Xia, Ming. 2000. "Political Contestation and the Emergence of the Provincial People's Congresses as Power Players in Chinese Politics: A Network Explanation." *Journal of Contemporary China* 9(24):185–214.

Xiao, Gang. 2004. "People's Republic of China's Round-Tripping FDI: Scale, Causes and Implications." Asia Development Bank Institute Discussion Paper.

Xu, Chenggang. 2011. "The Fundamental Institutions of China's Reforms and Development." *Journal of Economic Literature* 49(4):1076–1151.

Xu, Chenggang. 2015. "Rule of Law Is the Basis for Market Economy Development." *People's Daily Forum.* www.rmlt.com.cn/. Last accessed July 15, 2015.

Xu, Yiqing and Yang Yao. 2014. "Informal Institutions, Collective Action, and Public Investment in Rural China." *American Political Science Review* 109(2):371–391.

Yinger, John. 1995. *Closed Doors, Opportunities Lost: The Continuing Costs of Housing Discrimination.* Russell Sage Foundation.

Zhang, Changdong. 2010. "Good Governance through Taxation." Unpublished doctoral dissertation.

Zhang, Changdong. 2014. "Business in Politics: Private Entreprenuers in Local People's Congresses." *Academia Bimestrie* (2).

Zhang, Jianjun. 2013. "Competition, Promise, and Compliance: Motivations behind Chinese Entrepereners' Donation." *Management World* (9).

Zhang, Qianfan. 2012. *The Constitution of China: A Contextual Analysis.* Hart Publishing.

Zhang, Xueren and Ningsheng Chen. 2002. *The 20th Century's Constitionalism of China.* Wuhan University Press.

Zheng, Wenyang. 2014. "People's Congress Meeting–A History When People Decided." *China's People's Congress Journal.* www.npc.gov.cn/npc/zgrdzz/ 2014-08/01/content_1873088.htm. Last accessed October 7, 2018.

Zhong, Yang. 2003. *Local Government and Politics in China: Challenges from Below.* M.E. Sharpe.

Bibliography (with Chinese-Language References)

Cai, Dingjian. 1992. China's People's Congress System. *Social Science Academic Press*. 蔡定剑, 中国人大制度, 社会科学文献出版社.

Cai, Dingjian. 2006. Constitution: An Intensive Reading. *Law Press China*. 蔡定剑, 宪法精解, 法律出版社.

Cai, Dingjian. 2007. "People's Congress System Reform and Constitutional Development" *Love Thinking Blog*. 蔡定剑, 人民代表大会制度改革与宪政发展, 爱思想. www.aisixiang.com/data/31725.html. Last accessed June 22, 2015.

Cai, Dingjian. 2011. "The History and Current Situation of Political System Reform" *Yan Huang Chun Qiu (China through the Ages)*. 蔡定剑, 政治体制改革的历史与现状, 炎黄春秋.

Dai, Zhiyong. 2008. "Selective Law Enforcement" *Chinese Journal of Law (04)*. 戴治勇, 选择性执法, 法学研究.

Dong, Ming. 2005. "On the Current Political Participation of Chinese Private Economic Entrepreneurs." *Journal of Ningbo Municipal Party School* (01). 董明, 论当前我国私营经济企业主阶层政治参与, 宁波党校学报, 第一期.

Fan, Gang. 1995. "On New Norms on Public Revenue and Expenditure: Research and Thinking about a Few Cases of Township Income." *Economic Research Journal* (06) 樊纲, 论公共收支的新规范: 我国乡镇收入若干个例的研究与思考, 经济研究, 第六期.

He, Junzhi and Leming Liu. 2012. "New Features on the Procedure of Independent Candidates Participating in China's People's Congress Election." *Journal of Shanghai Administration Institute*. 何俊志, 刘乐明, 公民自主参选人大代表过程中的新特征, 上海行政学院学报.

Jiang, Jinsong. 2009. "The Development of People's Congress System since the Reform and Opening-Up" *Hunan Social Sciences (02)*. 蒋劲松, 改革开放以来人民代表大会制政体的成长, 湖南社会科学, 第二期.

Li, Hong and Enhua Gong. 2013. "The Association Study between Tax-Fee Burden and the Development Dilemma of Small and Medium Enterprises: Investigation and Analysis of Changzhou SMEs" *Development Research (02)*

179

李红, 龚恩华, 税费负担与中小企业发展困境关联性研究-常州市中小企业调研分析, 开发研究(02).

Liu, Zheng. 2004. "Debates and Practices on Unicameralism versus Bicameralism in Chinese History" *Journal: The People's Congress of China.* 刘政, 历史上关于一院制还是两院制的争论和实践中国人大. www.people.com.cn/GB/14576/28320/35193/35204/2674556.html. Last accessed October 7, 2018.

Mo, Fengqi. 2011. "Liang Wengen: The Richest Man" *Jinghua Weekly, 17.* 莫丰齐, 首富梁稳根, 京华周刊第17期. http://paper.people.com.cn/jhzk/html/2011-10/01/content_957818.htm. Last accessed October 7, 2018.

Organization Department of CPC Central Committee. 2013. "The Organization Department of CPC Central Committee Prints and Distributes the Notice of Opinions on Further Regulating the Issue of Party and Government Cadres Holding Posts in Business" "中共中央组织部印发关于进一步规范党政领导干部在企业兼职任职问题的意见的通知" http://pkulaw.cn. Last accessed June 22, 2015.

Wu, Gufeng. 2013. "Retired Senior Officials' Holding Posts in Business Drawing Attention" *The People's Daily.* 吴谷丰, 退休高官企业任职引关注, 人民日报 August 12, p. 11. http://finance.people.com.cn/n/2013/0812/c1004-22523681.html. Last accessed October 7, 2018.

Wu, Xiaobo. 2008. "Three Decades of Excitement: Chinese Enterprises in 1978–2008" Zhongxin Publishing House. 吴晓波, 激荡三十年: 中国企业1978–2008, 中信出版社.

Xu, Chenggang. 2015. "Constitutionalism and the Rule of Law are the Foundation of the Development of Market Economy" *People's Tribune.* 许成钢, 依宪、法治是市场经济发展的基础, 人民论坛网. www.rmlt.com.cn. Last accessed July 15, 2015.

Zhang, Changdong. 2014. "Business in Politics: Private Entrepreneurs in Local People's Congresses" *Academia Bimestrie* 02. 张长东, 在商言政: 地方人民代表大会中的民营企业家. 学海第二期.

Zhang, Jianjun. 2013. "Competition, Commitment, and Compliance: Motivations of Chinese Enterprises' Charitable Donations" *Management World* 09. 张建君, 竞争, 承诺, 服从: 中国企业慈善捐款的动机, 管理世界第九期.

Zhang, Xueren. 2002. *China's Constitutionalism in the 20th Century.* Wuhan University Press. 张学仁, 陈宁生, 二十世纪之中国宪政. 武汉大学出版社.

Zheng, Wenyang. 2014. "Conferences of Deputies of Various Circles to the People's Congress – A History of the People Beijing the Masters of the Country" Journal: *The People's Congress of China* (12) 郑文阳, 各界人民代表会议-一段人民当家作主的历史中国人大杂志, 第十二期. www.npc.gov.cn/npc/zgrdzz/2014-08/01/content_1873088.htm. Last accessed October 7, 2018.

Index

Other Books in the Series